Flexible Multilingual Education

NEW PERSPECTIVES ON LANGUAGE AND EDUCATION

Series Editor: Professor Viv Edwards, *University of Reading, Reading, Great Britain*

Two decades of research and development in language and literacy education have yielded a broad, multidisciplinary focus. Yet education systems face constant economic and technological change, with attendant issues of identity and power, community and culture. This series will feature critical and interpretive, disciplinary and multidisciplinary perspectives on teaching and learning, language and literacy in new times.

Full details of all the books in this series and of all our other publications can be found on http://www.multilingual-matters.com, or by writing to Multilingual Matters, St Nicholas House, 31-34 High Street, Bristol BS1 2AW, UK.

Flexible Multilingual Education

Putting Children's Needs First

Jean-Jacques Weber

MULTILINGUAL MATTERS
Bristol • Buffalo • Toronto

Library of Congress Cataloging in Publication Data
A catalog record for this book is available from the Library of Congress.
Weber, Jean Jacques.
Flexible Multilingual Education: Putting Children's Needs First/Jean-Jacques Weber.
New Perspectives on Language and Education: 38
Includes bibliographical references and index.
1. Multilingualism in children.
2. Multilingual education.
3. Children--Language. I. Title.
P115.2.W43 2014
404'.2083–dc23 2014001715

British Library Cataloguing in Publication Data
A catalogue entry for this book is available from the British Library.

ISBN-13: 978-1-78309-199-7 (hbk)
ISBN-13: 978-1-78309-198-0 (pbk)

Multilingual Matters
UK: St Nicholas House, 31-34 High Street, Bristol BS1 2AW, UK.
USA: UTP, 2250 Military Road, Tonawanda, NY 14150, USA.
Canada: UTP, 5201 Dufferin Street, North York, Ontario M3H 5T8, Canada.

Website: www.multilingual-matters.com
Twitter: Multi_Ling_Mat
Facebook: https://www.facebook.com/multilingualmatters
Blog: www.channelviewpublications.wordpress.com

Typeset by Deanta Global Publishing Services Limited.
Printed and bound in Great Britain by Short Run Press Ltd.

Contents

Acknowledgements

I would like to thank the following people: Kristine Horner for her invaluable help with everything; Marilyn Martin-Jones for her most useful comments on this project; and Anna Roderick for her support and editorial expertise. Moreover, the case-study chapters have been immeasurably improved by the expertise of the following scholars, who have all provided detailed and invaluable comments: Haley de Korne, David Li, Jinting Wu, Stefan Serwe, Ana Deumert and Mireia Trenchs-Parera. All remaining errors are, of course, my own.

Some of the material appeared in Jean-Jacques Weber and Kristine Horner, *Introducing Multilingualism: A Social Approach* (Routledge, 2012). The material is my own and is reproduced from the following pages of the above-mentioned publication: 44, 54, 58–61, 71–78, 96–101, 110–115, 123–128, 132–133, 136–142, 172–173. It is reproduced here with the kind permission of both Kristine Horner and Taylor & Francis.

1 Introduction

The important point, in the context of this book, is not so much whether or not the children's heritage and home background can be sustained by the school, but rather that children may be assisted to school success without downgrading their background and language

Edwards, 1989: 135

In line with the above quotation, this book adopts a perspective on multilingual education, which consistently puts children's needs first rather than languages. One consequence of this reorientation will be the transcending of arguments for or against a particular language and looking more holistically at what the resources are that children in a specific situation need for their educational and later professional success. As more and more children grow up multilingual in our globalized world, there is a need for more nuanced multilingual solutions in language-in-education policies.

This book therefore advocates flexible (rather than fixed) multilingual systems of education that build on children's actual home linguistic resources. It discusses the use of non-standard varieties in education, as well as the important issue of students' access to opportunities and resources. It includes numerous case studies from around the world: from the USA to Hong Kong, contrasting the highly restrictive language-in-education policies in parts of the USA (especially Arizona) with the move towards a more flexible multilingual system of education in Hong Kong; from Singapore to South Africa, exploring how these states deal with the challenge of building on children's repertoires which are often multilingual and heterogeneous (and do not consist of just one 'mother tongue'); from Luxembourg to three Autonomous Communities of Spain (Catalonia, the Basque Country and Galicia), focusing in particular on the differential access to English provided for migrant students in their multilingual education systems.

The argument made in this book is that flexible multilingual education is best for children, whereas fixed multilingual education based upon a discourse of ethnolinguistic essentialism confronts particular groups of students with obstacles similar to those found in monolingual education. Hence, language-in-education policies need to build upon all the resources in children's linguistic repertoires, and not just on a narrow range of standard varieties that are ascribed to them on the basis of their perceived ethnicity. The many case studies in the book reveal that this is the most promising approach towards the elusive goal of educational equity in our late modern age of globalization, migration and superdiversity (Vertovec, 2007).

In this introductory chapter, I first contrast the traditional approach to the study of bi- or multilingual education with the more innovative approach taken here. Next, I explain the difference between fixed and flexible multilingual education, and finally I show that many existing mother tongue and other multilingual education programmes are not flexible enough in the sense that they are informed by the assumptions of what can be referred to as the 'monolingual mindset' (Clyne, 2008).

Different Models of Bi- and Multilingual Education

A traditional approach to the study of bi- and multilingual education has been to distinguish between different models (see e.g. Baker, 2006, 2007). Bi- and multilingual education is often defined as involving the use of two or more media of instruction, and it is possible to differentiate between 'strong' or additive and 'weak' or subtractive programmes. While the latter aim at transitioning minority language students as quickly as possible from their minority language to the dominant language in a society, the former aim at developing both minority and majority languages as a way of fostering bi-/multilingualism and bi- or multiliteracies in students. These strong forms of bi-/multilingual education include heritage language education, dual language education (as found, for example, in the USA) and immersion education (e.g. in Canada).

One thing that may strike the reader here is that all the forms of strong bi-/multilingual education that Baker discusses are informed by an ideology of (parallel) monolingualism, in which languages are strictly compartmentalized (for further discussion, see the section 'Fixed vs. Flexible Multilingual Education'). In the typical Canadian immersion programmes, anglophone students are immersed – wholly or partly – in French, with the aim of developing in them a proficiency in both French and their 'mother tongue' (English). The same applies to some heritage language programmes such as Māori-medium education in New Zealand, though nowadays many of these programmes have shifted from an exclusive focus on the heritage language and reserve an increasingly important place in the curriculum for the study of academic English (see Chapter 3). In the typical dual language programmes in the USA (usually Spanish–English), Latino and Anglo-American students are taught about half their subjects through the minority language and the other half through the majority language (though different weightings are possible, too), with the aim of developing bilingualism and biliteracy in both language majority and minority students (see Chapter 5).

However, Baker (2007: 132) points out that there is variation within each model and that specific schools often apply a mixture of these models, as teachers endeavour to deal pragmatically with the challenge of implementing the model in their particular school environment. It is clear that such a pragmatic and flexible approach is highly desirable; thus, for instance, teachers have to be ready to adapt the model to a changing school population, by, for instance, increasing or decreasing the number of subjects taught through one or other language, depending on students' needs and interests. Or there may be a need to break through a language separation approach by flexibly switching between varieties or languages as a way of scaffolding students' learning. As a result, the boundaries between models become porous, and the gap between models and practices increases, so that the whole system of classification becomes less useful. A more promising approach may be to focus instead on the key principles underlying multilingual education.

Key Principles Underlying Multilingual Education

A principle-based approach to multilingual education has been adopted for instance by de Jong (2011), who identifies the following criteria as making multilingual education effective for as many students as possible, and in fact as being important in the schooling of all children:

* striving for educational equity
* structuring for integration
* affirming identities
* promoting additive bi-/multilingualism

Educational equity is the ultimate goal of all flexible multilingual education and can be defined as 'providing high-quality education and learning opportunities for students of different backgrounds' (van Avermaet et al., 2011: 1). It is based on the assumption that if there is an achievement gap between different groups of students, it is due not to the students themselves, but to inequities in the education system. De Jong's second principle, 'structuring for integration' is closely related to her first principle in its concern with desegregation, inclusion and equality of status, and hence could easily be included under the overarching equity principle. The third principle, affirming students' linguistic and cultural identities, involves building on all their resources, including non-standard, vernacular varieties. Finally, the promotion of additive bi- or multilingualism highlights the importance of the issue of access: in today's increasingly multilingual world, students need access to both minority and majority languages for all sorts of reasons, from identity-based ones to instrumental ones concerned with social mobility. Hence, looking at languages as being in conflict, and one language only being able to thrive *at the expense of* another, is not a very helpful or productive perspective in this respect. What is needed is a radical shift from an either-or to a both-and logic in thinking about languages and education (cf. Cummins, 2000: 28).

This book is primarily concerned with the key issues of building on children's linguistic resources and providing them with high-quality access to all the linguistic resources they need for educational and professional success. These major concerns inevitably put medium of instruction policies at the centre of our investigations, for the obvious reason that, as Tollefson and Tsui point out,

> medium of instruction policy determines which social and linguistic groups have access to political and economic opportunities, and which groups are disenfranchised. It is therefore a key means of power (re)distribution and social (re)construction. (Tollefson & Tsui, 2004: 2)

In the upcoming chapters, I therefore explore the medium of instruction debates in numerous multilingual countries around the world, from Singapore via South Africa to Hong Kong and others. What is striking are the great differences in the medium of instruction debates in these countries. To give just a few examples, in Singapore the medium of instruction is English, which is actually a second language for many of the students, whereas the official mother tongue is taught as a subject and only minimally used as a medium of instruction. Because of the importance of English in the Singaporean education system, a large part of the medium of instruction debates has been concerned with the role to be played by the nativized variety of English, namely, Singapore English or Singlish. In many South African schools, the medium of instruction is a local African language in the initial stages of education, but usually there is a switch to English halfway through primary school. Here, the debates are primarily concerned with whether it would be better to use the indigenous languages or English as the medium of instruction throughout primary education. In Hong Kong, on the other hand, Cantonese is the most usual medium of instruction in primary school, and the debate is largely focused on whether to use Cantonese or English in secondary education. Moreover, there is a further debate about whether Cantonese should be gradually replaced by Putonghua as the medium of instruction from primary education upwards, now that Hong Kong has become a part of the People's Republic of China.

All these and many other issues will be analysed in depth in the chapters that follow. But we can already note here that most of these medium of instruction debates are framed in terms of an either-or logic: Singlish or standard English, English or an indigenous South African language, Cantonese or English, Cantonese or Putonghua. The challenge will be to rethink these debates in terms of a radically different both-and logic. Finally, I also need to point out that, because of its focus on language in education, this book does not take into account other important social factors that influence the quality of education, such as educational infrastructures, the financial resources of schools, the availability and quality of teachers and of teaching materials, parents' involvement in their children's schooling or the families' social milieu.

Fixed vs Flexible Multilingual Education

In this book, I contrast fixed and flexible multilingual education systems, building on similar distinctions that have been made between separate and flexible multilingualism or homoglossic and heteroglossic multilingualism (Blackledge & Creese, 2010; García, 2009; Weber & Horner, 2012a). Fixed multilingual education is informed by a monolingual mindset or habitus (Clyne, 2008; Gogolin, 1994), and is often referred to in the literature as 'double', 'plural' or 'parallel' monolingualism (Heller, 2006; Otsuji & Pennycook, 2011). This is because in this conception languages are seen as being discrete, bounded entities. Monolingualism is looked upon as the norm, which can be expanded by learning one or several more of these entities ('languages'), which in this way are perceived as being easily countable; hence, the common definition of bi- or multilingualism as the ability to use two or more languages in communication.

Many of the discourses that circulate widely in contemporary society rely upon these basic and apparently commonsensical assumptions of the monolingual mindset. Let me just mention two such discourses here: first, the discourse of language endangerment (Duchêne & Heller, 2007), which needs to identify and name a particular 'language', so that it can then be split off from other 'languages' on what is usually a linguistic continuum and, as a separate and discrete entity, it can then be perceived as being in need of revitalization. At times, the motivation behind this can be an attempt to preserve the alleged 'purity' of the language and keep it from changing through contact with other languages in the sociolinguistic environment. Another widespread discourse is the discourse of ethnolinguistic essentialism, which links ethnicity with language. It is based upon such language ideologies as the one nation–one language ideology and the mother tongue ideology, with each human being assumed to have one and only one mother tongue as the norm.

Mother tongue education often relies upon one or both of these discourses and therefore constitutes a rather fixed type of multilingual education. It is usually concerned with, and committed to, the maintenance and revitalization of a particular endangered language. However, as we will see in the following section and in later chapters, it tends to be focused on the standard variety of students' assumed mother tongue and, in the process, frequently overlooks non-standard varieties; in the case of indigenous minority languages, it also frequently ignores the needs of particular groups of students in society, such as migrant students.

The multilingual mindset or habitus, on the other hand, relies upon very different assumptions. It problematizes the distinction between 'languages' and 'dialects', arguing that the distinction is of a political rather than a linguistic nature. It therefore takes a resource-based rather than a language-based view of multilingualism: all the linguistic resources in a person's repertoire, whether 'languages', 'dialects', registers, styles or accents are taken into account, at whatever level of proficiency she or he masters them (see Blommaert, 2010: 102). This implies that multilingualism rather than monolingualism is the norm; indeed, it is hard to imagine somebody who does not master, at least to some extent, more than one linguistic variety or register. Moreover, people's linguistic repertoires are highly dynamic in that they constantly have new linguistic experiences. In this way, the multilingual mindset puts language variation, contact and change at the centre of its preoccupations.

Flexible multilingual education is informed by the assumptions of the multilingual mindset. It builds on students' home linguistic resources (see Chapter 2), including non-standard varieties such as the urban vernaculars that are emerging in the metropolitan areas of our globalizing world. It provides high-quality access to *both* local, indigenous languages *and* global languages such as English, and hence access to the best possible educational opportunities for all children, including migrant students (see Chapter 3). Chapter 4 draws together these two primary concerns in order to further illustrate and define the nature of flexible multilingual education. These chapters are followed by extended case studies of different countries around the world which have multilingual education systems that, as we will see, range from highly fixed to more flexible.

Before we proceed, however, there is a need for a word of caution. While this book is in line with similar approaches advocating hybridity or translanguaging, it goes beyond many of them in its endeavour to set up an ethical and responsible theory of flexible multilingual education. Indeed, these approaches are often purely 'celebratory' and hence limited, in that they 'fail to address the issues underlying educational underachievement' (Edwards & Redfern, 1992: 51). Therefore, this book goes beyond a mere celebration of translanguaging and is fully aware of the dangers of romanticizing such practices because they can easily become 'socially disadvantageous' for the very children whom our proposals are most intended to help (Stroud & Wee, 2012: 106; see also the discussion in Chapter 7).

Mother Tongue Education or Flexible Multilingual Education

In this book, I argue that mother tongue education needs to be rethought and reoriented in the direction of a more flexible multilingual education. Instead of relying upon the problematic concept of mother tongue, it is more important to build on students' *actual* linguistic resources in a positive and additive way. With more and more children growing up multilingual in today's globalized world, their actual linguistic resources often cannot be reduced to a single mother tongue. Therefore, this book advocates openness to all varieties, including non-standard and vernacular varieties, and insists upon the importance of access to both minority and majority, local and global languages. It argues against the common assumption that mother tongue education is automatically and necessarily what is best for students, and calls for more flexible multilingual solutions in language-in-education policies.

Because of its focus on mother tongue, mother tongue education almost inevitably simplifies the linguistic reality of the actors concerned. Let us take heritage language education as an example. First, we note that often this is not mother tongue education in any literal sense, as the heritage language (e.g. the Māori language in New Zealand) may not be the home language but a second or foreign language for many children. Yet, as we will see in Chapter 3, Māori medium bilingual education achieves highly positive results even for those children who have to learn Māori as a second or foreign language. Such examples of heritage language education show that students can learn successfully through a second or foreign language as long as that language is present at least to some extent in their out-of-school environment.

However, both in mother tongue and heritage language education, students are sometimes taught the standard variety of what is assumed to be their mother tongue, even though this particular variety may not be present in their out-of-school environment. An example of this is Blackledge and Creese's (2010) study of how Bengali is taught to Bangladeshi migrants in the UK, whose home languages include Sylheti and English (see the discussion in Chapter 2). In such cases, learning their presumed mother tongue can be almost like learning a foreign language for the students. In these heritage language education programmes, teachers would need to build on all the languages involved – both Sylheti and Bengali, as well as English – in a positive, flexible and additive way, and make students aware of the differences between them.

Thus, we reach the conclusion that such mother tongue or heritage language programmes are often too fixed and that a better form of education for children is flexible multilingual education. However, it is frequently claimed that students' proficiency in their mother tongue is required *before* a second or foreign language can be learnt successfully, as it is high proficiency in the mother tongue that allows cognitive transfer from the L1 (the mother tongue) to the L2 (the foreign language being learnt). This hypothesis is relied upon when scholars argue that, in the education of language minority students, the use of the presumed mother tongue should be extended to a period of at least six years before the socially dominant language (often English) can be taught successfully. However, this is yet another problematic hypothesis relied upon by some advocates of mother tongue education. Importantly, it would discount the possibility of successful Māori-medium bilingual education for Māori children whose home language is English. It is also disproved by the other successful types of multilingual education discussed by Baker and mentioned at the beginning of this chapter, in particular dual language education. Indeed, in these programmes, majority and minority group students are taught both minority and majority languages from the very beginning of their education, and they all tend to achieve highly positive results.

There is therefore an urgent need to break through these myths underlying mother tongue education and to rethink these programmes in terms of greater flexibility. Mother tongue education is too strongly linked to the ideology of ethnolinguistic essentialism, assuming that (for instance) if you are Portuguese, then your mother tongue must be Portuguese, or if you are Tswana, your mother tongue must be Setswana. But in our multilingual world, more and more children have multilingual repertoires; they grow up with more than just one mother tongue. Thus, as will see in Chapter 9, there are many children with a Portuguese migration background growing up in Luxembourg whose home languages may or may not include Portuguese, but do include varieties of French, Luxembourgish or other languages. Yet, the official Luxembourgish language-in-education policy for these children simply assumes that their mother tongue is Portuguese and offers them a two-hour course per week taught through standard Portuguese in primary school, thus building on their assumed proficiency in this variety, as a – predictably not always very successful – way of 'integrating' them into the Luxembourgish school system. Along the same lines, in Chapter 8, I will discuss Cook's (2009) study of how Tswana students in South Africa are taught standard Setswana as their mother tongue. Yet, in their out-of-school environment, these students mostly use street Setswana, which is very different from the standard variety, and English. Hence, they often find English easier to learn than standard Setswana, which is assumed to be their mother tongue.

We can conclude that, all too often, mother tongue education as implemented by politicians, policymakers and teachers is informed by an ideology of fixed rather than flexible multilingualism in the following two senses:

- first, these programmes frequently ignore the variation inherent in all languages because of their exclusive focus on the standard variety;
- secondly, because of their overall commitment to the revitalization of the presumed mother tongue, they tend to downplay the importance of the question of access not only to local but also to global languages for all students.

More generally, educational programmes structured around a distinction between L1 and L2, etc., make less and less sense in today's world of globalization, migration and superdiversity, as the fact that not only the L1 (the 'mother tongue') but also additional languages may already be present in children's multilingual repertoires is frequently erased. Instead, what is increasingly needed is more inclusive and flexible programmes building on all the linguistic resources (or as many of the resources as possible) in children's repertoires. Such programmes are underpinned by an ideology of multilingualism as the norm, whereas mother tongue education is informed by a monolingualizing ideology.

What This Book Does

Many scholars have pointed out that there are vested interests underlying language-in-education policies. As Crawford (2000: 10), for instance, puts it, 'Ultimately language politics are determined by material interests – struggles for social and economic supremacy – which normally lurk beneath the surface of the public debate'. Focusing on the US context, Crawford (2000: 23) discusses 'the close ... connections between language restrictionists and immigration restrictionists'. Following Fishman (1992), he argues that there are 'middle-class anxieties about the declining quality of life, overcrowding, crime, rootlessness, and incivility, all of which find a scapegoat in our growing multiculturalism' (Crawford, 2000: 22). He concludes that 'the demand for language restrictions … is a demand to reinforce the existing social order' (Crawford, 2000: 27). Such anti-diversity attitudes and fears may be particularly strong in times of demographic fluctuations or economic crises. Hence, we cannot expect such feelings and anxieties to change easily or quickly, and yet this should not prevent us from making the case for greater social justice and educational equity. This is what this book does, by arguing that we can move towards these goals through the implementation of flexible multilingual education.

This chapter has touched on the fact that many multilingual education systems are too fixed and need to become more flexible in order to provide as many students as possible with both educational access and professional success. There is, of course, a basic contradiction here between educational access, which implies inclusiveness, and professional success, which inevitably involves selection and exclusion. But this contradiction between inclusion and exclusion can be, if not solved, at least mitigated by moving towards more meritocratic systems of education. As Lin puts it,

It is not so much a problem to have an elite in a society if everybody in the society has equal opportunities to enter the elite class … However, it is outright social injustice if only the children of the elite can become members of the elite. (Lin, 2001: 160)

In line with Lin's argument, let me restate the overall aim of this book here, which is to explore some of the most promising ways of moving towards the elusive goal of educational equity. The book focuses on academic discourses about multilingual education in a wide range of countries in order to find out what issues have been raised in recent scholarship, what the key debates are, what has been praised and what has been criticized. Through such a comparative study of many different countries, the aim is to distil what seem to be the most effective policies in multilingual education. While respecting the sociohistorical specificities of each context, the numerous and detailed case studies will allow us to derive a blueprint of what constitutes flexible multilingual education and, ultimately, to provide an account of multilingual education which puts children and their interests and needs first, rather than languages.

Part 1

2 Using Non-standard Varieties in Education

Decades after the publication of the seminal volumes of Trudgill (1975) and Cheshire *et al.* (1989) on dialect and education, the main issues remain largely unresolved: it is still usually the case that, when a language is taught at school, it is only the standard variety that is taught. As for the non-standard varieties which are frequently used as home languages by students, they tend to be negatively valued by teachers or even banned from classrooms. The main argument used for banning these varieties from classrooms is the 'interference argument': continued use of the non-standard variety 'interferes' with students' acquisition of the standard variety, leading them to confuse the two varieties, especially if they are closely related linguistically.

Fortunately, however, not everybody agrees with these assumptions. In many schools, non-standard varieties are positively built on as a means of leading students towards acquisition of the school standard. In fact, researchers have shown that such use of the students' non-standard home varieties in education has positive results; for instance, in relation to English-dominant environments, Siegel (1999: 710) mentions 'greater participation rates, higher scores on tests measuring reading and writing skills in standard English, and increases in overall academic achievement'. Particularly effective are awareness programmes which make students aware of the differences between the varieties, which in turn leads to a decrease in interference.

In this chapter, I discuss these issues of language variation with reference to indigenous minority languages, immigrant minority languages and societal majority languages. First, I examine the debates on the standard that often arise in situations of indigenous minority language revitalization. I contrast situations where the standard language and purism ideologies prevail (e.g. Quechua and Breton) with the Corsican approach of *polynomie*, which is informed by an ideology of linguistic tolerance. With regard to immigrant minority languages, we will see that here, too, the standard language and purism ideologies often prevail, even in extracurricular language learning and teaching environments such as the complementary school system in the UK.

In the case of majority languages, we find a major split depending on whether the non-standard variety is used by the dominant group in society or by an oppressed group. I look at how Swiss German and Cypriot Greek are successfully built on in the Swiss and Cypriot education systems in order to lead students towards acquisition of standard German and Standard Modern Greek. In contrast, non-standard varieties such as African-American English (AAE) or Singlish (Singapore English) tend to be denigrated or banned from classrooms, as will be shown in the discussion in Chapter 5 (on the USA) and Chapter 7 (on Singapore). In the final sections of this chapter, I examine the slowly increasing use of pidgins and creoles in education, with a specific focus on Seychellois Creole, Hawai'i Creole English and Nigerian Pidgin English.

Standardizing Indigenous Minority Languages

How (not) to standardize 1: Quechua

Quechua (or Kechwa) is an indigenous language spoken by over 10 million people in Peru, Ecuador, Bolivia, as well as in Colombia, Argentina and Chile, though with much smaller numbers of speakers. Apart from the authentic (*auténtico*) varieties used by mostly older, rural speakers, there is also a standard variety taught at schools: Unified (*unificado*) Quechua. While the *auténtico* varieties are often mixed with Spanish, the *unificado* standard constitutes an attempt to go back to the traditional, 'pure' Quechua of the past, free from Spanish influence. However, the search for such a 'pure' standard has led to major debates, including in particular the question of whether Quechua should be written with five vowels, like Spanish, or only three vowels (i, a, and u; see Hornberger, 1995).

On the one hand, Peruvian linguists, mostly from universities in Lima, have argued for the three-vowel position, with 'i' pronounced as /e/ and 'u' pronounced as /o/ when they occur in proximity to 'q'. On the other hand, members of the Peruvian Academy of the Quechua Language in Cusco, which was founded in 1953 with the explicit aim of promoting Quechua, take up a position of resistance against the domination of the Lima linguists. The academy members are used to writing Quechua with five vowels and are reluctant to change; they argue that five vowels are needed since all five vowels are pronounced.

In their discussion of these debates, Hornberger and King (1998) suggest a solution based on linguistic tolerance. They argue that the most important thing is to encourage the greatest possible use of Quechua in whatever form, with Unified Quechua varieties potentially used more in formal, written communication and authentic varieties more in informal, spoken communication. They also insist that it is essential for schools to build on the children's actual home linguistic resources. Excellent work in this respect was done as part of the Experimental Bilingual Education Project of Puno, Peru, in the 1980s (Hornberger & López, 1998). Field-based studies were carried out into the varieties of Quechua used at home by five- to six-year-olds, and the results of these studies informed curriculum development and classroom materials production (Hornberger & López, 1998: 213).

Furthermore, Hornberger and King (1998) warn that the opposite attitude of linguistic intolerance can lead to community polarization and jeopardize the chances of revitalizing the Quechua language. An example of such community polarization is discussed by Wroblewski (2012). His study focuses upon language attitudes of indigenous speakers in Tena, the provincial capital city of the upper Napo River region in Ecuador (as we will see in Chapter 4, the language is known as Quichua or Kichwa in Ecuador). Wroblewski found active resistance against Unified Quichua, which was seen as something alien and imposed from outside, and support for the local Tena Quichua dialect, which was considered to be emblematic of local Amazonian identity and ethnicity.

How (not) to standardize 2: Breton

Just like Quechua/Quichua, Breton has recently undergone a transformation from spoken vernacular to written standard. Breton is a Celtic language spoken in Brittany, especially the western part, and exists in a number of regional varieties. In a country where one language, namely French, is all-powerful, the number of Breton speakers has been steadily declining and the traditional forms of the language can be considered endangered. Since the 1970s, the language revitalization movement has fostered the creation of a new standard, usually referred to as *néo-breton*, which is now taught especially in the Diwan schools, private schools providing immersion education in Breton. *Néo-breton* is thus the educated variety mostly used by young, middle-class people in urban areas, whereas the traditional varieties are mostly spoken by older, working-class people in rural areas. Because of the considerable differences between *néo-breton* and the traditional varieties, the former is sometimes unintelligible to native speakers of Breton and, moreover, the rural native speakers of Breton sometimes (are made to) feel that their Breton is inferior, 'bad' or 'incorrect':

There was, among these native-speakers, a growing awareness that their Breton was 'mixed' with French, a fact which 'those people' [i.e. speakers of *néo-breton*] often discussed. Their daily Breton was not really 'good Breton' ... because *'deformet eo toud'* (it's all deformed). (McDonald, 1989: 285)

On the other hand, the differences between *néo-breton* and the traditional varieties can also imply that the former is looked upon as an artificial or non-authentic variety. This is something that happens quite frequently when indigenous languages are standardized: we have already seen the example of Quechua/Quichua in the previous section and, to give just one more example, in Chapter 10, I discuss the case of standard Setswana, which is taught in schools in some parts of South Africa but which is very different from the vernacular or 'Street Setswana' spoken by most people. In this way, standardization, instead of contributing to language maintenance, can potentially reinforce the tendency towards language shift if people fail to identify with or if they feel alienated from the standard variety. As we will see, this seems to be happening with standard Setswana. As for Breton, language activists claim that, since the traditional varieties are on the whole only spoken by older people, it was essential for language revitalization to develop a variety that schools could pass on to the younger generation. In other words, the 'price to pay' to keep Breton alive may be the disappearance of the traditional varieties of Breton. And because it is used by a new generation of young speakers, *néo-breton* may be the variety with the best chance of survival.

At the same time, it should be clear that learning Breton at school is not sufficient to ensure the survival of the language. The question is whether it will also be transmitted as a home language from one generation to the next. Note that this is not a matter of choosing Breton instead of French – an unlikely choice, considering the powerful position of French in France. It is much more a question of whether *néo-breton*-speaking parents will raise their children bilingually in French *and* Breton. But if it succeeds, the story of the survival of Breton will be, as Bentahila and Davies (1993) point out, not so much a story of language revitalization but of language transformation.

Corsican and the polynomic paradigm

In the case of the revitalization of Quechua/Quichua and Breton, we found that there are winners and losers: some speakers are included, but others are excluded. This is what Shohamy (2008) refers to as the costs of language policy. It is therefore important to make an effort to include all varieties and all speakers of a language. My example to illustrate this is the revitalization of Corsican.

Like Breton, Corsican is an endangered regional language of France that exists in a number of varieties. But unlike with Breton in Brittany, where the revitalization movement tried to impose a new standard upon on the community of speakers, Corsican has traditionally been constructed as a 'polynomic' or pluricentric language. The polynomic approach involves a positive response to linguistic variation, advocating linguistic tolerance and respect for all the different varieties of Corsican and thus attempting to include all the speakers of Corsican in the revitalization project. No single linguistic norm is considered to be the only 'correct' one. In this way, the ideology of polynomy is the very opposite of the standard language ideology, and, as a result, the teaching of Corsican in Corsican schools, informed as it is by the former ideology, is very different from the teaching of French, which is informed by the latter.

In her ethnographic study of language ideologies in Corsica, Jaffe (2005) notes that Corsican tends to be taught in a more communicative way than French does, with much less emphasis on spelling and grammar. Moreover, Corsican spelling conventions as defined in the 1973 manual *Intricciate è Cambiarine*, which is widely used in educational contexts, are informed by the polynomic principle: they are variable rules sensitive to 'dialectal' variation. In other words, the spelling of words is dependent on their pronunciation. Jaffe (2005: 290) gives the example of the pronoun *we*, which in Corsican is written *noscia* if it is pronounced /noša/, but is written *nostra* if it is pronounced /nostra/. Jaffe also records that the two teachers in the classrooms that she observed always responded positively to dialectal variations in their students' oral and written productions. She argues that this may be due to the fact that in teacher training the polynomic approach has been, as it were, 'normalized' for Corsican (Jaffe, 2005: 296).

Thus, the Corsican language teachers legitimated multiple pronunciations and multiple spellings. Here are some of the things that one teacher said in classroom situations:

Ciò chè vo dite, pudeti scrivela. (If you say it, you can write it [the way you say it]).

Vo ùn seti micca di u mo paesi, un sò micca di u vostru … dite a vostra, dicu a meia, ùn hè micca quistione di impone. (You aren't from my village/town and I'm not from yours … you say it your way and I say it my way, there's no question of imposing [one spelling or pronunciation]). (Jaffe, 2013: 6)

According to Jaffe (2013: 6), the second example illustrates particularly well 'the principles of reciprocity and respect: no speaker, not even a teacher, has the authority to impose his or her variety on another'.

However, there were also limits to the polynomic approach. Whereas *polynomie* as dialectal diversity was widely accepted by teachers, *polynomie* as a result of language contact was not so easily accepted. Jaffe (2008, 2011) recounts an episode where the local carpenter, Mr Ottaviani, was invited to the school as an 'authentic' speaker of Corsican. He talked to the students about his tools but used mixed Corsican–French, for instance saying 'u crayon' (the pencil; from French) instead of 'pure' Corsican 'a minna' (Jaffe, 2008: 229). Interestingly, Jaffe (2008: 230–231) notes that the words the teacher wrote on the board were only the 'pure' Corsican words and none of Mr Ottaviani's loanwords. She comments as follows:

> Within the school, the teachers were also trying to counteract the dominance of French in the children's lives and practices, which made French influences on their own (or others') Corsican problematic. (Jaffe, 2008: 232–233)

There is a conflict here between authenticity and authority: though Mr Ottaviani is an authentic speaker, the teachers have the authority to decide what good or bad Corsican is. Jaffe (2011: 220–221) expresses the hope that this conflict could be solved within the framework of a plurilingual European citizenship, which would constitute the basis for a more flexible approach to multilingualism and would recognize all language practices, including those marked by contact phenomena such as Mr Ottaviani's, as authentic. She also notes that a more flexible approach is easier for teachers to take as soon as the hegemonic pressures of French are no longer present. Thus, for instance, in bilingual Corsican–French schools that also teach Italian as a first foreign language, she found students engaging in school projects 'in which the fluidity of language boundaries between Corsican and Italian is the object of play, appreciation, and exploration of what it means to have a multilingual repertoire' (Jaffe, 2011: 221).

Immigrant Minority Languages and Complementary Schools in England

In England, education policy related to issues of linguistic and ethnic diversity has been strongly influenced by the Swann Report, *Education for All*, published in 1985. It addressed the needs of bilingual students, especially those of Caribbean and South Asian descent, though it failed to endorse any form of bilingual education. It stressed the need to teach English as a second or additional language by relying on bilingual support staff. Thus, bilingual minority students are given language support by an English as an additional language (EAL) teacher working collaboratively with the class teacher, as a way of helping these students to cope with the English-only mainstream classroom (Creese 2005).

However, in the early 1990s, issues of diversity were increasingly sidelined with the introduction of the national curriculum, along with national testing for 7, 11 and 14 year olds. Instead, more emphasis was put on the acquisition of standard English (without taking into account ethnic and linguistic diversity), and a discourse of blaming the victim became commonplace: if students did badly in the new system, it must be that they themselves were to blame. The New Labour government of Tony Blair, elected in 1997, raised expectations that it would at last tackle educational exclusion. In practice, however, its National Literacy Strategy of 1998, with the 'Literacy Hour' as its centrepiece, only reinforced the free-market ideology of the education system and the accompanying emphasis on imparting standard English (see e.g. Harris *et al.*, 2002).

The marginalization of minority communities and their languages is reflected in the fact that these communities have been left to themselves to organize classes in their own languages outside the state education sector. Such community language classes, which usually run in the evenings or at the weekend, are frequently referred to in the UK as 'supplementary' or 'complementary' schools. Moreover, these complementary schools tend to see themselves as teaching not only proficiency in the community language but also the cultural values of the community. In this section, I report on the interesting results of a recent study of complementary schools by Blackledge and Creese (2010), who carried out ethnographic work in classrooms where community languages such as Turkish, Bengali, Gujarati, Cantonese and Mandarin were taught. I focus in particular on a number of issues about the nature of language and heritage arising in connection with, first, Turkish and then, in greater detail, with Bengali, the official language of Bangladesh.

In all the complementary schools where Blackledge and Creese (2010: 24), together with their co-researchers, investigated linguistic practices and the construction and negotiation of identities, they found a pervasive tension between 'two ideological positions: one characterized by heteroglossic, flexible linguistic production which indexed multicultural cosmopolitanism, the other rooted in linguistic affiliation to national and cultural heritage'. They refer to these positions as flexible and separate bilingualism, a distinction which is very similar to the one I have drawn between flexible and fixed multilingualism in Chapter 1. Separate bilingualism tended to be the institutional ideology of the schools, with teachers and administrators looking upon the separation or compartmentalization of languages as necessary to ensure the maintenance of the minority language. However, actual classroom practices, not only of the students themselves, but also in teacher– student interactions, tended to be much more mixed, with both English and the minority language being flexibly drawn upon to get the classroom work done. Moreover, we will see that, when teachers tried to enforce the ideology of separate bilingualism, this often met with contestation and resistance from students.

Cypriot Turkish: The dominance of the standard language and purism ideologies

I start with a brief example which shows that language hierarchies informed by the standard language and purism ideologies can be found not only in mainstream education but also in heritage language education. The example is derived from the research project mentioned in the previous section, involving ethnographic work in a Turkish complementary school in London, which was attended by a large number of students with a Cypriot-Turkish background (Lytra *et al.*, 2010). In one particular student–teacher interaction, the student relies on gestures to let the teacher know that she needs a pen. The teacher uses this opportunity to teach the students the Turkish word for 'pen', and praises the student for avoiding the use of the Cypriot-Turkish word *penna*. Lytra *et al.* (2010) argue that the teacher here insists on the separation of *temiz Türkçe* (clean, uncontaminated or standard Turkish) and the Cypriot-Turkish variety used as a home language by most of the students, and sets up a linguistic hierarchy between them:

> In this example, the teacher and pupil privilege the use of the standard Turkish word *tükenmez* over the Cypriot-Turkish equivalent *penna* for <pen>. These linguistic hierarchies are rooted in the marginalized position of Cypriot-Turkish and the stigmatization of regional varieties of Turkish, particularly regional accents, with respect to standard Turkish. (Lytra *et al.*, 2010: 30)

Bengali or Sylheti?: Student contestation and resistance

In their study of Bengali complementary schools in Birmingham, Blackledge and Creese (2010: 111) quote an example where a teacher insists on the students speaking Bengali 'because tumi Bangali' (because you are Bengali). But her demand meets with student resistance, with one student insisting on the right to choose between languages ('miss you can choose') and adducing the example of a member of her family who, while of Bangladeshi heritage, consistently code-switches into English: 'My aunty chose it, she speaks English all the time' (Blackledge & Creese, 2010: 111). This example illustrates the clash between the ideologies of separate (or fixed) and flexible bilingualism. What is particularly interesting here is that while explicitly adhering to the ideology of separate bilingualism, the teacher actually mixes English and the minority language in her own linguistic practice when she says, 'because tumi Bangali'.

Another interesting example given in Blackledge and Creese (2010: 173) is where a teacher pronounces a student's name in the Bengali way as /Jaara/, and one of the other students corrects him in the following way: 'Z-a-h-r-a. In school we call her Zahra, in school we call her Zahra'. /Zahra/ is the anglicized pronunciation of the name, which is widely used in the mainstream school that these students attend. Thus, the student seems to resist the complementary school ideology of keeping the minority language separate from English. In general, these examples show that complementary schools often attempt to impose fixed, reified 'heritage identities' upon the students, but the imposition of these heritage values is sometimes contested and flexibly renegotiated by the students.

However, this is only the first half of the story. Apart from keeping the heritage language separate from English, many complementary schoolteachers and administrators also attempted to keep the standard variety of the heritage language separate from non-standard varieties. Bengali is the standard language, while many students actually use a non-standard language (Sylheti) as their home language (alongside English). But many teachers insisted on teaching the students what they considered to be the 'pure' form of the language, and looked down upon the variety spoken in the students' families. In this way, the complementary schools reproduced the mainstream society's ideology of purism: just as mainstream society values standard or 'proper' English above non-standard varieties, the complementary schools valued standard or 'proper' Bengali above Sylheti.

In fact, in the eyes of many teachers, standard Bengali had come to represent the 'heritage' of the Bangladeshi nation. They looked upon it as 'a vital symbol of the founding of the Bangladeshi nation' because of the tragic pro-Bengali protests back in 1952 in which 'the "language martyrs" were killed while demonstrating against the imposition of Urdu as the national language by West Pakistan' (Blackledge & Creese, 2010: 188–189). When Bangladesh split off from Pakistan in 1971, Bengali (also called Bangla) was chosen as the official language, although many languages are spoken in the country. As a result, the complementary school teachers felt they had to protect the purity of Bengali by keeping it separate not only from English but also from other languages of Bangladesh such as Sylheti. One school administrator said that 'Sylheti should not be allowed to "contaminate" the standard form' (Blackledge & Creese, 2010: 169). Another one insisted that 'when you talk about language it means Bengali, Sylheti is not a language' (Blackledge & Creese, 2010: 170). On the whole, the representatives of the institution, who were themselves speakers of standard Bengali, emphasized the difference between Bengali and Sylheti, as well as the superiority of the former. This notion of superiority was also frequently extended to the speakers of the standard variety: they considered Bengali to be the language of educated people, while they looked down upon speakers of Sylheti as uneducated, poor and lower-class people.

Interestingly, these prejudiced assessments were contested by the speakers of Sylheti (some parents, the students themselves), who sometimes looked upon speakers of Bengali as snobs and show-offs. At the same time, the speakers of Sylheti tended to emphasize the similarities between Sylheti and Bengali, and they sometimes even considered the two varieties to be more or less identical. These diverging ideological positions thus raise questions both about what constitutes 'a language' and what constitutes 'heritage'. And on the whole, it is the young students in Blackledge and Creese's study who show us the most flexible and sophisticated responses when they contest and subvert the adults' essentialized notions of language and heritage.

Vernacular Varieties of Societal Majority Languages

Swiss German

Switzerland's multilingualism is based on a strict principle of territoriality: the four national languages, German, French, Italian and Romansch, are official regional languages in different parts of the country. In their education system, the Swiss traditionally learn the official language of their territory as their first language (L1) and another Swiss national language as their second language (L2) – though we will see that this is in the process of changing.

Thus, for instance, in the German-speaking part of Switzerland, the schoolchildren traditionally learn L1 German and L2 French. The complicating factor in the German-speaking part of Switzerland is the widespread use of non-standard German varieties, usually referred to as Schwyzertüütsch (Swiss German). According to Watts (1999: 69), Swiss German has served as the most powerful marker of local Swiss identity at least since World War II, and its symbolic value is perceived to be much higher than that of standard German in all domains except the written medium. Many Swiss

Germans look upon Swiss German as their mother tongue, while they refer to *Schriftdeutsch* (written or standard German) as their first foreign language. Watts reaches the interesting conclusion that there is no danger of the Swiss German varieties dying out and that

> it is the oral forms of language which guarantee survival, not the written forms. In fact, Switzerland might even give the lie to the hypothesis that only a written standard can guarantee the survival of a language. (Watts, 1999: 95)

At the same time, however, the Swiss German varieties are seen as obstacles to communication in the other parts of Switzerland. For instance, the French Swiss usually learn standard German as their L2, yet they often find it easier to communicate with the German Swiss in English (usually learnt as their third language [L3]). This is because many German Swiss resent using standard German and prefer to use their Swiss German varieties which, however, are difficult for the French Swiss to understand. So, it is not surprising that English thrives in such a situation.

Yet, it was not in French-speaking Switzerland but in the heartland of German-speaking Switzerland that an initiative was first taken that upset the Swiss language policy balance. At the beginning of the 21st century, the canton of Zurich introduced English as the first foreign language in its primary schools (instead of French), thus giving priority to English over the Swiss national languages. This caused controversy leading to a major language ideological debate frequently referred to as the *Sprachenstreit* (language strife; see Stotz, 2006). According to Grin and Korth (2005: 79–80), questions such as the following were raised as part of these debates: Will English become the lingua franca of Switzerland? Will this undermine Swiss national unity? Is the future of the country endangered?

Another ongoing debate in German-speaking Switzerland is the use of Swiss German or standard German as the medium of instruction in pre-school education. This is linked to the question of whether Swiss German or standard German is the language of 'integration'. In the canton Zurich, for instance, the medium of instruction in kindergarten was largely Swiss German up to 2000. However, after the publication of the rather unsatisfactory results of the first Programme for International Student Assessment (PISA) tests in 2001, more emphasis was put on standard German, though in practice many teachers and students continued to use a lot of code-switching between the two varieties. Ten years later, on 15 May 2011, the wheel had turned again, with the adoption of the citizens' initiative *'JA zur Mundart im Kindergarten'* (YES to the dialect in preschool education), with 54% of the votes. According to the manifesto of this initiative, Swiss German is to be used as the default medium of instruction in preschool education, with the double aim of developing 'bilingualism in the one language' (*zweisprachig in der einen Sprache*; Schwarzenbach, 2011: 4) in all children and enabling migrant children to 'integrate' into Swiss society in the best possible way.

Despite these ongoing debates about language-in-education policy in German-speaking Switzerland, the school system has been highly successful in building on students' Swiss German varieties and developing in students a high level of proficiency in standard German. A major reason for this may well be that the Swiss German varieties are positively valued throughout society and that they are used by speakers of all social classes. In the following section, I look at a very similar sociolinguistic situation in the Greek-speaking part of Cyprus.

Cypriot Greek

From 1878 to 1960, Cyprus was a British colony, when an independent Cypriot state, the Republic of Cyprus, was established. The official languages of the Republic of Cyprus are Standard Modern Greek and Turkish, though people mostly use local varieties of Greek or Turkish. However, in 1974, a war broke out between the Greek-speaking and Turkish-speaking communities, which led to the geographical separation of the two communities. This means that Cypriot Greek is now widely used in the Greek-speaking part of the island, whereas Cypriot Turkish is used in the north of the island, where the Turkish-speaking community lives. While earlier in the chapter, I discussed an example involving the use of Cypriot Turkish, in this section I focus on the Cypriot Greek community. Its members' identities are closely linked with the use of both Cypriot Greek and Standard Modern Greek. The relative values attached to each of these varieties are directly connected with the political dimension of whether Cyprus is seen as 'a part of the Greek nation or an autonomous independent state', whether the Greek Cypriots see themselves as 'being more Greek and less Cypriot or the opposite' and whether they look upon Turkish Cypriots 'as being the enemy, the brothers or an equal ethnic group in Cyprus' (Ioannidou, 2007: 167). It would seem that in recent years, there has been a gradual strengthening of Greek Cypriot identity, along with an ongoing revalorization of Cypriot Greek in society.

One noticeable aspect of this is the increasing interest on the part of Cypriot sociolinguists in 'bidialectal' education. Until recently, official language-in-education policies had always advocated the use of Standard Modern Greek in schools, while Cypriot Greek was excluded from the classroom environment. However, this policy could easily lead to feelings of disenfranchisement and linguistic insecurity among students. As two of Ioannidou's (2007) informants – both 10- to 11-year-old students in an urban primary school – put it:

> Agis: When I speak Greek I feel, how can I say it, I FEEL LIKE I AM A STRANGER because most of us in Cyprus, we speak Cypriot, miss, this ain't my real language.
> Menelaos: I feel more comfortable using Cypriot because I know it better than Greek, and sometimes when I speak Greek I get confused so I can speak Cypriot more easily, I speak Cypriot much better, definitely. (Ioannidou, 2007: 188; capital letters in original)

In practice, therefore, many teachers and students rely on extensive code-switching between Cypriot Greek and Standard Modern Greek. Yiakoumetti (2006) discusses ways of building on these code-switching practices: if seen in a positive light, Cypriot Greek can be strategically employed by teachers in order to make their students aware of both the similarities and the differences between the two varieties and, ultimately, to lead them towards (even) higher proficiency in the standard. Yiakoumetti carried out a pilot project along these lines in some Cyprus schools, and the results were convincing:

> The evidence indicates that focusing bidialectal students' attention on the formal properties of their two dialectal varieties facilitates an increased rate of second-dialect development. Moreover, the project confirmed that the ability to consciously identify differences between two varieties enhances performance in the variety which is targeted for improvement. (Yiakoumetti, 2006: 312)

Thus, the use of Cypriot Greek in the classroom had positive effects on students' learning of the standard, leading to less, rather than more, 'dialectal interference'. Under the influence of such well-informed sociolinguistic studies, there has been an increasing emphasis on the importance of fostering a metalinguistic awareness in students with regard to the two varieties, Cypriot Greek and Standard Modern Greek, which are in daily use in society. According to Ioannidou (2012: 224), the new 2010 curriculum for the first time explicitly addresses the issue of language variation and stresses the need for the pedagogical use of Cypriot Greek in the classroom in order to 'enhance [students'] competence both in the standard language and in the dialect'.

Towards an Increased Use of Pidgins and Creoles in Education

Seychellois Creole

Just like Yiakoumetti's project trialling the use of Cypriot Greek in class-rooms in Cyprus, many successful educational programmes have built on students' proficiency in pidgins or creoles in an additive way over the last few decades. I discuss the case of pidgin and creole languages in the final section of this chapter, because they are often perceived, even by their own speakers, as non-standard varieties. Their use in education has helped with the revaluation of these languages, though others are still widely stigmatized. The main creole languages which are systematically used in education are Seychellois Creole in the Seychelles, Haitian Creole in Haiti, Tok Pisin in Papua New Guinea and Papiamentu in the Netherlands Antilles and Aruba.

In this section, I focus on Seychellois Creole (often called Seselwa) in the Seychelles, a chain of islands in the Indian Ocean. The Seychelles gained independence in 1976, after periods of French and British colonialism. Seychellois Creole is a French-based creole, which is spoken by over 90% of the population as their native language. The government of the newly independent state took the landmark decision to make Seychellois Creole its third official language, alongside English and French. In 1981, Seychellois Creole was introduced as a medium of instruction primarily in the first four years of education, with a gradual shift to English as the medium of instruction from Year 3 onwards and with French also being used as an additional medium of instruction at a later stage.

This trilingual system of education has been highly successful, leading to 'significant increases in rates of graduation, proficiency, literacy, and continuing education' (Laversuch, 2008: 379). Nevertheless, there have been criticisms of the use of creole in education, and a more monolingual type of education in English only has been advocated. In fact, it seems that the government has recently taken some steps in this direction; in particular, the 2001 Creole Curriculum policy document of the Ministry of Education has restricted the use of Seychellois Creole as a medium of instruction to the first two years of education and, moreover, French is now taught only as a subject (i.e. it is no longer used as a medium of instruction; Laversuch, 2008: 382).

These changes have reinforced the dominant role of English in the education system. They are in line with societal attitudes that look upon English as the language with the highest instrumental value and as the key to upward social mobility. Indeed, English is not only important in the tourist industry, alongside French, but it is also increasingly used for doing business not just with the UK and the USA but also with many other countries such as China. French, on the other hand, suffers from society's negative perceptions of it as the language of colonial oppression, because the period of French colonialism was experienced by most Seychellois as far more oppressive than the period of English colonialism. Finally, it should be remembered that Seychellois Creole is used far more than English and French, but it is often seen as a language 'appropriate only for informal, private uses' (Laversuch, 2008: 387).

For these reasons, it is easy to predict that if there were a shift to English-only monolingual education, many Seychellois students would face great difficulties at school. The present system of multilingual education is much better suited to this multilingual society: it builds on children's home linguistic resources as the best possible way of leading them towards proficiency in English and French. The only issues of concern are, first, the flexibility of the system and secondly, the role of French. Concerning the flexibility of the system, it may be possible to introduce an even more gradual shift in the medium of instruction from Seychellois Creole to English; as for French, its role as a medium of instruction has already been curtailed and its future place in the education system depends on what role it will continue to play in the Seychelles society as a whole.

From Hawai'i Creole English to Nigerian Pidgin English

The state of Hawai'i recognizes two official languages: English and Hawaiian, a Polynesian language. Moreover, many people use Hawai'i Creole, an English-based creole, as one of their home languages, and there is a wide range of immigrant minority languages such as Tagalog, Ilokano and Samoan. Hawai'i Creole English is still widely stigmatized in Hawaiian society, though there have been numerous endeavours to re-evaluate the language. In the area of education, Siegel (1999, 2010) discusses a number of programmes involving the successful use of Hawai'i Creole English, which have been run in Hawai'i since the 1980s. They include Project Holopono ('success') and Project Akamai ('smart'), both of which involved contrastive analysis of the linguistic features of Hawai'i Creole English and (standard) English. In another programme of writing workshops for second graders speaking Hawai'i Creole English, the children were encouraged to write in whatever linguistic variety they preferred and gradually became more proficient in written standard English 'through a process of modelling and recasting rather than correction' (Siegel, 1999: 708).

According to Siegel (2006, 2010), the most promising programmes are critical awareness programmes that involve both studying the differences between the varieties and analyzing the roles that these varieties play in society. A recent educational programme for heritage language speakers in Hawai'i – that Siegel does not mention – is the Studies of Heritage and Academic Languages and Literacies (SHALL) project set up by Davis (2009) and colleagues. It attempts to bring about more equitable educational practices for all students by putting them into the roles of critical researchers. Thus, for instance, in a Hawaiian high school the participating students were mostly speakers of heritage languages such as Ilokano and Samoan, as well as Hawai'i Creole English as their L1 and L2. They took combined heritage and academic English language classes and, as part of their coursework, they explored the marginalization of (in particular) Hawai'i Creole English (referred to as 'Pidgin' in the following quotation) in such institutional settings as school. The aim was to help students develop their heritage, local and academic English language abilities and identities, all at the same time, through activities such as the following:

> Students engaged in textual analysis through oral history assignments in which they used their heritage language and/or Pidgin to interview family or community members. They then translated the interview into academic English and conducted analyses of the syntactic, phonological and lexical similarities and differences between their heritage language and English. This and other comparison and contrast assignments helped students develop metalinguistic awareness of academic English rhetoric as well as promoted new or enhanced multilingual literacy practices. (Davis, 2009: 214)

In this way, participants were enabled to gradually move from 'at risk' and 'failing' to 'successful and capable' student identities. In fact, in all the programmes discussed in this section, it was found that the approach of building on students' home varieties in a positive and additive way led to a significant improvement in their academic performance, including their proficiency in standard English.

However, many other pidgins and creoles are widely stigmatized in society and are not used in education. One example is Nigerian Pidgin English, which is widely spoken in Nigeria but is not officially recognized and plays no (official) role in education. Nigeria is a highly multilingual country with English and three regional indigenous languages – Hausa, Yoruba and Igbo – as its main languages. While English is used by the educated elite, Nigerian Pidgin English often functions as an interethnic lingua franca in urban interactions, as the language of trade in marketplaces and as the language of entertainment and culture in the media and literature.

As with Singlish in Singapore, more and more people actually speak Nigerian Pidgin English, either as their L2 or even their L1; yet it is stigmatized as 'bad' English and has a low status because it is mostly associated with poor and uneducated speakers. According to Adegbija (2004: 226), it is a 'solidarity and intimacy language' and 'the most effective language of national mobilization and motivation at the grassroots level'. He therefore concludes that, given its 'widespread and far-ranging functions in the nation, Nigerian Pidgin deserves mention in Nigeria's language policy provisions' (Adegbija, 2004: 227). Wolf and Igboanusi (2006: 346) are even more explicit in stating that for many children the use of Nigerian Pidgin as their L1 in early education would be a pedagogically sound measure. Indeed, it is important to take into account all the children's linguistic resources and to build the best possible education system on these foundations. However, as we have seen in this chapter, it is much easier to get politicians, policy makers and teachers to act upon this principle if the vernacular variety in question is valued positively in society, as is the case with Swiss German, than if it is stigmatized, as is the case with Nigerian Pidgin English.

Conclusion

In all the contexts that we looked at in this chapter, there seems to be an urgent need to move towards multilingual pedagogies and teaching methods that are more tolerant of linguistic variation. This is the case not only for indigenous and immigrant minority languages but also for societal majority languages. An attitude of linguistic tolerance is always the best way of empowering learners and helping them to acquire the standard variety. While this is most easily achieved with vernacular varieties of societal majority languages used by the dominant group, the negative attitudes quickly resurface in the case of non-standard varieties used by oppressed groups in society, such as Nigerian Pidgin English, AAE (see Chapter 5) and Singlish (Chapter 7).

The most successful pedagogical approaches in this respect involve putting students into the roles of critical researchers in an attempt to bring about more equitable educational practices (as in the SHALL project in Hawai'i discussed above). They can be encouraged to critically explore the marginalization of vernacular varieties in such institutional settings as school, and their denigration in society as a whole. They can write texts using their own voice, and then translate them into more academic language. In the process, they can analyse the phonological, syntactic, lexical and pragmatic differences between standard and non-standard varieties. The overall aim would be to enable students to develop their heritage, local and global language abilities, and in the process to foster successful student identities.

As a way of building on students' home linguistic varieties, teachers should be encouraged to use code-switching between varieties, whether 'languages', 'dialects', registers or styles. Even if students' home variety is negatively valued in society (as with AAE), teachers can still build on the variety in a positive way in the classroom and use it strategically as a way of scaffolding students' learning and facilitating their access to academic standard discourses. Where students' home variety is more positively valued (as with Swiss German and Cypriot Greek), it will be more socially acceptable for teachers to officially include the variety in classroom work. I conclude that, to different degrees depending on the social situation, the Corsican paradigm of *polynomie* and its associated ideal of linguistic tolerance could usefully be applied to language learning and teaching in general.

3 The Issue of Access

In this chapter, I explore the question of access to high-quality language teaching and learning. First, I critically discuss the restrictive language-in-education policy of francophone Canada and its impact upon minority language students. Then, I analyse the Welsh language situation in order to show how difficult it is to find the right balance between choice and compulsion. My argument is that what is of prime importance is access rather than choice (see further discussion of this issue in Chapter 10), and my next example in this chapter is the Māori community in New Zealand and how their students' access to English has been improved by the gradual shift from fixed Māori-medium to more flexible bilingual education programmes. The final example of some inadequacies in the teaching and learning of English in Malaysia further illustrates the importance of quality of access for all students.

Issues of Access in the Education System of Francophone Canada

The Canadian policy of bilingualism and multiculturalism

According to the Canadian 2001 census data (as reported in Duff, 2008: 74), Canada has about 30 million inhabitants, 17.4 million of whom have English as their first language (L1) and 6.7 million have French as their L1. Other important 'mother tongues' include Chinese (various varieties of Chinese), Italian and German. The largest indigenous languages are Cree (about 70,000 speakers) and Inuktitut (about 29,000 speakers). Canada has a federal government and is divided into 10 provinces and 3 territories. The provinces have jurisdiction over education, and the territories, too, have gradually gained the right to deal with matters of education. The fact that English and French are the official languages goes back to a history of colonization by Britain and France.

In the 1960s, the French-speaking province, Quebec, started the 'Quiet Revolution' movement in order to gain more power and control for francophones. This led to the passing of the Canadian Official Languages Act in 1969, which enshrined French–English bilingualism, requiring all federal institutions to provide services in both the official languages and ensuring the right to L1-medium education for francophone minorities outside Quebec as well as anglophone minorities in Quebec. From the 1970s, Canada also pursued a policy of multiculturalism, which eventually led to the passing of the Multiculturalism Act in 1988. Canada thus sees itself in terms of the 'mosaic' metaphor rather than the US metaphor of the 'melting pot'. Whereas the melting pot metaphor suggests assimilation, the Canadian metaphor of a cultural mosaic promotes – nominally at least – respect and support not only for the two official languages but also for all the languages and cultures in Canada. The ideology is one of cultural pluralism within the official bilingual framework. At the same time, it should be noted that the Canadian multicultural policy has often been accused of being rather superficial and merely celebratory (see e.g. Bannerji, 2000).

In the area of education, French immersion programmes have been implemented throughout the country since the 1960s. One of the aims is to allow anglophone majority group children to learn French, using a content and language integrated learning (CLIL)-type of instruction, with various school subjects such as biology and history taught through the medium of French. As a way of validating the official policy of multiculturalism, such immersion programmes were gradually extended to the indigenous languages. Children are frequently taught in their indigenous language as the primary medium of education during their first few years of education or, if they no longer speak it at home, immersion programmes are used in an attempt to revitalize the language (see Burnaby, 1996).

Quebec francophone nationalism

French is the majority language in Quebec, but it is a minority language in Canada as a whole. As a result, many Quebeckers feel that French is endangered and needs to be protected against English and to be defended in what some Quebeckers see as hostile anglophone surroundings. For this reason, Quebec has opted for a policy of French monolingualism, which goes against the federal Canadian policy of bilingualism and multiculturalism. Quebec francophone nationalism has been on the rise since the 1960s, often with a separatist agenda. Two referenda were held on the question of Quebec's sovereignty in 1980 and 1995, but neither of them were passed.

In the 1970s, Quebec adopted restrictive language policies in order to preserve and promote the use of French. In particular, Bill 101 (Charter of the French Language, 1977) included a number of restrictive clauses, for instance, forcing 'allophones' (new immigrants whose mother tongue is neither French nor English) to enrol their children in French-medium schools and requiring all commercial signage to be in French only. Restrictions were even placed on the amount of time allocated to English instruction in French schools, which effectively made bilingual education impossible (Lamarre & Dagenais, 2004: 59). These clauses were sources of tension and led to legal challenges, as a result of which some aspects of Bill 101 were ruled to be unconstitutional. Consequently, some of the language restrictions were gradually relaxed in the 1990s (see May, 2001: 229).

With both francophones and allophones forced to attend French language state schools, access to English language state schools is limited to the anglophone minority in Quebec. To get around this, some parents enrolled their children in a private English language school for one year, after which they could legitimately apply to be admitted to an English language state school. However, since private schools tend to charge high fees, this was an option only open to well-off parents. As a way of putting an end to this practice, the Quebec government has adopted a further set of controversial laws aimed at further restricting parents' right to choose (for details, see Duchêne, 2012).

According to May (2001), the nationalists believe that for French to have a chance of survival, societal (and institutional) monolingualism in French is necessary in Quebec:

> Advocates of Bill 101 argue that the only way that individual bilingualism can be maintained and fostered is by, counterintuitively, setting strict limits on the extent of institutional bilingualism. (May, 2001: 231)

The advocates of Bill 101 argue that because of the all-powerful position of English in Canada as a whole, people will acquire English in any case and thus achieve individual bilingualism in French and English. However, many students' difficulties with academic English show that this does not work automatically and, as a result, the Quebec government has been considering the introduction of English immersion in the last year of primary school – a policy which is strongly resisted by some because they see it as a threat to the position of French. Furthermore, as Quebec has a lot of control over its immigration policy, there has also been a deliberate attempt to attract immigrants from French-speaking countries such as Haiti and the Democratic Republic of the Congo (formerly Zaire). But, as Edwards (2009: 185) notes, even though these immigrants speak French, this policy has led to increased intolerance, xenophobia and racism in society.

Youth bilingualism in Montreal

In 2009, a controversy broke out during the days leading up to Quebec's National Day celebrations, the *Fête de la St-Jean* (see Warren & Oakes, 2011:

12–13). One of the scheduled events, *L'autre St-Jean*, included a couple of anglophone musicians on the programme, who were due to perform in English. At the last minute, the decision was made to ban them from appearing, on the part of people who felt strongly that the whole of the St-Jean celebrations should be in French. This decision polarized the two communities: many anglophones felt discriminated against, and many members of the francophone community saw the anglophones again as 'the enemy'. Interestingly, however, the francophone community was divided between those 'who demanded that the French language be used exclusively in the celebrations' and those who favoured a more 'inclusive, pluralist Quebec, where French is the common, the most used, but not exclusive language' (Warren & Oakes, 2011: 13).

Despite these ongoing antagonisms and the official French-only policies, French–English bilingualism seems to be inexorably on the rise as far as linguistic practices are concerned. This is most obviously the case among young people in the Montreal area, which is the economic hub of Quebec and therefore also more cosmopolitan and heterogeneous than the rest of Quebec. According to Oakes and Warren (2007: 147), young people frequently engage in 'fluid, adaptive and varied bilingual or multilingual practices in a range of public spaces, from cafés and shopping centres to local health centres and public transport'. This applies to young people from all three communities: francophone, anglophone and allophone. Both francophones and anglophones are increasingly bilingual in French and English, while allophones are often tri-/multilingual in French, English and their heritage language(s). With their heteroglossic practices, these young people break down the traditional linguistic, ethnic and spatial boundaries of the city (see also Lamarre & Lamarre, 2009). Therefore, Warren and Oakes (2011: 16) conclude that it may be English–French bilingualism, rather than French only, that 'is acting as a positive force for unity in spite of periodic tensions that serve to "reactivate" the linguistic and cultural boundaries' between francophones and anglophones.

A French language school in anglophone Ontario: Individual bilingualism through institutional monolingualism

We find the same language policies and ideologies, as well as the same gap between policies and practices, in the educational setting of a French language school in anglophone Ontario. The francophone community in Ontario constitutes about 4.8% of the total population of Ontario. Heller (2006) has carried out a thorough ethnographic investigation of French language minority education in Ontario, showing how francophone state schools attempt to achieve individual (French–English) bilingualism through a policy of institutional monolingualism (in French). She also reveals how both francophone Canada as a whole and these francophone schools in particular were forced to adapt to the new global economy of services and communication.

The schools use French as the sole medium of instruction and in this way an attempt is made to turn the schools into French-only environments in order to ensure the survival of the French language and of the French-speaking communities. In a way, Quebec's territorial nationalism is here appropriated but simultaneously transformed into a form of institutional nationalism, via the creation of institutions (schools) run by and for francophones. The ultimate aim is to develop individual bilingualism in French and English in the students, with the assumption – already mentioned above – that they will acquire English in any case through living in an anglophone society, even if it is only taught as one subject among many others at school. Moreover, French–English bilingualism is understood as double monolingualism, with the students encouraged to keep the two languages separate, to avoid code-switching and, in particular, to cut all Anglicisms out of their French.

However, in order to survive, the schools have also had to attract English-speaking students as well as migrant students, both French-speaking migrants and allophones (who speak French though neither French nor English is their 'mother tongue'). In the French language high school in the Toronto area that Heller (2006) studied, Heller and her co-researchers found a highly heterogeneous school population consisting of the following three groups:

- speakers of French as their L1;
- middle-class anglophones wanting to become bilingual in English and French because such linguistic capital provides access to desirable jobs especially in the public sector;
- new immigrants from Somalia, Haiti, etc., who are speakers of French as their L1 or their second language (L2).

The school offered two streams which reproduced social stratification: a more advanced stream, where many of the middle-class francophone and anglophone students could be found, and a more vocational or 'general' stream, attended by many working-class French-Canadians, as well as Somalis, Haitians, and other new immigrants. The school tried to enforce the use of French, though this had the consequence that students frequently used English in 'backstage' events (i.e. not to the teachers but among themselves); in Heller's (2001: 389) words, English became 'available as a means of contesting [the school's] authority'.

However, there was also a clear difference between the advanced and 'general' classes as far as the French-only policy was concerned. In the latter classes, a much wider range of vernacular and contact varieties of French was used, and there was frequent code-switching into English by both students and teachers. In fact, only in the advanced-level French classes was the school ideology of institutional monolingualism in French strictly adhered to. Indeed, in these classes, teachers were found to insist on the 'right' kind of French, namely, standard Canadian French, while both 'the old imperialist-imposed standard of European French and the still-stigmatized Canadian French vernaculars' (Heller, 2001: 391) were rejected.

Thus, the school relied upon the twin ideologies of monolingualism and language quality (Heller, 2006: 78) in a continuing endeavour to create a French-only zone. However, the teachers, who were expected to implement the system of linguistic surveillance, were fighting a losing battle due to the importance of English in Canadian society and the school's need to accept anglophone students as a way of boosting its student enrolment. As a matter of fact, English was often used as a lingua franca among the students. In this situation, it is not surprising that the efforts of teachers of French focused primarily on eradicating all traces of contact with English. Heller (2006) provides numerous examples of teachers correcting their students' use of English loanwords and refers to this as *la chasse aux anglicismes* (the hunt for Anglicisms).

Exclusion through French, inclusion through English

At the same time, Heller shows that even though the school was supposed to be a French-only monolingual zone, students who entered the school with a high proficiency in French and a low (or no) proficiency in English often found themselves excluded and marginalized. This was often the case with French Canadian students from Quebec, as well as French-speaking immigrant students primarily from Somalia and Haiti. The former group found that, with the school's insistence on standard French, their own vernacular varieties of Canadian French were sometimes stigmatized both by teachers and other students. The same frequently happened with the varieties of French spoken by the Haitian and Somali students; moreover, these students' feelings of marginalization and alienation were compounded at least initially by the fact that they found it difficult to understand the Canadian French varieties used by many teachers and students.

Both the French Canadian and the francophone immigrant groups were also surprised to discover the important role played by English among the students, at least outside the official spaces of classroom teaching, and they quickly realized that they would need English in order to make friends. Interestingly, if bridges were built and new friendships were formed, this often happened through a shared interest in hip-hop music. Heller shows how this shared music culture not only especially helped the Somali students to improve their English but it also made it easier for these previously marginalized students to be fully included in the school community.

According to Heller (2006: 214), the contradictions between official policies and actual practices reflect the overall dilemma faced by the school of how to reconcile (French Canadian) authenticity with pluralism. The school had been born out of the ideology of linguistic nationalism, prevalent in Quebec since the 1960s, in an attempt to preserve an endangered language (French) and to resist the hegemony of English. However, the old politics of identity has been radically transformed in the new and changing global economy of services and information. As a result, the school has had to adapt itself to the growing heterogeneity of its student population. Thus, for instance, with the increasing number of Somali students, it became more problematic for teachers to present French as an oppressed language, since for these students it was the opposite, namely, the language of oppression. But what most students seemed to share was a belief in French as a means of social advancement in Canadian society. In this way, language was commodified, and the old politics of identity was gradually replaced by a new politics of linguistic capital. The school put greater value on standard French, even at the risk of losing (some of) the authenticating value of the French Canadian vernacular. The old vision of the *francophonie de souche* (local francophone communities with 'roots') gave way to a new vision of *francophonie internationale*.

A difficult situation for migrant students

We have seen how the migrant students in Heller's study managed to improve their conversational English through a shared interest in hip-hop culture, and as a result they gradually felt more included. However, for these students it is also important to acquire a high level of proficiency in academic English, which is needed both for higher education and employment in Ontario and anglophone Canada as a whole. As Hambye and Richards (2012: 179) point out, this group of students want to acquire French–English bilingualism primarily for economic reasons and not because of a sense of belonging to the Franco-Ontarian community. Yet, the schools, as we have seen, are constructed as monolingual French spaces, which is considered necessary in order to protect French, and English is looked upon as a threat:

'The Francophone identity-building mission of the school seems to be only successful through the oppression of English' (Hambye & Richards, 2012: 179).
Hence, the migrant students

> may have less access to opportunities to learn and practise English than other Franco-Ontarian families who have nothing to lose in pretending that only French matters ... Bilingualism, in Francophone schools, so it seems, is not accessible for everyone. (Hambye & Richards, 2012: 180)

Yet, for these migrant students it is vital to learn not only French but also English for educational and professional success. Hambye and Richards give examples of students who have difficulty in developing high levels of proficiency in academic English in their francophone schools. Consequently, if they want to continue their education beyond the secondary level, they must do so in francophone institutions, which may be positive from the point of view of the francophone community but from the point of view of the students, most of them would prefer to 'have the choice of language of instruction at the institution of their choice' (Hambye & Richards, 2012: 180).

Finally, Hambye and Richards note that migrant students' home languages – if different from French – are not valued in the francophone schools. They conclude that 'it is as if languages, unlike cultures, are not cumulative and as if the protection of French works only through the symbolic negation of the existence of English and other languages in the school milieu' (Hambye & Richards, 2012: 181). There are some similarities here with the situations in Catalonia and Luxembourg (to be discussed in Chapters 9 and 10), in particular with regard to the issue of migrant students' access to learning English.

Education and Access in Wales

Iaith Pawb: The vision of a truly bilingual society

After a long period of linguistic repression due to language policies decided upon by Westminster, the Welsh language experienced a revival from the 1960s onwards. Milestones in the revitalization of Welsh include the promotion of Welsh as a 'core subject' in the national curriculum (1988); the 1993 Welsh Language Act, which established the parity of Welsh and English; and devolution in 1999 and the formation of the Welsh National Assembly. In 2003, the Welsh Assembly government published a policy report in which it set out its vision for the future of Wales as a truly bilingual society. It envisages Wales as a place where people will be able to choose freely how they want to live their lives linguistically: through English only, through both English and Welsh, or through Welsh only. The last option is impossible or at least very difficult at present, since many people in Wales are not (yet) fluent in Welsh.

The report is entitled *Iaith Pawb*, which means everybody's language. This obviously refers to Welsh, which the Welsh Assembly government hopes will become everybody's language in the future. Musk (2006: 164) comments as follows: 'Welsh is explicitly named *iaith pawb* "everyone's language", although in reality *English* is (if not by preference, then at least by practice)'. However, as Musk also points out, English is simply taken for granted and it is hardly mentioned in the report. Nor, by the way, are other languages, such as immigrant minority languages, taken into account.

The report constructs an inclusive vision of Welsh as everybody's language. According to Musk, this is part of a globalizing discourse that commodifies languages and perceives them as cultural capital, but it is combined in the report with a more exclusive nationalist discourse that presents Welsh as being iconic of 'our' national identity:

> by constructing Welsh as an 'essential', 'integral' and 'enduring component' of the 'social fabric' and 'national identity' of Wales, the Welsh are depicted as a homogeneous and unified collectivity. Interestingly, however, there is no specific mention of English in these first two paragraphs [of the report], although today English would in fact be a more unifying language than Welsh. (Musk, 2006: 161)

The report emphasizes people's right to choose Welsh over English, though it stops short of introducing new legislation to enforce this right: it asserts that the government will strongly encourage, but not compel, businesses to provide bilingual services (i.e. not only in English but also in Welsh). The narrow line between choice and compulsion has also been a recurrent topic of debate in the area of education, to which we now turn.

The tension between compulsion and choice

As a result of positive political developments, more and more Welsh-medium nursery schools, primary schools and secondary schools opened in the 1960s and 1970s. Schools that are referred to as Welsh-medium are in fact bilingual schools that usually teach more than half of the subjects through Welsh and the remaining subjects through English. Interestingly, more and more parents – including English-speaking parents – choose to enrol their children in Welsh-medium nursery and primary schools. A number of factors have been put forward to explain the success of these schools, including in particular the high quality of education imparted by the schools and the new instrumental value of Welsh for employment, especially in the public sector.

According to Jones and Martin-Jones (2004: 53), '440 [primary schools in Wales in 2000–2001] out of a total of 1,631 schools (27 per cent) were using Welsh as the sole, main, or partial medium of education'. Jones and Martin-Jones' phrasing here highlights the fact that there are different models of bilingual education. The authors distinguish in particular between 'designated' bilingual schools, aimed primarily at English-speaking children, which use Canadian-type immersion, and 'traditional' or 'natural' bilingual schools for native Welsh speakers, which cluster in rural heartland Wales (Jones & Martin-Jones, 2004: 53). However, they also point out that increasingly in these schools, there are students with very different degrees of proficiency in Welsh and that, as a direct consequence of this, code-switching between Welsh and English is widespread in Welsh-medium classrooms (Jones & Martin-Jones, 2004: 56–57).

Despite the remarkable successes in the revitalization of Welsh, there are also clear limitations. Jones and Martin-Jones explain that the language is reproduced through school, but it is used less and less as a home language. Moreover, many students who are fluent in Welsh choose English-medium education at secondary level (Jones & Martin-Jones, 2004: 55–56). Does this mean that the position of Welsh is in need of further strengthening? Since 1999, Welsh has been a compulsory subject at both primary and secondary level. However, it is only a 'core subject' in the Welsh-medium primary schools, whereas in the English-medium schools it is taught as a 'foundation subject' and is not used as a medium of instruction. Should it become a core subject and a medium of instruction in all primary schools in Wales? The answer to this question depends on what our primary concern is: do we want to ensure by all means the maximum possible revitalization of the Welsh language? Or are we primarily concerned with offering all children in Wales the best possible bilingual education that enables their educational success and opens up the widest possible range of employment opportunities? Ultimately, our language-in-education policy decisions will depend on what or who we put first: the children or the Welsh language. And if we go for the former, then we will have to acknowledge that parents and students should have a say in the decision about which option is the best one for them. As Petrovic and Majumdar (2010: 14) state, 'the challenge of the participatory ideal is to avoid restricting legitimate parental autonomy while combating hegemonic conditions'.

But even if we are primarily concerned with the Welsh language, we need to remember that too much compulsion can backfire. To give an example, Musk (2010) organized focus group discussions with students at a designated bilingual secondary school in Wales. He found students complaining about teachers 'preaching' to them about using Welsh and about English being bad (Musk, 2010: 58). This led to students rebelling against teachers' authority and using English as a deliberate reaction. He concludes that there must be better, 'alternative ways of making Welsh "cool" in order to persuade pupils to speak it' (Musk, 2010: 58). Furthermore, in another paper, Musk (2012) shows how the students' informal Welsh is mixed with English and differs from formal, 'pure' Welsh as promoted by schools and the Welsh Language Society. The purist norm is resisted and contested by the youngsters, who look upon their own linguistic practices not as 'bad' Welsh but as 'natural, cool or hip Welsh' (Musk, 2012: 666).

Similarly, Selleck (2013) carried out an ethnographic study of language ideologies in two secondary schools in south-west Wales, one English-medium and the other Welsh-medium. While the 'English' school relied on an ideology of flexible multilingualism, allowing for 'individual autonomy over language choice' (Selleck, 2013: 27), the 'Welsh' school promoted a monolingual ideology (of Welsh only) and an ideology of separate bilingualism (keeping Welsh and English separate). As a result of this insistence on the use of Welsh, 'bilingualism is problematized and indeed devalued within the school context' (Selleck, 2013: 32), with the justification that this is necessary for the revitalization of Welsh. As Shohamy (2008) puts it, these are the 'costs' of revitalization. However, because the ideology of separate bilingualism leads to a strong sense of 'us' (Welsh speakers) vs 'them' (the others), Selleck (2013: 38) wonders whether the cost 'might be too high, in view of the within-community divisions it is likely to promote'. She therefore raises the question whether 'a more open ideology (flexible bilingualism)' would be better at 'sav[ing] the language' in the long term (Selleck, 2013: 38).

Issues of Access in Maori Education in New Zealand

A revitalization success story

Māori became an official language of Aotearoa (New Zealand) – alongside English – in 1987. According to May (2001: 293), this makes New Zealand 'the *only* example where the first language of an indigenous people has been made an official state language', since other indigenous languages such as Sámi in Norway or Basque in Spain only have 'regional official status'. After a long period of colonial oppression and assimilationist policies in education, Māori had become a highly endangered language. But the introduction of Māori-medium schooling from the 1980s onwards has led to the successful revitalization of the language. In 1982, the first Māori-medium preschools (*Te Kōhanga Reo* 'language nests') were established, largely run by the Māori communities themselves. These preschools providing immersion in the Māori language were so successful that the provision of Māori-medium education was rapidly extended to primary level and beyond. In 1985, the first Māori-medium primary schools (*Kura Kaupapa Māori* 'Māori philosophy schools') opened, and the first Māori-medium secondary schools and tertiary institutions followed in 1993–1994. They, too, are, at least to a certain extent, under community control, and it would seem that this degree of local control is one key factor that has contributed to the programme's overall effectiveness.

All in all, the development of Māori-medium education, whose aim is for the children to achieve biculturalism and (additive) bilingualism in Māori and English, has been such a resounding success that other communities have adopted the 'language nest' teaching and learning philosophy, both in New Zealand and beyond. Thus, May (2001) comments as follows on the language and education provision for Pacific Islanders (Samoan, Tongan, etc.) who migrated to New Zealand from the 1960s onwards:

> Māori-medium education appears to have provided a template that other minority groups are moving increasingly to adopt … These developments are reflected in the nascent emergence of comparable Pacific Islands preschool language nests (modelled on *Te Kōhanga Reo*). (May, 2001: 305)

Moreover, language nest education has been adopted by other language minority communities around the world, notably in Hawai'i, where Hawaiian-medium language nest preschools were established from 1984 and have since been extended all the way up to higher education in what constitutes another highly successful revitalisation movement; similar initiatives were taken in other parts of the world for children speaking minority languages, including some Native American languages, as well as Sámi and Karelian.

However, it needs to be added that, despite all of these achievements, it is still a moot point whether Māori will be effectively revitalized. Indeed, because of the all-powerful position of English in New Zealand society, it is not clear whether Māori will become (one of) the home language(s) of many Māori again or whether it will remain a (mere) school language.

From Māori-medium to bilingual education

It is important to realize that the high-level Māori immersion pro-grammes implemented in the 1970s and 1980s were not a form of mother tongue education in any literal sense. Many students had English as their home language, hence the emphasis was placed on revitalizing Māori. Moreover, there was an assumption that English would be automatically acquired by the students due to the all-pervasiveness of this language in students' out-of-school environment and its dominant position in New Zealand society as a whole. Hence, the Māori-medium programmes were not bilingual education programmes either, since they sometimes even pro-hibited the use of English to a large extent in order to focus exclusively on Māori revitalization. Thus, for instance, Hornberger (2006: 288) recalls vis-iting a Māori-medium school that enforced a Māori-only policy:

The *whanau* [extended family] leader asks me 'What do you think of bilin-gual education?' As I formulate my answer and engage in further dialogue with him, it suddenly dawns on me that for him, bilingual education and Māori immersion are opposites, while for me they are located on a con-tinuum. Māori-only ideology is of such integral and foundational impor-tance to Māori immersion that the use of two languages (English and Māori) suggested by the term bilingual is antithetical to those dedicated to Māori revitalization. (Hamilton, author's field notes, 28 June 2002)

Other scholars, too, such as May and Hill (2008: 92) have warned that 'this is where the wider aims of Māori language revitalization and the need to "ring-fence" Māori from English within the educational system may well run counter to the best educational interests of the students'.

As a result, there has been a gradual realization that students also need to study academic English. There has been a shift from the absolute prioriti-zation of Māori to putting students first and building on their actual home linguistic resources. On the whole, Māori-medium schools nowadays offer more balanced, additive bilingual programmes, endeavouring to develop students' bilingualism and biliteracy in both Māori and English. While the debate between those who put students' interests first and those who prioritize the revitalization of the Māori language is ongoing, many school programmes seem to have adopted the former perspective. As Hill and May (2011) put it, the policy emphasis has changed

from a sole focus on Māori language revitalization to one that more actively foregrounds biliteracy. This illustrates a gradual but still uneven move away from Māori-medium programmes that proscribe English to ones that include academic English as an important dimension of their programmes, *even if* English-language instruction is more circumscribed than bilingual programmes elsewhere. (Hill & May, 2011: 180)

We can conclude that, ultimately, this is not so much an issue of choice or of linguistic human rights (the right to be educated in either Māori or English), but rather it is about providing students with high-quality access to both languages. In the following section, I focus in greater detail on this notion of quality of access, in relation to the situation in Malaysia.

Education and Access in Malaysia

Pragmatic nationalism: Bahasa Malaysia and English in the Malaysian system of education

Malaysia, a British colony until 1957, is a highly heterogeneous, multi-ethnic and multilingual country with about 100 languages. It consists of two geographical parts: Peninsular Malaysia and East Malaysia, which comprises the states of Sabah and Sarawak on the island of Borneo. As in Singapore, there are three main ethnic groups: the Malays together with other indigenous groups, the Chinese and the Indians. As a result of interethnic conflicts in the late 1960s, the government implemented the *Bumiputra* (son-of-the-soil) policy, which privileged ethnic Malays in the areas of education and employment.

The newly independent country focused on nation building through the imposition of Bahasa Malaysia (the language of Malaysia, also known as Malay) as the national language. Whereas during the colonial period there were schools with English, Malay, Chinese and Tamil as medium of instruction, the 1963 National Language Act enforced a switch to Bahasa Malaysia as the medium of instruction in public education, with English taught as a subject. This was promoted as a form of mother tongue education, though in fact Bahasa Malaysia is not the 'mother tongue' for many children and it was rather the nationalist impulse that drove the reform:

this so-called 'mother-tongue' education policy should better be termed 'national language' education policy, as Bahasa Malaysia is linguistically different from vernacular Malay and is not the mother tongue of the majority of Malays. (Lin & Man, 2009: 112)

Nor is it the mother tongue of the many indigenous minority groups living mostly in East Malaysia.

However, by the 1990s, the nationalist fervour had subsided somewhat and a more pragmatist orientation had taken over, as the government felt that Malaysia was lagging behind in the competitive race in an increasingly globalized world. The pragmatist ideology won over the nationalist one or rather it led to a new, compromise ideology of 'pragmatic nationalism' that included high proficiency in both Bahasa Malaysia and English (Martin, 2005: 93). In a first step, in 1993 the government introduced English as the medium of instruction in science and mathematics in colleges and universities, both as a way of improving students' proficiency in the language and allowing state institutions of higher education to compete more successfully with the increasing number of private English-medium universities.

In a second step, the regulation concerning the use of English as the medium of instruction in science and mathematics was extended to the whole of public education in 2003. What was introduced, in other words, was a form of bilingual education with a clear separation between science subjects taught through English and all other subjects taught through Bahasa Malaysia. But this medium of instruction reform led to major problems, especially in rural schools with mostly indigenous students, where both teachers and students often had no or very little proficiency in English. As a result, the government has now decided upon a gradual return to Bahasa Malaysia as the medium of instruction for science and mathematics too, which has been implemented since 2012. This, however, does not mean that the government has given up on its aim of improving Malaysian students' level of proficiency in English; it is just that it has decided upon a different way of achieving this, with English being introduced already in preschool.

Quality of access vs safetalk practices

Quality of access to the dominant language(s) in society is of paramount importance to all students but especially the most marginalized and underprivileged students in impoverished rural areas. Even if the latter have access (to, for example, English), it is often limited to what Chick (1996) and Hornberger and Chick (2001) refer to as 'safetalk', namely, the highly limited language used by teachers in the classroom when they do not want to take any risks but follow prescribed ('safe') routines and patterns. In this section, I critically discuss an example of safetalk practices in the Malaysian system of education.

Martin (2005: 88) highlights the 'unequal access to English-language education in Malaysia between urban and rural areas'. Shortly after the 2003 switch to English as the medium of instruction for science and mathematics,

he carried out an ethnographic study of English lessons in two rural classrooms in Sarawak, East Malaysia. Both schools are located in areas where
mostly indigenous people live, speaking their own indigenous languages:
one school is a primary school in an area where the main language of communication is Sa'ben, and the other is a secondary school in an area where
the main language of communication is Kelabit. He found that mostly
English and Bahasa Malaysia were used in the classrooms, with Kelabit also
used in the secondary school, while Sa'ben was conspicuously absent from
the primary classroom. In both schools, he found that students' contributions, whether in English or Bahasa Malaysia, were overwhelmingly limited to minimal, one-word responses. In other words, the teacher–student
interactions that predominated in these classrooms were of the kind that
Hornberger and Chick (2001) refer to as 'safetalk': that is, cued responses
and chorus-like answers, with students often repeating key lexical items
after the teacher. Although there was extensive code-switching between
English and Bahasa Malaysia (and Kelabit in the secondary school), there
was no exploratory talk of the type that is so important to learning, where
teacher and students 'engage critically but constructively with each other's
ideas' (Mercer, 2004: 146).

Martin shows that the most common form of student–teacher interaction in the classroom consisted of highly traditional initiation–response–
feedback (IRF) exchanges, as in the following examples:

Exchange 1
    Teacher: **apa yang dia makan itu?** <*what is he eating?*>
    Student: bread
    Teacher: bread

Exchange 2
    Teacher: **apa itu?** <*what's that?*>
    Student: **roti** <*bread*>
    Teacher: **itu yang kita panggil** bread <*that's what's called* bread>
    (Bahasa Malaysia – bold; English – plain; Martin, 2005: 80)

Code-switching between English and Bahasa Malaysia is used here to
scaffold students' learning but only in a highly limited way:

[the use of Malay] is only to annotate the English text, and it does
not appear to hand over any speaking rights to the pupils … [There
are only] one-word responses from pupils and no meaningful discussion in response to the questions posed in the textbook … [Malay is]

used simply to gloss words or statements that appear in the text, and not in any communicative or exploratory way. The brief analysis of the lesson shows that the classroom is a very tightly controlled environment, with the pupils positioned as recipients of teacher-mediated text. There is little active participation from the pupils. (Martin, 2005: 87)

These safetalk practices thus constitute a form of classroom interaction that allows a minimal kind of participation without loss of face for the students and (especially) the teacher. However, such safetalk practices do not contribute to student emancipation but, on the contrary, to the continuing marginalization of the language minority students and their communities. According to Hornberger and Chick (2001: 51), safetalk 'creates a space where the students know more or less what to expect and how to behave in class, but where a high price is paid in terms of (a lack of) learning'. Ultimately, what these students need is more and better access to all the languages, from their home language(s) via Bahasa Malaysia (if it is not a home language) to English. The use of their home languages in the classroom would empower them and allow them to engage in extended exploratory talk; as for English, the quality of teaching would need to be improved in order to develop in students a high level of proficiency – which is what the Malaysian government is attempting to do with its latest reforms, including introducing English at preschool level.

Similar safetalk practices have been reported in many classrooms in the underprivileged parts of the world (e.g. Brock-Utne [2005] on Tanzania and South Africa; Williams [2006] on Malawi and Zambia). Often, these school systems switch to the dominant language (e.g. English) as the medium of instruction after about three years, though the sudden switch is difficult to manage for many students and teachers, whose proficiency in English is not high enough. In such situations, mother tongue education advocates usually recommend delaying access to the dominant language as the medium of instruction until secondary school. However, many students in underprivileged parts of the world only attend primary education. Hence, if, for instance, English is only taught minimally as a subject in primary education and it is not used as a medium of instruction until secondary education, these students will miss out almost completely, and the school system risks reinforcing the social stratification between English-speaking elites and non-English-speaking subalterns. For this reason, it may be preferable to attempt to improve teacher training and the quality of English language teaching, and to implement a very slow and gradual change from L1 to L2 as the medium of instruction from an early stage.

Conclusion

In this chapter, we have seen how a focus on one particular language (e.g. French in francophone Canada or Welsh in Wales) can lead to a polarization of communities (speakers of French vs English in Canada, speakers of Welsh vs English in Wales), each using a discourse of linguistic rights to defend their interests or privileges. Underlying these discourses is a dichotomizing (Manichean) view of languages in conflict, such that one language can only flourish *at the expense of* the other. In such conflictual situations, the needs of students are often overlooked, especially those of migrant students, as in the Canadian case.

We have also looked at what has been done in Māori education in New Zealand in order to provide students with high-quality access to English, the dominant language in society. In contrast, the Malaysian education system is one of many that still need to break through safetalk practices and enable more effective and more equitable learning. These topics will be discussed further in later chapters: the impact of restrictive educational policies and practices upon minority group students is the main theme of Chapter 5, and the question of access to *both* local languages *and* English comes up in one way or another in all the case studies in Part 2. But first, in Chapter 4, I bring together the main concerns of Chapter 2 (building on non-standard varieties) and Chapter 3 (providing high-quality access) as a way of further illustrating what constitutes flexible multilingual education.

4 What Makes and Breaks a Good Language-in-Education Policy?

A Social Perspective

Makoni and Mashiri (2007) point to the urgent need for a change of perspective in language policy and planning, as well as sociolinguistics:

> The position we are adopting is the converse to conventional models of language planning, whose main goals are to promote the status of languages ... The models assume that, by changing the status of a language we will be able to alter [people's] social and economic status. We are arguing that changes in the status of language can occur as a result of changes in the social, political and economic status of its speakers. The converse does not necessarily occur. People's socio-economic status will not necessarily improve because the status of their languages has been changed. (Makoni & Mashiri, 2007: 64)

This book hopes to contribute to such a change in perspective in the area of multilingual education. Accordingly, there is a need to move beyond an exclusive focus on linguistic human rights, as it marginalizes social issues and, moreover, often does not even lead to a satisfactory solution on the linguistic level: indeed, because of the problematic concept of 'mother tongue', schools sometimes teach the standard variety of the assumed mother tongue without building on children's actual vernacular resources or varieties (see below; also Chapter 8). Thus, it is important for sociolinguists to prioritize social aspects over linguistic ones, and to always put people first before languages. With this basic concern in the foreground, we explore a number of sociolinguistic situations in very different parts of the world: Zimbabwe, India, Ecuador, France, Australia and Japan.

The chapter starts from a key social issue: the Great Divide between the haves and the have-nots, and the dichotomy between the former's elite bilingualism and the latter's mass bilingualism. It first considers how underprivileged students can be enabled to break through this divide by developing their multilingualism and multiliteracies in both local indigenous languages and a global language such as English. The case studies in this part include Zimbabwe and India. In the second half of the chapter, we consider a number of countries with rather flexible or progressive language-in-education policies, where, nonetheless, language minority students find it extremely difficult to break through the Great Divide and to be education-ally successful. This may be due to powerful institutional ideologies (as in France) or to other social factors such as emigration (in Ecuador). The final case studies of Australia and Japan illustrate the potential for shifts between more fixity and more flexibility, and show that flexible and progressive language-in-education policies constantly need to be fought for, because of ever-changing political and economic priorities.

The Long Way Towards Flexible Multilingual Education

Drawing together the discussions in Chapters 2 and 3, I argue that a good language-in-education policy builds on students' actual linguistic resources (e.g. the urban vernaculars in Zimbabwe) and provides access to both local indigenous languages and a global language such as English. Whereas Chapter 3 focused mostly on the question of access to English for immigrant minority groups (e.g. in francophone Canada) and indig-enous minority groups (e.g. in New Zealand), I now widen the scope to include all children and consider their access to both local languages and English in societies – such as Zimbabwe and India – where English is not only perceived as the national lingua franca and the language of inter-national relations, but also as the key to social mobility and economic advancement.

Zimbabwe: A story of urban vernaculars and English

Rhodesia became Zimbabwe when it eventually gained independence from Britain in 1980, putting an end to white domination. However, Robert Mugabe's post-independence politics, which included the seizure of land from white farmers, led to Zimbabwe's 'ostracization' (Makoni, 2011: 440) by the Western powers. This plunged Zimbabwe into a severe economic crisis in the 1990s, accompanied by rapid urbanization, social deprivation and political oppression. It also had the consequence of Zimbabwe turn-ing to China for economic and other support, which explains the growing importance of the Chinese language in Zimbabwe. Indeed, Chinese is now taught as a foreign language in some secondary schools and universities in Zimbabwe; the University of Zimbabwe, for instance, offers a degree-level course in Chinese.

The main languages in education are English, the former colonial language, which still plays a key role in contemporary Zimbabwean society, as well as Shona and Ndebele. Makoni *et al.* (2006) point out that the standard varieties of Shona and Ndebele taught in schools are not most students' 'mother tongues' but rather the varieties constructed and codified by European missionaries and other governmental agencies during the colonial period. In that way, standard Shona and Ndebele are as much colonial or European constructions as English is, and many students find them as difficult to learn as 'foreign' languages. In the Education Act of 1987, it was specified that students should become bilingual in English and Shona or Ndebele. Moreover, English was to be used as the medium of instruction from fourth grade if not earlier. The 2006 Education Act modified this slightly by further specifying that, if English is not chosen as the primary medium of instruction, it should be taught as a subject from first grade onwards. Furthermore, the aim now is to make students tri- or multilingual by developing their proficiency in English, Shona *and* Ndebele.

The 2006 Education Act also goes further than the 1987 Education Act by reclassifying a number of minority languages as indigenous languages which can be taught at school and/or used as media of instruction. Under the influence of the work of the Zimbabwean Indigenous Languages Promotion Association (ZILPA), these 'new' indigenous languages include Shangani, Tonga, Venda and Nambya, though others, both smaller minority languages and those looked upon as 'immigrant languages', are still excluded (Makoni, 2011: 443). In sum, schools are required to teach English, Shona and Ndebele, and they may additionally teach one or more of the new indigenous languages.

However, the school curriculum does not include the new urban vernaculars, such as chiHarare, which is widely used in the capital city, even though these vernaculars have become the 'mother tongues' of an increasing number of mostly young urban residents. The spread of such urban vernaculars in large cities throughout Africa is discussed in greater detail in the chapter on South Africa. In Zimbabwe, as in South Africa and many other African countries, these urban vernaculars are valued and celebrated in popular culture, but they are denigrated in schools, where an ideology of linguistic purism still prevails (Makoni *et al.*, 2010. 2). Makoni *et al.* argue that urban vernaculars should be used as (additional) media of instruction in education for the following three reasons among others:

a)   unlike the standard varieties of indigenous languages, urban vernaculars cut across ethnic boundaries, and hence do not reflect a rigid ethnic identity but rather convey an urban identity (Makoni *et al.*, 2010: 2)

b)   many students find the standard varieties of Shona and Ndebele taught at school largely incomprehensible (Makoni *et al.*, 2010: 3)
c)   in highly multilingual contexts, the imposition of a 'single standard language in a classroom setting is an aberration' (Makoni *et al.*, 2010: 11)

As a result, the picture that is frequently painted by Zimbabwean sociolinguistics of a conflict between English and the indigenous languages is a gross oversimplification. As Makoni *et al.* (2006: 390) argue, it is the 'urban vernaculars, much more than English, that have begun to replace chiShona and isiNdebele as first languages'. Along the same lines, Kadenge and Nkomo (2011) take issue with the view that what is needed in Zimbabwe is the promotion of indigenous languages such as Shona and Ndebele *at the expense of* English. Instead, they argue that English and indigenous languages complement each other: Zimbabwe needs to develop a 'multilingual national language policy' (Kadenge & Nkomo, 2011: 258) to promote the indigenous languages *and* to improve the learning and teaching of English. They summarize their argument as follows:

The point being made is that while promoting and developing indigenous languages is a noble idea, it may fail to have the envisaged positive socioeconomic, cultural and political impacts, as long as it is not undertaken alongside efforts to harness English as one of the important languages in the country's linguistic profile. (Kadenge & Nkomo, 2011: 261)

While the use of urban vernaculars and indigenous languages as media of instruction in Zimbabwean schools can help with educational opportunities, the use of English as a medium of instruction is equally important in order to help students break through social class barriers and access the global economy. Ideally, the education system would build on children's actual linguistic resources and varieties (in particular, the urban vernaculars) as a way of leading them towards the standard varieties (of Shona, Ndebele and English) that they need to acquire for educational and later professional success.

India: No life without English?

Let us start with two quotations describing the Great Divide in different societies of the world:

With a dominant presence of English, all multilingual societies in South Asia characteristically show signs of a hierarchical multilingualism with

English (and, in some cases, a major national language) at the top of the hierarchy, with other major languages in the middle rungs and with ITM [indigenous and tribal minority] languages at the bottom ... The linguistic double divide in the hierarchical power structure of languages leads to deprivation and impoverishment of languages, threats of language shift, and endangerment and identity crises for the ITM languages. (Mohanty, 2010: 140)

Great Divide ideologies are implicit and explicit in current U.S. media of instruction policies, and they are constructing two kinds of people: those with and without access to opportunity and resources. Despite the calls of conservative politicians to 'leave no child behind' – codified in Federal education policy under President George W. Bush – an unconscionable number of English language learners, students of color, and working-class children are, in fact, being left behind. (McCarty, 2004: 87)

As I have already said, this book puts people first before languages. Therefore, I follow McCarty rather than Mohanty in the above quotations: the Great or Double Divide is primarily between people and only derivatively between languages. It is people who suffer from 'deprivation and impoverishment' or from 'identity crises', and the people who are most deprived and impoverished are often also those whose languages are most marginalized. In India, this is the case with tribal communities whose languages are not included in schools. But the most urgent issue is to help these people out of poverty and deprivation, even if, as Labov (2008) points out in reference to the US context, this should be at the cost of further endangering their languages (see Chapter 5). Only focusing on their linguistic rights and trying to elevate the status of their languages will not, necessarily or automatically, raise their socio-economic status (as pointed out by Makoni and Mashiri in the quotation at the very beginning of this chapter).

Before returning to these controversial points, we need to provide some background on the sociolinguistic situation in India. India is a country marked by high levels of both individual and societal multilingualism. It has 2 official languages at the federal level (Hindi and English), and a further 21 officially recognized languages at the level of the individual states. In education, 33 languages – including English – are used as media of instruction (Mohanty, 2006: 267, 275).

There was local resistance, especially in non-Hindi-speaking areas, against the imposition of Hindi as the national or official language, which led to the compromise of the Three Language Formula being adopted as the cornerstone of Indian language-in-education policy: the first language (L1) is supposed to be the 'mother tongue', though in fact it is usually the official regional language of the state; the second language (L2) tends to be English; and the third language (L3), which is most often only added as a subject at secondary level, is Hindi or, in states where Hindi is the official regional language, it is Sanskrit or another Indian language. The Three Language Formula is not always applied rigorously; for instance, in non-Hindi-speaking states such as Tamil Nadu, often only Tamil and English are taught. It is interesting to note that English is thus placed higher in the hierarchy than Hindi. Indeed, English is the language of the educated elite, whose children often study in English-medium schools. These schools are mostly private schools, charging high fees; they are clustered especially in urban areas and constitute about 10% of the total number of schools in the country (at primary level; see Annamalai, 2004: 184). The other 90% of primary schools are state schools, clustered in rural as well as urban areas, and frequently use an Indian language as their medium of instruction (usually the official regional language).

This means that often the indigenous languages of tribal children are not used at school, and they find it very difficult to learn through two languages that they may not be familiar with, namely, the official regional language and English. Some linguistic minorities have engaged in political activism and have been successful in getting their indigenous language accepted as the medium of instruction in their schools, whereas other groups with less political clout have failed. Furthermore, other groups have campaigned for English as the medium of instruction, as they feel convinced that if their children were educated through English rather than the official regional language or their own minority language, they would have better chances of social mobility (Annamalai, 2004: 189–190).

But even children whose language is used as the medium of instruction at school come up against linguistic barriers. As Khubchandani (2003) points out, there is frequently a wide gap between the standard varieties of Indian languages taught at school and the varieties actually used in the home environments. Because of these unresolved issues, there is often limited instruction in Indian classrooms as well as high educational failure rates. From what has just been said, it should be clear that mother tongue education is too fixed a model and it cannot solve all the problems. The main issue is social inequality and how this is perpetuated by the split between elite bilingualism, which is taught in English-medium, high-quality and high-cost schools, and mass bilingualism, imparted in Indian language medium, low-cost and frequently also low-quality schools. It is difficult to even suggest a way out from a linguistic perspective. In light of the increasing diversity in most Indian classrooms, a bi- or multilingual medium of instruction policy (in one or more local languages and English) may be more appropriate for many children than a single medium of instruction, which in any case often does not correspond to the children's home linguistic resources. Another important suggestion made by Annamalai (2004: 191–192) would be to improve the quality of English teaching, but he adds that perhaps the most pressing issue is to raise literacy levels, by teaching as many children as possible to read and write, whether it is in their 'mother tongue', the official regional language or English – with the best choice here depending on which languages are already present in the children's linguistic repertoires, which tend to be highly multilingual.

That English should not be excluded here has been emphasized by scholars such as Rao *et al.* (2010: 122), who argue that 'exposing children to English right from their preschool years or even before should … be viewed as a positive influence on success in literacy', as well as Vaish (2005), who shows how English can enable the underprivileged and disenfranchised to access the global economy. More particularly, Vaish (2010) discusses a number of modifications made to the Three Language Formula in the last 10 years or so in state primary schools, though only in urban areas: nowadays, more and more English-medium programmes are offered with English as the medium of instruction from the beginning. Actually, these are dual medium programmes, with some subjects taught through English and others through Hindi. But what these programmes involve is more access to English, since they offer an extra six years of English language teaching – something that was previously only available in expensive private schools. In this way, these new English-medium programmes begin to break through the Great Divide by offering greater educational and professional opportunities for the urban disadvantaged, though not yet for the rural poor (Vaish, 2010: 137). This again shows that as sociolinguists, we need to be open to the positive contributions that (knowledge of) every language can make, rather than framing our arguments in terms of pitting one language against another.

Some Obstacles On the Way

In the remainder of this chapter, I look at education systems that, at least in theory, provide students with more or less flexible bi-/multilingual options, offering access to both local and global languages; for instance, Ecuador has introduced bilingual intercultural education and France offers minority language sections including, for instance, an Arabic language section. However, we will see that in practice this may turn out very different from what was intended in theory. Finally, in the last part of the chapter, I discuss the interplay between political priorities and economic factors, and their positive or negative impact upon language-in-education policies.

Ecuador: Quichua maintenance and emigration

Like India and Zimbabwe, many Central and South American countries illustrate the Great Divide between the elite (in this case, Spanish–English) bilingualism of the upper and middle classes and the mass bi-/multilingualism of the lower classes. In Ecuador, for instance, many lower-class people are indigenous people speaking an indigenous language as well as Spanish and some English. The most widely used indigenous language is Quichua or Kichwa (known as Quechua or Kechwa outside Ecuador), spoken by about 10 million people not only in Ecuador but also in Peru and Bolivia (King, 2001: 7). However, like most indigenous languages, it is endangered, as its speakers are tending to shift towards greater use of Spanish.

In Ecuador, the second half of the 20th century saw the development of bilingual education for indigenous communities. In the 1980s, a progressive policy of bilingual intercultural education was adopted with Quichua as the medium of instruction and Spanish as 'the language of intercultural relations' (King, 2001: 42). However, the reality on the ground can be very different, as King (2001) found out. In the two indigenous communities that she studied, the majority of the children did not have Quichua as their primary home language and were more proficient in Spanish than in Quichua; moreover, the amount of Quichua that they learnt at school was extremely limited and did not extend much beyond a purely symbolic use of the language. King discusses several factors responsible for this gap between policy and practice: language use and attitudes in the communities, language teaching methods in the schools, varieties of Quichua and the linguistic consequences of emigration.

Language use and attitudes in the two communities

King's study focuses on one particular group, the Saraguros of the southern Ecuadorean highlands. She studies two communities, Lagunas, a more urban and economically successful community, and Tambopamba, a more rural and remote community. In Lagunas, Spanish is the main language of home and community, and many parents are not very familiar with the Quichua language. While Quichua is used less and less for communicative purposes, its use has become highly symbolic and indexes ethnic identity. There is, therefore, great interest in teaching it to children at school and in this way revitalizing the language.

The more remote Tambopamba community is a community bilingual in Spanish and Quichua, where Quichua is still used quite frequently as the language of everyday communication. Here, the rural lifestyle is seen as indexical of ethnic identity, and so the Quichua language plays a much less important role as a symbolic resource than it does in Lagunas. However, for this reason, there is also a declining interest in Quichua in Tambopamba. Spanish is looked upon as the language of social mobility and economic success, and many parents want their children to develop the necessary skills in Spanish rather than in Quichua. Thus, ironically, there are more revitalization efforts in Lagunas, where Quichua is no longer used much, than in Tambopamba, where it is still in daily use.

Language teaching at schools

Both Lagunas and Tambopamba have community-run elementary schools, with many indigenous teachers genuinely concerned about the revitalization of Quichua. Yet, in her study, King found very limited instruction of Quichua, with a focus on receptive rather than productive skills. Spanish was used almost exclusively as the medium of instruction in the schools, as well as being regularly used in both teacher–student and student–student interactions. As for Quichua, it was mostly limited to symbolic uses in greetings or short announcements – which reflect the way it is used in the Lagunas community. Although there was slightly more spontaneous use of Quichua among students in the Tambopamba school – reflecting these students' greater exposure to Quichua outside school – their proficiency in Quichua was also mostly of a receptive kind and was not expanded on by the school. Hence, in both schools, the children had very limited competences in Quichua, and King (2001: 187) concludes that it is unlikely, in the current environment of both home and school, that Quichua will develop into the 'everyday, unmarked language of the community'.

Varieties of Quichua

As discussed in Chapter 2, languages exist in a number of varieties; in the case of Quichua, these are on the one hand the varieties used by mostly older native speakers and are often referred to as 'authentic Quichua', and on the other hand standardized or 'Unified Quichua' as taught in schools. Paradoxically, 'authentic' Quichua varieties are heavily influenced by contact with the Spanish language and contain many Spanish loanwords, whereas Unified Quichua is often looked upon as the more 'pure' variety that is free from Spanish influence (King, 2001: 95). In the Lagunas community, where Quichua is mostly used for symbolic purposes, it is Unified Quichua that is seen as being indexical of ethnic identity. In Tambopamba, on the contrary, it is authentic Quichua that is still widely used for everyday communication. These speakers of authentic Quichua often find Unified Quichua to be artificial or even unintelligible. Quichua speakers in

Lagunas, on the other hand, tend to have learnt it at school, and hence use Unified Quichua and look down upon authentic Quichua as 'bad' Quichua (King, 2001: 195).

King concludes that, for a more successful revitalization, there would be a need to establish Quichua language nests, along the lines of the highly successful Māori immersion programmes in New Zealand, and to involve the elders of the communities, so that the children would be exposed to authentic as well as Unified Quichua, 'which might eventually help to close the real and perceived gaps between the two varieties' (King, 2001: 221). This is necessary, King argues, as otherwise purist attitudes can inhibit speakers or even polarize communities.

The linguistic consequences of emigration

In a highly innovative study, King and Haboud (2011) investigate the impact of migration upon the sending community rather than the host community. They explore how large-scale emigration from Ecuador in the late 1990s affects the language competences and practices of those who are left behind. Their focus is in particular on children growing up with grandparents in the community, while their parents work in the USA or Spain and send remittances back home. King and Haboud note that the resulting shifts in childhood patterns have an effect on the children's Quichua language maintenance and language learning opportunities.

Thanks to the remittances from abroad, many young people are now freed from traditional agricultural work and household chores. The youngsters, who are more financially independent, spend more time at school as well as hanging out in town. The result of this has been a loss of discipline and a rise in gangs, as well as alcohol and drug abuse – at least according to the adults that King and Haboud interviewed. In these youngsters, lack of respect (especially for their grandparents) seems to be caused at least partially by the emotional hardship of being separated from their parents.

It is important to be aware of these changing patterns of childhood and adolescence in order to understand their implications for Quichua language maintenance and revitalization. As King and Haboud point out, it could be thought that, as the grandparents are often quite fluent in Quichua, the children would acquire the language from them. However, the opposite seems to be the case: 'rather than grandparents socializing children into ways of speaking Quichua, grandparents' influence is greatly diminished in many homes, and instead children are socializing them to use Spanish' (King & Haboud, 2011: 151–152).

As a result, Quichua is being used less and less in the home and is becoming more and more just a school language. But even in the domain of the school, Quichua is increasingly sidelined, as Spanish and English progressively dominate. For in the eyes of many youngsters, it is Spanish and English that they will need if, like their parents, they will emigrate one day in search of better educational or professional opportunities. In this way, King and Haboud (2011: 155) conclude that 'even progressive language policy to support an Indigenous language such as Quichua can be simply overwhelmed by large-scale global forces'.

France: Language choice and institutional ideology

France is a country not only with a highly centralized education system but also with a dominant language ideology, namely, the one nation–one language ideology. Indeed, the whole concept of the French nation has been constructed around (the use of) the French language. Hélot (2003: 257) critically discusses the clear status hierarchy of languages within the French education system, with the French language at the top, of course. Below it are ranked foreign languages (with English as the most popular choice among students and their parents), regional languages (Breton, Corsican, Basque, Catalan, Occitan, etc., which had been marginalized and repressed for a long time) and at the bottom of this hierarchy, the so-called 'languages of origin' or immigrant minority languages (such as Arabic, Turkish, Russian, Mandarin Chinese, Vietnamese and Japanese, which are still marginalized today).

It is only since the year 2000 that the state school system has been opened to a wider range of language learning opportunities. Partial immersion is now offered in regional languages in the areas where these languages are spoken, with one interesting exception being Alsace, where High or Standard German is taught in these bilingual programmes rather than Alsatian. These programmes run from preschool to primary and even secondary education, with about half of the school subjects being taught through the regional language as the medium of instruction and the other half through French. Students in all other French primary schools also take a foreign language but only as a subject. Then, in secondary school, they can apply to the 'European' or 'Oriental' sections, where the foreign language is used as the medium of instruction for one or two non-language subjects taught through the methodology of content and language integrated learning (CLIL).

In the European sections, the language taught through CLIL methods is usually a major European language, with English being chosen by the vast majority of students. Non-European languages are offered within the Oriental sections, though these have not had much success, unlike the European sections. Hélot (2008a, 2008b) gives the example of Arabic, which has been included as a foreign language option at primary level and as part of the Oriental sections at secondary level. However, despite the fact that there are over two million speakers of Arabic in France and that they constitute the biggest migrant group (from North African countries such as Algeria, Tunisia and Morocco), few students have taken up the Arabic language option and very few schools offer it (see Hélot, 2008a: 66; 2008b: 217). Hélot provides the following figures for the whole of the country: in secondary education, 55 students attended the Oriental section in Arabic in 2002, and only 16 in 2005 (Hélot, 2008a: 66; 2008b: 212); as for primary schools, only three schools offered Arabic as a foreign language in 2006, one in Montpellier and two in Paris, and only 0.2% of students chose it as their foreign language (Hélot, 2008b: 217). The reasons given by Hélot for this rather shocking state of affairs include the low status of Arabic in French society, the fact that schools often teach classical Arabic rather than the vernacular varieties spoken in students' homes and that the language is taught at beginner level instead of building on students' home linguistic resources (Hélot, 2003: 272).

Hélot (2008b: 213) explains that both the regional language partial immersion programmes and the European and Oriental sections function within mainstream schools. This means, for instance in the case of a European section, that students are part of a regular class with whom they take all their subjects except for the (advanced) foreign language course and the couple of other courses taught through this language. For the latter courses, they leave their mainstream class and join the foreign language section that they have chosen, which could be, for instance, the English language section. In this way, no state schools in France are fully bilingual schools; there are only some bilingual classes functioning within otherwise mainstream French-medium schools. Hélot (2008b: 213) notes that this is due to the principle of equality that is fundamental to public education, as well as the strong ideological belief that there is a need to defend the central position of French in the education system. Fully bilingual schools and total immersion programmes could be seen as threatening the position of French, and hence, also threatening 'national unity', as a result of which such schools can only be found in the private sector (i.e. the Diwan schools in Brittany, as mentioned in Chapter 2).

However, despite the principle of equality that informs state education in France, it should be clear that the way these new policies concerning European sections have been implemented is basically elitist (Hélot, 2008b: 214). Indeed, only the 'best' students are admitted to these sections, depending on their grades in French, mathematics and the foreign language that they have chosen. This is a form of elite bilingualism, where bi- or multilingualism is seen as an extra resource giving top students even better chances in their educational and professional careers. This is very different from the way the bi-/multilingualism of migrant students is perceived: these students' multilingualism is seen as a problem, causing an educational 'deficit', which can only be remedied through teaching them French as much and as quickly as possible. Their home languages are largely ignored by the education system and the aim is, ironically or tragically, to cure them of their bi-/multilingualism and turn them into monolingual speakers of French. Paradoxically, it is only after the successful achievement of this first step that they can then start learning foreign languages again at school and, if they are good enough, actually be admitted to the European section, where they will acquire elite bilingualism as a resource!

Hélot (2008b: 214) insists that the European sections 'are not elitist by nature', but 'it is the way they are implemented' that makes them elitist. The Oriental sections, on the other hand, are a total failure due to the overall institutional ideology of French education and society which only values French and denigrates migrant languages such as Arabic.

The Role of Political and Economic Priorities

1991 in Australia: The year when it all changed

In the previous sections, we have seen how even rather flexible or progressive language-in-education policies can be undermined by social factors such as powerful institutional ideologies (in France) or patterns of emigration (in Ecuador). In this section, I look at how such policies can be scuppered by changing political and socio-economic priorities, and my example is Australia.

Australia has had a long history of linguistic repression and racism, from the 19th-century policy of removing Aboriginal children from their families for the purpose of assimilation into white society, to the 20th-century White Australia policy and the infamous Australian Dictation Test. Its primary aim was to keep out Asian immigrants by subjecting them to a dictation test 'in a language that the undesirable immigrant did not speak, thus ensuring failure on the test' (McNamara, 2009: 224). As for Aboriginal peoples and Torres Strait Islanders, they were only granted full citizenship rights in 1967. But from this time onwards, Australia has set up a far-sighted, progressive policy of linguistic pluralism and multiculturalism. The first indigenous bilingual schools opened in the Northern Territory in 1973, though mostly only of the transitional type. By 1990, Aboriginal communities were given more control over these schools and, consequently, they have been able to introduce more maintenance types of bilingual education.

Such maintenance and revitalization programmes were urgently needed, as many Aboriginal languages had already disappeared or were in the process of disappearing. However, bilingual education programmes do not provide easy solutions for this issue of language shift. In these programmes, regional lingua francas are frequently taught, as a result of which young people may switch from the local clan language to the wider lingua franca (Lo Bianco & Rhydwen, 2001: 399). This is reinforced, as Lo Bianco and Rhydwen (2001: 399) point out, by changing patterns of settlement, with people who speak different clan languages increasingly living together. The authors conclude that clan languages are threatened by these regional lingua francas more than by English, while also noting that the lingua francas include English-based creoles, in particular Kriol in north Australia and Torres Strait Creole in the Torres Strait Islands and parts of north Queensland (Lo Bianco & Rhydwen, 2001: 400).

Despite the challenges faced by bilingual education programmes and language revitalization movements, they have been relatively successful due to the progressive policies of pluralism and multiculturalism during the 1970s and 1980s. The largely implicit language policies of these decades eventually crystallized in the first explicit official language policy, the 1987 National Policy on Languages. This document, also known as the Lo Bianco report (after the name of its author, the sociolinguist and language policy expert Joseph Lo Bianco), for the first time formally recognized the indigenous Aboriginal languages. It developed a far-reaching vision of social justice, and promoted access to English for all, support for Aboriginal and Torres Strait languages and acquisition by all schoolchildren of a language other than English (see Herriman, 1996: 49).

Unfortunately, however, the National Policy on Languages was replaced by a very different policy after only four years, namely, a government White Paper entitled 'Australia's Language: The Australian Language and Literacy Policy' (1991; note the highly significant change in the title from 'languages' in the plural to 'Australia's *language*' in the singular). Yet, there had been no change in government to cause this shift in language policy: the Labour Party was in power continuously from 1983 to 1996. But there was an overall shift in the policies of the Labour government, away from the earlier concerns with pluralism and multiculturalism, and towards a new politics of 'economic rationalism' combined with 'labourism' (Moore, 2000: 42). The emphasis was put on much narrower concerns such as accountability, cost efficiency and employment skills. As a result, the Australian Language and Literacy Policy moved away from the broad vision of social justice articulated in the National Policy on Languages and placed more emphasis on the acquisition of basic literacy skills – by which was meant exclusively literacy in the English language. As Lo Bianco and Rhydwen (2001: 418) argue, literacy became 'the Australian variant of English-only' (see Chapter 5 on English-only policies in the USA). A negative consequence of this was the large-scale restructuring of the field of English as a Second Language (ESL): from seeing ESL as a core element of bilingual education, practitioners were now forced to offer a much narrower and more instrumental form of ESL with an almost exclusive focus on literacy skills (see Moore, 2000).

The backlash against pluralism and multiculturalism gained ground throughout the 1990s, fuelled by an economic crisis and rising unemployment. The second half of the 1990s saw the election of a new Liberal–National government committed to further downsizing in areas such as education, as well as the rise of Pauline Hanson's 'One Nation' party with its anti-Aboriginal and anti-immigration policies. In this hostile atmosphere, and due to the gradual reduction or even removal of funding for indigenous bilingual education programmes, it became increasingly difficult for such programmes and the associated language revitalization movements to continue their work.

One territory in particular that introduced numerous cuts in this area was the Northern Territory, as a result of which a number of bilingual programmes were discontinued and the overall quality of education decreased considerably. Ironically, though, the resulting underachievement of Aboriginal students was blamed on bilingual education and there were repeated calls, especially in the media and among politicians, for increased English language instruction. In 2008, the Northern Territory government effectively abolished bilingual education by introducing a new policy that required English to be used as the sole medium of instruction in schools during the first four hours of each day. This is very similar to other restrictive, English-only policies such as those recently implemented in Arizona (see Chapter 5) and, just as in Arizona, there are numerous associations campaigning for the rehabilitation of bilingual education. In this way, we have seen in this section that the year 1991 marked a shift in Australia from a highly progressive to an increasingly restrictive language-in-education policy. It reached its nadir with the 2008 decision of the Northern Territory government, which had first introduced bilingual education in the 1970s, but is now implementing English-only programmes that close down educational opportunities for Aboriginal children.

Japan: Opening the nation?

The forces of globalization and migration that have led Australia to 'close up' as a nation can also have the opposite effect of a nation 'opening up' (Anderson, 1991; Horner, 2007b). The final case study in this chapter is Japan, which for a long time has constructed itself as a closed nation, a highly homogeneous and monolingual state, with the Japanese language as the key symbol of Japanese identity. Coulmas (2002: 221) describes it as an 'ideology of social and ethnolinguistic uniformity', arguing that 'ethnolinguistic homogeneity has been cultivated as a pivotal element of Japan's self-image' (Coulmas, 2002: 219–220). However, in the second half of the 20th century, Japanese society changed as a result of the processes of globalization. With migration mostly from other Asian and Latin American countries, the society has become more diverse both linguistically and culturally. There is also more tolerance of indigenous minorities and their languages, such as Ainu and the Ryukyuan languages (especially Okinawan), which previously had been ruthlessly suppressed.

Thus, the Ainu Cultural Protection Act of 1997 for the first time explicitly acknowledges the diversity that exists in Japan. Its aim is to protect the Ainu language and culture as a valuable part of the Japanese heritage, though it stops short of recognizing the Ainu people as a distinct ethnic group, which, according to Liddicoat (2013: 209), would have destabilized the ideology of Japan's ethnolinguistic homogeneity. Coulmas (2002: 221) comments as follows on these developments: 'The notion that a democratic society should make allowances for minorities and speakers of other languages is gaining ground, however slowly'. He also notes that even the term for Japanese as the national language (*kokugo*) 'has come under attack as being linked to exclusionist and intolerant attitudes' (Coulmas, 2002: 220).

English in particular has come to play an increasingly important role in Japanese society. Hino (2009: 105) lists the following landmarks in the opening up of Japan's language policies to the English language:

- in 2000 there was a proposal by a government-affiliated policy council to adopt English as the second official language of Japan (which, however, did not go through);
- in 2003 the Ministry of Education published the Action Plan to Cultivate 'Japanese with English abilities';
- in 2008 it was decided to start the teaching of English in elementary school instead of junior high school, although only in the last two years of elementary school.

Hino (2009: 107) also discusses the tendency in Japan to teach English as an international language, what he calls a 'de-Anglo-Americanized' version of English that can be used to express Asian values and Japanese identity. This is reminiscent of varieties such as Singlish (or Singapore English, discussed in Chapter 7), which is also seen as a vehicle for the expression of a specifically Singaporean identity. However, in Singapore, Singlish is denigrated by the government, which insists on the teaching of standard English. The difference with Japan is that Singlish is a fully nativized variety of English used for intranational communication in Singapore, whereas the international variety of English taught in Japan is only meant for communication with the outside world. In other words, the concern in Japan seems to be for an international variety of English that can express Japanese values but is close enough to the standard to maintain communicative intelligibility.

In this way, English proficiency has gradually come to be included in the concept of Japanese identity. At the same time, Hashimoto (2009) points out that the 2003 Action Plan to Cultivate 'Japanese with English abilities' also has limitations, in that it constitutes an attempt to find a balance between the need to maintain a specifically Japanese identity and the need for more English in an era of globalization. It is an endeavour 'to prevent the power of English from undermining Japanese culture and traditions' (Hashimoto, 2009: 37), by constructing it as a language with a primarily instrumental value and thus containing its spread. A further limitation, not mentioned by Hashimoto, is that so far Japan has only opened up to English and not (yet) to other languages that are part of the diversity of contemporary Japanese society, in particular immigrant minority languages such as Korean, Chinese, Portuguese and Spanish. It may be worth adding here that the speakers of Korean and Chinese belong to long-established ethnic minority communities, who are, to a large extent, linguistically assimilated, while the speakers of Portuguese and Spanish are mostly Brazilian and Peruvian descendants of Japanese emigrants.

We have seen how Japan is beginning to open up, though in very limited ways, under the pressures of democratization, internationalization and globalization. However, as we have seen in the case of Australia, the forces of globalization are a double-edged sword that can also lead to the opposite process of closing the nation. As researchers, it is our responsibility to work towards the opening of nation states, with the ultimate goal of getting such countries as Australia, Japan and France to adopt flexible and inclusive language-in-education policies and to break through their institutional ideologies which only value one language (English, Japanese, French) at the expense of all others. We have to highlight that young people nowadays want and need access to multiple languages for personal development, educational achievement and professional success, as in India and Zimbabwe where they need *both* English *and* local indigenous languages (including urban vernaculars), or in Ecuador where they need Quichua *plus* Spanish *plus* English.

Conclusion

In this chapter, we have looked at the question of what makes and what breaks a good language-in-education policy from a primarily social perspective. We argued first that good policies are informed by a both-and rather than either-or logic, developing in students high levels of proficiency in both local indigenous and dominant global languages. Next, we showed how good policies can be undermined by such social factors as emigration or powerful institutional ideologies. Finally, we illustrated the key role of political and economic priorities, as a result of which policies constantly oscillate between the polar opposites of opening vs closing the nation.

These topics will be discussed further in the chapters of Part 2, especially the chapter on the USA, where many Latino students in Arizona's increasingly fixed and restrictive school system are denied the possibility of learning through Spanish, and the chapter on Hong Kong, which has recently moved in the opposite direction towards a more flexible multilingual system of education providing students with access to Cantonese, Putonghua and English.

Part 2

5 The United States of America

According to Wiley (2002), the main concern of US bilingual education policy has been how to manage societal multilingualism. The USA has traditionally seen itself as a society of immigration, with immigrants being assimilated into the American melting pot. Hence, most bilingual education programmes from the early 20th century to the present have been of the transitional type, with a focus on Spanish, the home language of the biggest minority group. Hispanic and Latino students are 'transitioned' as quickly as possible from Spanish to English, with the ultimate aim of assimilation and eventual monolingualism in English. In other words, this is a type of subtractive bilingual education, where language minority students are supposed to be weaned away from their minority language and towards the dominant language.

The most favourable time for bilingual education was in the late 1960s, at the time of the civil rights movement, when the Bilingual Education Act of 1968 was passed. However, in the 1970s and 1980s, there was a gradual shift away from strong types of bilingual education of the maintenance type and towards more and more transitional bilingual programmes or English as a Second Language (ESL) programmes. But even the weak transitional forms of bilingual education came under increasing attack from the 1980s onwards. The strong anti-immigration feeling and the concomitant suspicion of all forms of bilingual education in the USA peaked at the turn of the millennium. The English-only movement (see below) constructed Latinos – and their language, Spanish – as a threat to mainstream America. Ironically, a discourse of endangerment spread about English, the global language, which, it was claimed, was being threatened by Spanish. Moreover, it was argued in a deliberately erroneous way that bilingual education supported minority languages (especially Spanish) *at the expense of* English. Any form of bilingual education came to be seen as a threat to national unity, and new legislation was passed in a number of states (California, Arizona and Massachusetts), replacing transitional programmes with English immersion programmes.

It was in this near-hysterical atmosphere prevailing in 2001 that the Republican President George W. Bush transformed the Bilingual Education Act into the English Language Acquisition Act as part of his new No Child

Left Behind policy, which introduced mandatory high-stakes testing in English for all children. As a result, many of the remaining transitional bilingual education programmes were discontinued, Spanish was increasingly banned from the classroom, and English immersion programmes were implemented. The results have been catastrophic for many language minority students, leading scholars to rename the Act 'No Child Left Untested' (Crawford, 2004) or 'English Language Learners Left Behind' (Menken, 2008).

But speakers of Spanish are not the only group of students who are chronically underserved by the US mainstream system of education. Other groups of students whose needs are not met and who, as a result, consistently underachieve are Native American and African-American students. The 1968 Bilingual Education Act was intended to help students with a non-English language background (e.g. speakers of Spanish and Native American languages), but it did not apply to children who speak a non-standard variety of English. Yet, it has been suggested that children in the latter category, and especially those speaking African-American English (AAE) at home, are perhaps in an even more difficult position within the US school system. Not only is there a whole history of slavery, denial of civil rights and economic marginalization behind many speakers of AAE, but there are at least two further reasons: first, they may find it difficult to differentiate between the standard school variety and their own non-standard varieties of English, and secondly, there is a very negative perception of non-standard varieties or 'dialects' such as AAE in society (Conklin & Lourie, 1983: 246–247). Because the societal perception of 'dialects' is even more negative than that of 'foreign' languages, this should be a good reason to move away from the categorization of AAE as a 'dialect'. Moreover, if AAE had been recognized as a variety in its own right (i.e. as a 'language'), then the measures specified in the Bilingual Education Act would also have applied to its speakers. These were some of the motivations behind the Oakland school board's decision to declare AAE a language in 1996. In the following section, I briefly summarize the controversy that followed on from this, widely known as the 'Ebonics debate'. After that, I try to understand why even US (socio)linguists were so reluctant to accept AAE as a language separate from English. Finally, I argue that a pedagogical–linguistic solution to this issue needs to be complemented by social change in order to achieve any degree of success.

In the second and third parts of this chapter, I discuss the issues connected with the education of Native American and Latino students. While the second part emphasizes achievements in Native American education, the third part highlights the opposite movement, namely, regression in language-in-education policies targeted at Latino students, with a special focus on recently introduced restrictive English-only policies in Arizona. In the last few sections of the chapter, I examine the advantages and disadvantages of dual language education, a highly promising model which could point the way forward for language minority education not only in the USA but also in many other countries around the world.

African-American Students

The Ebonics debate

A major controversy, usually referred to as the Ebonics debate, erupted in the USA in December 1996 concerning the nature and use of AAE or African-American Vernacular English (AAVE). In light of the continuing difficulties of African-American children in the school system, the Oakland school board in California put forward a proposal to use AAE as an integral part of these children's language education. The basic idea was to value the children's home variety in a positive way and to use it as a bridge leading them to better acquisition of standard English.

However, there was a huge outcry in the media, with many voices (journalists, politicians, members of the general public) complaining that the use of what some of them referred to as 'slang' would mean condemning these children to educational failure. Actually, the Oakland board of education was attempting to do just the opposite, namely, to give the children better chances of educational success by building in a positive way on their home linguistic resources. But because of the political and media outcry they were eventually forced to withdraw their proposal.

One of the most hotly debated issues was whether AAE is a language or a dialect or merely 'slang'. The Oakland school board had initially suggested that it was a language. Many contributors to the debate indignantly rejected this and vilified AAE by referring to it as 'wholly unintelligible', 'slang' and even 'gibberish'. What they revealed in the process was not only their prejudiced minds but also a blatant lack of linguistic understanding. Indeed, a linguistic variety cannot possibly be reduced to 'slang', which is largely a matter of vocabulary. Moreover, slang terms such as *booze* (for drink) or *dough* (for money) can, of course, be used in any variety of English, including standard English. Slang expressions change rapidly, and yesterday's slang terms have either disappeared or – like the two above – entered the (informal) standard vocabulary. But, even more interestingly, the whole debate illustrated what I discussed in Chapter 1, namely, how sets of linguistic resources are *constructed* as a language or a dialect. What the Oakland school board had tried to do was to construct the children's home linguistic variety as a language, as a way of valuing it more positively, thereby implementing of mother tongue education. But this construction was rejected as illegitimate for political reasons and the traditional construction of AAE as a 'dialect' of English was upheld.

Schmid (2001) compares the situation of African-American schoolchildren moving from AAE to standard English with that of Swiss German children moving from their Swiss German 'dialect' to standard German (see Chapter 2). She finds both similarities and differences between the two situations; for instance, both Swiss German and AAE are key markers of group identity but, unlike AAE, Swiss German is positively valued in society as a whole and is used by speakers of all social classes. Perhaps for this very reason, the Swiss education system is much more successful than the US one in helping children to transfer from the 'dialect' to the standard. The Swiss situation proves that the underlying idea of the Oakland school board's proposal was a sound one:

> Mastering the standard language is easier if the differences in the vernacular and standard language are made explicit rather than ignored. This lesson was at the heart of the Oakland school board's proposal. Their educational reform that attempted to use AAVE to teach standard English is supported by the Swiss case. (Schmid, 2001: 150)

In the Ebonics debate, the media wholly misrepresented and distorted this key issue. The Oakland school board was accused of wanting to 'imprison' African-American children within their 'dialect', by denying them access to standard English. However, it was not an issue of whether these children should learn AAE or standard English, as if these were exclusive choices. Obviously, the Oakland school board wanted the children to learn standard English, but the question they raised was what was the best way for African-American children to learn standard English. The answer they suggested was one that would be endorsed by the vast majority of applied linguists around the world, namely, by taking the children's home linguistic resources into account and valuing them positively. Thus, for instance, McWhorter (1998) makes a number of suggestions about how this could be achieved, including the following:

- train schoolteachers in the systematicity of black English;
- institute Afrocentric curricula at predominantly African-American schools;
- allow young African-American students to speak in their home dialect in class.

Such a teaching methodology would, in McWhorter's (1998: 254) eyes, 'promote the fluently bicultural identity necessary for African-Americans to succeed in this country'.

Language or dialect?

In her book *The Language Wars*, sociolinguist Robin Lakoff provides an informed account of the Ebonics debate; however, her account is marred by her reliance on a *linguistic* distinction between language and dialect, with mutual intelligibility as its main criterion. This leads her into an untenable position, such as when, in referring to Swedish and Norwegian, she claims that 'by strictly linguistic definition they are dialects of a single language' (Lakoff, 2000: 235). She oscillates between an allegedly scientific definition of the two terms (in her discussion of Swedish and Norwegian) and a more popular definition, as when she concedes that, in the end, people or at least linguists have 'a pretty good idea' of what a language is and what a dialect is (Lakoff, 2000: 236).

Lakoff (2000: 245) claims that describing AAE as a non-standard dialect of American English 'is not to make any sort of political statement – it's just a definition'. Whether something is a language or a dialect, she alleges, is not a matter of 'political expediency' but 'requires close and careful study of the complete grammatical systems of both objects under comparison' (Lakoff, 2000: 245). Yet, towards the end of her chapter, she seems to contradict herself by acknowledging that there is some 'political involvement' in the distinction between language and dialect (Lakoff, 2000: 248).

The non-linguistic nature of this distinction has already been discussed in Chapter 1, where we saw that, in fact, political involvement is what makes one variety a language and another a dialect. But what interests us here is the following question: if the societal perception of dialects is so negative, even more negative than that of foreign languages, why does it seem so difficult even for linguists to move away from the categorization of AAE as a dialect? Perhaps a hint towards an answer can be found in Baugh's (1998) discussion of the difference between Hawai'i Creole English and AAE, and why it has been possible to recognize the former as a language, whereas the latter must perforce remain a dialect. Baugh (1998) argues as follows:

> Because Hawai'i is insular, its language difficulties are confined to the state, in physical isolation from the mainland. The linguistic legacy of slavery is far more pervasive throughout the mainland, and can be traced prior to the birth of the nation. (Baugh, 1998: 294)

Because of this fundamental difference, it has been possible to implement bilingual policies to help speakers of Hawai'i Creole English achieve educational success (see Chapter 2), but not the speakers of AAE. Baugh's discussion reveals the extent to which this is a political and ideological issue and not a linguistic one: recognizing AAE as a language would be seen as a threat to national unity. As Wiley and Lukes (1996: 514–515) put it, 'the dominant groups succeed in attributing the status of language to their own variety while ascribing the status of dialect to those of others'. In this way, we see how linguists such as Robin Lakoff can be – however unwittingly – complicit in this process.

Prioritizing the social over the linguistic

To return to our basic concern, namely, the educational underachievement of African-American students within the US system of education, the question is how we can harness the vernacular in order to teach the standard. One of the most promising approaches would be a 'dialect awareness' programme (Wolfram, 2010) involving some form of contrastive analysis, which is basically what the Oakland school board wanted to do: teachers need to positively value students' home variety and explain which variety (home or school) is appropriate in which contexts (see also Rickford, 2005: 29). This is because speakers of AAE often find it difficult to differentiate between what is standard and what is non-standard. As Wolfram and Schilling-Estes (1998) put it,

> When two systems are highly similar … it is sometimes difficult to keep the systems apart … In some ways, it may be easier to work with language systems that are drastically different, since the temptation to merge overlapping structures and ignore relatively minor differences is not as great. (Wolfram & Schilling-Estes, 1998: 287)

It should be noted here that the point made by Wolfram and Schilling-Estes is a more general issue concerning the language learning of closely related varieties, whether these are perceived as dialects or languages. Thus, just as it may be difficult for learners to differentiate between AAE and standard American English, it can be equally difficult to differentiate between Dutch and German, or Swedish and Norwegian.

It would therefore be important to implement language-in-education policies building on students' knowledge of AAE and leading them towards mastery of standard English, along the lines of the Oakland school board's proposal. However, we should be aware that such measures are not enough;

in fact, they are bound to fail unless there are also social changes. In his discussion of the Ebonics controversy, McWhorter (1998: 255) reminds us that if US society really wants to solve the issue of the underachievement of children speaking AAE at home, it will also have to tackle 'the ills of poverty, drug abuse, and societal alienation'. Labov (2008), too, in a critique of sociolinguistic discourses of language endangerment, argues that we should endeavour to 'save' people rather than linguistic varieties, even if the former might have the effect of endangering the latter. He illustrates his point in relation to speakers of AAE: as a way of improving social conditions for those who are trapped in the cycle of poverty and unemployment, one key measure would be to work towards a reduction of residential segregation in US inner-city areas. In turn, this could lead to more contact between speakers of AAE and speakers of other varieties such as standard American English, as a result of which AAE could *become* an endangered variety:

> At that point, AAVE as a whole might be in danger of losing its own distinct and characteristic forms of speech. I am sure that many of us would regret the decline of the eloquent syntactic and semantic options [of AAVE] that I have presented here. But we might also reflect at that time that the loss of a dialect is a lesser evil than the current condition of an endangered people. (Labov, 2008: 235)

Labov's point about saving endangered people rather than endangered languages is a challenging one for linguists, and it applies not only to children who speak a non-standard variety of English but also to children with a non-English language background. In the remainder of this chapter, we focus on the latter category, discussing first the situation of Native Americans and then, in much greater detail, that of Latinos.

Native American Students

There are large numbers of bi- and multilingual speakers in the USA, but their proficiency in languages other than English is generally not valued in society. Moreover, official language policies such as the No Child Left Behind policy only emphasize English language proficiency and tend to look upon other languages merely as an obstacle to learning English. For this reason, many speakers of heritage languages shift to English and lose proficiency in their home language. Since the 1990s, however, there have been some signs of a revival in the learning of heritage languages, especially Native American languages. In particular, the federal

Native American Languages Act of 1990 and the Esther Martinez Native American Languages Preservation Act of 2006 officially recognize the right to use indigenous languages in such contexts as education; moreover, the number of supportive state-level policies is also increasing (de Korne, 2010, 2013).

In this section, we look at the situation of Navajo, a Native American language used in the south-west of the USA (mostly Arizona, New Mexico and Utah). Like all Native American languages, Navajo and its speakers have undergone a long history of linguistic repression:

> The present situation of Navajo is part of a larger process of language shift engulfing all Native American communities ... Of 175 Indigenous languages still spoken in the United States, only 20 are being acquired as a first language by children. The causes of language shift in Native American communities include a history of genocide, the seizure by whites of Indigenous lands, and explicit federal policies designed to eradicate Indigenous languages and to 'remake American Indian children into brown White citizens'. (McCarty et al., 2008: 161)

Navajo, with almost 178,000 speakers who are bilingual in Navajo and English, is one of the few Native American languages still acquired as a home language by children.

As part of their ethnographic research project, McCarty et al. (2008) found evidence of contradictory language ideologies on the part of Navajo speakers, in the sense that the language was simultaneously valorized and stigmatized. Young people in particular saw it as linked to their identity while feeling that it was an endangered or even dying language. They frequently used a discourse of both language pride and language shame. On the one hand, they were proud of Navajo as their own language. But, on the other hand, they also looked on Navajo as belonging to the past; for them, it indexed lack of education, poverty and backwardness, due to a process of internalization of the discriminatory ideologies present in US education and society. English, on the contrary, was linked with 'modernity, opportunity, and success' (McCarty et al., 2008: 168). As a result, many young people actually tried to hide their proficiency in Navajo, preferring to use English instead. Yet, their attitudes towards English could be equally contradictory: it was not only seen as the language of modernity but sometimes also as the language of colonization and oppression.

The research of McCarty et al. (2008) aims at raising the status of Navajo by involving young people in local activities connected with the project:

Carefully listening to youth discourses opens up new understandings of language shift dynamics and new possibilities for language education programs and practices. We are hopeful that these possibilities will continue to unfold and that they will actively involve youth and the generation of young parents, not only as language learners but as language planners, researchers and educators in their own right. (McCarty *et al.*, 2008: 170)

By working with the community in this way, it may be possible to set up flexible bilingual programmes that will foster the maintenance and revitalization of Navajo, as well as students' academic achievements in the dominant language, English. McCarty (2012, 2013) discusses such a programme at a highly successful K-5 public magnet school, the Bridge of Beauty (Puente de Hozho) School in Flagstaff, Arizona. The school is situated near a reservation, and the school population is made up of Native American, Latino and white students. Both Navajo and Spanish are widely used in the school alongside English. The school builds on the students' heteroglossic repertoires in Navajo, Spanish, English and/or other languages, all of which are seen as resources for learning. According to school co-founder Michael Fillerup (quoted in McCarty, 2013: 147), the aim is to create a school culture in which 'diverse languages and cultures [are] regarded as assets rather than deficits, as things to be desired and augmented rather than eliminated or suppressed'. At the same time, emphasis is put on the students' acquisition of standard English, since the school will only be allowed to continue its bilingual programmes if its students score well enough on the standardized tests in English mandated by both federal and state policy. The school's results have been highly promising, in that its students have consistently outperformed their peers in Arizona's English-only programmes (McCarty, 2012: 9). Unfortunately, however, most Native American and Latino children do not attend such schools and so, in the following section, we will see how many Latino students, instead of being able to develop in rich multilingual environments such as that of the Bridge of Beauty School, suffer from restrictive English-only policies.

Latino Students

The English-only movement and the fear of Spanish

According to Wiley and Lukes (1996), the dominant language ideologies in the USA are an ideology of English monolingualism and the standard language ideology, and these are linked to such concepts as 'national unity'.

These ideologies underpin US language policies, and it should be clear that bilingual education does not fit into this model. Hence, as has already been mentioned, if bilingual education is practised at all, it tends to be of a transitional type with an emphasis on English immersion.

In fact, any social phenomenon that breaks through the boundaries of these ideologies tends to be perceived as what McCarty (2004: 72) refers to as a 'dangerous' difference in society that needs to be contained. This explains some of the attitudes towards bilingual education. It also explains why the Ebonics controversy developed into a veritable 'language panic' (Hill, 2001). As Native American communities have been the victims of such containment policies for centuries and most Native American languages are now only used by comparatively small and isolated groups, these languages are no longer the targets of national language panics. But Spanish, with its constantly increasing number of speakers across the USA, is recurrently the target of such panics, and this will be the focus of the following sections. The reactions against these social phenomena which are perceived as threatening include such containment measures as anti-bilingual and anti-immigration legislation, English-only mandates, high-stakes (standardized) testing in English and other accountability measures in education, as well as phonics-based literacy teaching (in the English language, of course; see McCarty, 2004: 75).

Such measures are frequently advocated by the English-only movement, which is spearheaded by two associations: US English and English First. US English was founded in 1983 by Senator Samuel Hayakawa, as well as John Tanton, who also founded the Federation for American Immigration Reform, an association aiming to limit immigration to the USA. As for English First, it was founded by Larry Pratt, the president of Gun Owners of America. The English-only movement is lobbying for a constitutional amendment which would designate English as the sole official language of the USA. Such a move is needed, they argue, in order to protect English, which is currently threatened by other languages, especially Spanish.

While the English-only movement has not been successful at the federal level, it has achieved much better results at state level; many states have now declared English to be their sole official language. It has also been successful in its fight against bilingual education. Most bilingual programmes in the USA have been of a limited, transitional type (transitioning students mostly from Spanish to English), yet the English-only movement worked hard to restrict bilingual education even further. Ron Unz, a Silicon Valley businessman, led campaigns against bilingual education in such states as California, Arizona and Massachusetts. This has entailed the passing of California's Proposition 227 ('English for the Children') in 1998, Arizona's Proposition

203 in 2000 and Question 2 in Massachusetts in 2002, the effect of which has been to restrict even transitional bilingual programmes and to replace them with ESL programmes. Furthermore, a similar effect has been achieved at the federal level by former President Bush's No Child Left Behind policy, which transformed the Bilingual Education Act into the English Language Acquisition Act.

These anti-bilingual education measures have had much popular support, as can be seen from the votes in California, Arizona and Massachusetts. But we may wonder why so many Americans feel that English, the dominant global language, is threatened by Spanish, and why they fear that English might actually die out and be replaced by Spanish. Undoubtedly, these fears need to be understood as a response to (biased) media coverage of an increase in the number of poor immigrants, mostly from Mexico. In other words, language is used as a proxy in what is largely an anti-immigration feeling and movement, which, furthermore, tends to gain in strength in times of economic recession.

Restrictive English-only policies in Arizona

As a prime example of restrictive English-only policies, I focus on Arizona in this section. It may be useful to start with a brief historical overview as a way of providing some background for understanding the current situation. In 1845, Texas was annexed by the USA, which led to the Mexican–American war of 1846–1848. In 1848, after the war, further territories that were annexed included Arizona, New Mexico, California, Nevada and Utah. As a result, in the south-west, a power struggle developed between the white Anglo-Americans and the Hispanic Americans, who were Spanish settlers and colonists. In the New Mexico territory in particular, this led to a scission between Arizona, where Anglo-Americans formed the majority, and New Mexico, where Hispanic Americans formed the majority. At the beginning of the 20th century, there was a plan to unite Arizona and New Mexico into one state, but it was rejected by Arizona because of a racially motivated fear concerning their English language school system. The separation became definite in 1911, with New Mexico becoming the 47th state in the union and Arizona the 48th state (Stull, 2012: 22).

While New Mexico has had a bilingual Spanish–English system of education throughout its history, Arizona introduced the infamous 'Mexican rooms', similar to the low-quality Mexican schools in Texas and California, where Spanish-speaking students were separated from their Anglo-American peers. Paradoxically, even though the stated aim was 'Americanization', it was felt necessary to segregate the Latino students in order to teach them

English and ultimately to suppress Spanish. This language-in-education policy continued until 1951, when an Arizona federal court decision, *Gonzales v. Sheely*, outlawed the segregation of Latino students because of its harmful effects (Gándara & Orfield, 2012: 12).

Despite this, Arizona has continued as one of the states with the most restrictive language policies. In 1988, English was declared the official language of Arizona; in 2000, Proposition 203 (English Language Education for the Children in the Public Schools) was approved by a majority of voters and led to the replacement of bilingual education with ESL programmes. Furthermore, in 2010, Arizona introduced one of the toughest immigration laws in the USA, and it adopted a statute outlawing ethnic studies programmes in K-12 classrooms, as well as removing teachers with allegedly 'heavy' accents from classrooms with English Language Learners (ELLs) and requiring them to take 'accent-reduction' courses (Stull, 2012: 23).

Proposition 203 led to the introduction of a policy of Structured English Immersion, consisting of teaching Latino students English as quickly as possible, using English as the sole medium of instruction and ignoring their first language (Spanish), even though such a policy has frequently been shown to be pedagogically ineffective and to increase social and educational inequalities. In 2008, the English Language Learners Task Force developed uniform guidelines, and all school districts were required to abide by these guidelines (Long & Adamson, 2012: 39). The Arizona Department of Education even threatened to impose sanctions, 'given well publicized defiance [of this policy] by several school districts' (Combs, 2012: 77). The new policy consists of a four-hour English Language Development block for all ELLs. Each day, they are separated from the mainstream students, grouped into proficiency levels and taught English, with the time to be spent on each language skill specified in a detailed curriculum. It has been argued that the four-hour a day English Language Development block is a way of recreating the 'Mexican rooms' and that Latino students are again being segregated on the basis of race (e.g. Gándara & Orfield, 2012: 15).

It has also been argued that the segregation of ELLs has negative effects and that ELLs going through the four-hour English Language Development block show lower levels of academic achievement than other ELLs who stay in the mainstream classroom (e.g. Rios-Aguilar *et al.*, 2012). This is because English Language Development classes focus on teaching English language forms and discrete skills (in particular, phonology, morphology, syntax and vocabulary), and there is no teaching of academic content (mathematics, science, social studies, etc.) which, however, is crucial for ELLs' educational success. As a consequence, there are 'restricted opportunities for creative student talk [and] academic discourse' (Long & Adamson, 2012: 44, 49), unlike in task-based communicative or bilingual programmes, which allow students to 'develop their command of English *and* their subject matter knowledge' (Long & Adamson, 2012: 46).

Furthermore, the four-hour English Language Development block segregates Latino students from their English-speaking peers, who could otherwise provide much of the language practice needed for fast and efficient language acquisition (Long & Adamson, 2012: 42). This throws doubt on the stated aim of the policy that ELLs should reach a high enough level of English in order to be transitioned into mainstream classrooms after just one year. Moreover, such a policy of segregating students can 'have negative linguistic and cultural consequences' (Long & Adamson, 2012: 42). In light of all these problematic aspects, it might be interesting to note that there is an opt-out possibility for parents. However, not many parents have been able to avail of this option because, in line with the restrictive nature of all aspects of this policy, it is extremely difficult to get waiver requests approved and, moreover, enough waivers must be approved in order to justify forming a special classroom.

Another highly restrictive aspect of this policy concerns teacher training. Since 2006, Arizona requires all its schoolteachers to have a teacher preparation endorsement in Structured English Immersion for working with ELLs (Arias, 2012: 14). The prescriptive curriculum of this programme 'reflects the state's restrictive language policy and promotes a monolingual ideology which is pedagogically detrimental to ELLs' (Arias, 2012: 6). As the syllabus has to be approved by the state, this means that institutions of higher education are required by law to reproduce an English-only ideology of linguistic assimilation in their teacher training courses (Arias, 2012: 5). Because the teacher preparation endorsement in Structured English Immersion is limited in time, it cannot deal with the wider sociopolitical dimensions of language use but is restricted to the issue of teaching discrete linguistic skills and in the process transmits restrictive language policy values to pre-service teachers. It can lead to deficit views of ELLs as it encourages 'teachers to think that simple methods and procedures will fix ELLs' "problems"' (Olson, 2012: 179). And if these 'simple methods' do not fix the 'problems' of Latino students' underachievement, then the implication is that it must be because these students are deficient. What this simplistic English-only approach does not encourage teachers to do is to critically examine the restrictive ideologies underlying 'the policies, programmes and mandated curriculum that fail to recognize ELLs' cultural repertoire of skills and knowledge' (Olson, 2012: 179).

Dual language education

Despite the continuing history of linguistic repression in the USA, it is interesting to note that dual language programmes are exempt from the law and continue to exist even in states such as Arizona, California and Massachusetts with their restrictive English-only and anti-bilingual education policies. In fact, there is a growing number of such programmes, especially in California, which may be due to the fact that, while transitional bilingual programmes for migrant students only are negatively perceived, dual language programmes tend to be seen as a valuable option for both migrant and mainstream students. Indeed, these programmes bring together English learners and native English speakers with the aim of developing (usually English–Spanish) bilingualism and biliteracy in all students. Both languages are used as media of instruction and share roughly equal instruction time. It is often middle-class parents who see the instrumental value of such an education for their children. A further positive aspect of these programmes is that, by bringing together (usually) Latino and Anglo-American students and putting them in an environment where they learn from each other, this can lead to desegregation and anti-racism (de Jong *et al.*, 2010). Thus, dual language programmes combine the educational goal of high academic achievement with the more social goal of intercultural understanding.

One issue with dual language programmes is that they are often informed by the standard language ideology and do not sufficiently take into account language variation and the children's non-standard home varieties. Therefore, Rubinstein-Avila (2002) insists on a need for greater flexibility in these programmes. She discusses a dual language programme in a school in Massachusetts serving English-speaking and Portuguese-speaking students. The latter group includes speakers of Iberian Portuguese, Brazilian Portuguese and Cape Verdean Creole, with a growing number of the students at the school having recently immigrated from Brazil. The question of which standard, Iberian or Brazilian Portuguese, the tests were going to assess became quite a heated issue among the teachers (Rubinstein-Avila, 2002: 81). Eventually, the teachers agreed to avoid using certain 'problematic' words in the tests (i.e. words with a different meaning in Iberian and Brazilian Portuguese; Rubinstein-Avila, 2002: 82). At the same time, Rubinstein-Avila notes that speakers of Cape Verdean Creole were consistently marginalized, as their varieties were not taken into consideration by the teachers. Rubinstein-Avila (2002: 84) concludes that 'a critical look at language variety is crucial in dual-immersion programmes'.

The same also happens with the vernacular varieties of Latino students, which are often stigmatized by their teachers as well as the other students. Latino students are sometimes marginalized and can feel alienated in Spanish classes because of the language ideologies prevalent there. According to Valdés *et al.* (2008: 125), these ideologies reproduce the 'nation-imagining' beliefs and values of mainstream US society, a society that views itself as monolingual and English speaking, and that is highly suspicious of bilingualism and other languages. The Spanish programmes simply transmit this ideology of monolingualism within the context of Spanish studies, in that they subscribe to the ideal of the monolingual and educated native speaker, whose standard Spanish is looked upon as the only 'correct' form of the language. As a result, many Spanish teachers feel the need to protect the language from 'contamination' by the mixed or contact varieties used by Latino bilinguals. Parodi (2008), on the other hand, emphasizes the need to change such teacher attitudes and argues that Latino students not only need to be given help with standard, academic Spanish but at the same time should also be encouraged to maintain their vernacular home varieties. This is the only way, Parodi insists, of helping them to deal with the stigma attached to their varieties in society and to overcome their linguistic insecurity in educational contexts – a solution which is reminiscent of the dialect awareness programmes advocated by Wolfram and others for speakers of AAE (discussed earlier in this chapter).

Despite these, at times, unresolved issues, dual language programmes seem like a beautiful flower blooming in the educational wasteland of restrictive, English-only policies. However, it is important to add that this flower blooms in areas that are not accessible to all students, as, for instance, Palmer (2010) shows in her study of an elementary school in northern California with a dual 'strand' programme. In other words, dual language here is not a whole-school programme as there is only one dual language class at each grade level in an otherwise English-medium mainstream public school. The student population is divided between African-Americans, Latinos and whites. Yet, there are hardly any African-American students in the dual language strand. Palmer explores the question of why these students seem to be excluded. She argues that it is largely due to 'deficit attitudes' (Palmer, 2010: 96) shared by many teachers towards these students. There is a widespread assumption that African-American students 'would not be interested in dual-language education' and that such programmes 'might not even be appropriate for black students' (Palmer, 2010: 108–109). Underlying these teacher beliefs is, according to Palmer (2010: 109), a racist attitude towards African-American students who are seen as being 'in need of remedial, as opposed to enrichment, experiences'.

However, academic research points in exactly the opposite direction. After reviewing studies of students in dual language programmes who are from a low socio-economic background or who have minority ethnic group status (including those speaking non-standard varieties of the majority language, such as AAE), Genesee (2008) concludes as follows:

> Practically speaking, the available evidence does not justify arbitrary exclusion of majority language students who face special learning challenges from dual language programmes on the assumption that they are incapable of benefiting from academic instruction through a second language, or that they will be held back in native language and academic development as a result of such instruction. (Genesee, 2008: 41)

Whose story is it anyway?

The story I have told in this chapter is one of linguistic repression and social oppression of minority communities by the white, Anglo-American middle and upper classes. The fierce repression of indigenous Native American languages has nowadays given way to the repression of immigrant languages. Or is it simply a continuation of the same policy, except that nowadays most Native American languages no longer pose a threat to white America? Even the brief interlude initiated by the civil rights movement of the 1960s only led to the implementation of a rather 'spineless' Bilingual Education Act (1968), which mostly fostered weak bilingual programmes of the transitional type or ESL programmes. The importance of making ELLs proficient in English as quickly as possible was increasingly emphasized during the 1970s and 1980s, so that by the 1990s the stage was set for the implementation of increasingly restrictive English-only policies. It is ironic that the only bilingual programmes that are allowed to flourish are dual language programmes, which bring together ELLs and native English speakers. They flourish mostly in middle-class areas where white Anglo-American parents see the instrumental value of such a bilingual (mostly English–Spanish) education for their own children. With such a focus on instrumental values, it is no wonder that these programmes tend to be informed by the standard language ideology and largely ignore linguistic variation among language minority speakers (as discussed in the previous section). It is also not surprising that African-American students are frequently excluded from these programmes, since they might be seen as detracting from the instrumental value of the programme (also discussed above). We reach the conclusion that bilingual education is only supported if it is perceived by middle-class parents as beneficial to their own children. But this implies severe limitations: extending such programmes to schools in lower-class areas or to large numbers of African-American students might be a far less attractive prospect in the eyes of many middle-class parents and policymakers.

Hence, dual language programmes tend to increase mostly in middle- and lower-middle-class areas. On the other hand, they are usually not available in lower-class areas and thus do not help with the education of the most underprivileged and disenfranchised children. It is for reasons such as these that Valdés (1997) has warned against making dual language education available to large numbers of white Anglo-American students. As they do not contribute to the education of the most marginalized children, these programmes may just have negative social effects in the sense of making the Spanish language a commodity available to large numbers of middle-class students, thereby reducing the value of the one advantage that lower-class Latino students enjoy on the employment market, namely, their proficiency in Spanish (alongside English).

At the same time, however, this does not mean that we should reject dual language programmes *en bloc*. On the contrary, they constitute an extremely attractive and successful model of bilingual education, and it is up to researchers in the area of multilingual education to develop this model further and make it more flexible, so that it can be applied across the whole school population of the USA and no group of children is any longer excluded from it.

Lessons to be Learnt from the US Experience

In this concluding section, I briefly summarize the main points that can be learnt from the US experience:

- it is important to build on students' home linguistic resources, whether these are perceived as 'dialects' or 'languages', in order to lead them towards acquisition of the school standard;
- especially in the case of closely related varieties (such as AAE and standard English), it is essential for the teacher to help students differentiate between their vernacular variety and the standard variety;
- linguistic measures need to be complemented by social changes if they are to achieve real success;
- instead of being able to develop in rich multilingual environments, many Native American, Latino and other students with home languages other

than English suffer both psychologically and academically from restrictive English-only policies;

- a promising option is dual language education, though such programmes
  need to become more flexible (in terms of linguistic variation) and more
  inclusive (of all students);
- the relative success of dual language education reveals a somewhat disturbing political dimension: bi- and multilingual education seems to be
  supported only if it is perceived by middle-class parents as beneficial to
  their own children.

6 Hong Kong and China

This chapter focuses on the People's Republic of China as well as, more particularly, Hong Kong. In 1997, Hong Kong changed its status from a British colony to a Special Administrative Region of China. Under the principle of 'one country, two systems', it has been allowed to keep a different political system from mainland China. While China as a whole has a population of over 1.3 billion, Hong Kong has about 7 million inhabitants. As we will see, both Hong Kong and China as a whole are multilingual areas of the world, and both have implemented bi- or multilingual education systems. I first discuss language and education in Hong Kong, and then, in the second half of the chapter, I turn to an investigation of language-in-education policies and issues in mainland China.

Hong Kong

The language situation in Hong Kong

Two languages are recognized as official in the Basic Law of Hong Kong: Chinese and English, where Chinese is normally understood to refer to Modern Standard Chinese as the written version and Cantonese as the spoken one. At the same time, Putonghua (Mandarin), which is the spoken form of Modern Standard Chinese and the national language of China as a whole, has been vigorously promoted since the 1997 changeover of sovereignty. The official policy is for all Hong Kongers to become biliterate and trilingual: biliterate in Chinese and English, and trilingual in Cantonese, Putonghua and English.

With regard to English in Hong Kong, it has played a highly controversial role as the colonial language. As in many other countries around the world, the colonial language was reserved for a small elite of local administrators who were allowed privileged access to an English-medium education, whereas all other colonial subjects were only given access to frequently second-rate types of vernacular education. According to Pennycook (2002), the British colonial government in Hong Kong promoted vernacular Chinese education as a way of inculcating the conservative ideals of Confucian ethics and thus enhancing the colonial domination of its subjects: 'Conservative Chinese education was the colonial route to the making of docile bodies'

(Pennycook, 2002: 108). Pennycook's analysis of vernacular education as a form of governmentality and surveillance leads him to the following important conclusion:

This understanding of increased modes of surveillance brings into question [the] widely held view of language policy that mother tongue or vernacular education is necessarily preferable to education in other languages. (Pennycook, 2002: 108)

It is this historical background, as well as the continuing socio-economic importance of English in Hong Kong society, that explains why English-medium education is in such high demand nowadays. Yet, after Hong Kong's return to China in 1997, the government introduced a streaming system, channelling large numbers of students into Chinese-medium secondary education. Lin (2001) argues that this policy reproduces social stratification in Hong Kong society: only the children of the wealthy, English-oriented elite gain access to the prestigious English-medium schools. As a result, there is a widening gap between a middle- and upper-class elite, whose children study at English-medium schools, and most other parents, who are forced to send their children to Chinese-medium schools. In this way, the present system perpetuates the social injustices of the colonial system (Lin, 2001). Therefore, Lin advocates instead a more flexible, bilingual English–Chinese educational system for all students at all levels of education. As we will see, the Hong Kong government has, to some extent, responded to these criticisms by allowing more English-medium instruction (EMI) in Chinese-medium schools since September 2010.

Bilingualism and identity in Hong Kong

Hong Kong society is ethnically quite homogeneous: over 93% are ethnic Chinese, with Cantonese as the home language of most of them. They tend to use Cantonese in everyday interactions, whereas English is limited to specific institutional contexts including school in particular. Thus, most Hong Kong Chinese are bilingual in Cantonese and English, though there are clear social class differences here. Many lower-class people only know Cantonese, whereas the middle classes, who often went through English-medium education, are much more proficient in English and also use a lot of code-switching between English and Cantonese. As Lin (2001: 160) puts it, there is an 'uneven distribution of English linguistic capital among different social groups in Hong Kong'.

Furthermore, Lin (2006) notes that Cantonese–English mixed code, which is in fact a linguistic continuum of different styles of speaking, can be seen as indexical of Hong Kong identity. There is a continuous

> intertwining of Cantonese and English words in the everyday public and private life of Hong Kong people, and these 'non-pure' linguistic practices seem to be playing an important role in marking out the hybridized, multilingual Hong Kong identity – they seem to serve as distinctive linguistic and cultural markers of 'Hong Kong-ness'. (Lin, 2006: 288)

Lin adds that this hybrid Hong Kong identity is often marked by a lack of acceptance of British colonial rule before 1997 as well as ambivalent feelings about 'Socialist China domination' since 1997 (Lin, 2006: 288). In this way, 'the distinct local identity of the people of Hong Kong' has been shaped by resistance to both British colonialism and Chinese nationalism (Tsui, 2007: 138), while at the same time it may be mixed with such factors as nostalgia for the past and the desire for a larger share in China's economic boom.

As a way of illustrating the bilingualism of Hong Kong society, I refer briefly to a small-scale linguistic landscape study by Scollon and Scollon (2003). The authors contrast street signs, signs in a shopping mall and signs for the Mass Transit Railway (MTR) system. Whereas on the street signs and the shopping mall signs, English is on top and Chinese below, the MTR signs are just the inverse, with Chinese on top and English below. Scollon and Scollon argue that the street signs constitute a carry-over from the era of colonialism, and the shopping mall signs refract an ideology of globalization (English as the global language, Chinese as local). On the other hand, the MTR signs are more pragmatic and instrumental, primarily addressing the users of the transport system, the huge majority of whom are Chinese speaking.

Is Hong Kong ethnically homogeneous?

As in any society, there are ethnic minority groups in Hong Kong, one of the biggest of which is the South Asian group, whose members have migrated from a wide range of countries including India, Pakistan, Nepal and Thailand (Gu & Patkin, 2013: 132). They tend to be fluent in English, as well as other languages such as Punjabi, Urdu and Hindi, but often they are not very fluent in Cantonese or Putonghua. For those who migrated during the colonial period, life was made easier by the fact that English was the most important language, which allowed them upward mobility. However, since the 1997 handover of sovereignty to China, Chinese (Cantonese and also Putonghua) has played an increasingly important role, which has caused some problems for South Asian children enrolled in Chinese-medium education, as no special support is provided for these children in mainstream schools. Especially at primary level, there are few schools with English as the medium of instruction, and most of these are private schools charging high fees, which many South Asian parents cannot afford. It is estimated that about 30,000 students from this group are attending educational institutions in Hong Kong, many of whom are at risk of failure 'due to language barriers' (Tsung, 2009: 183). As a way of dealing with this predicament, over the last few years the government has opened about 30 'designated schools' using mostly English as their medium of instruction and teaching Chinese as a second language, specifically 'to cater for the needs of South Asian children' (Gao, 2011: 255). However, Gao (2011: 258) maintains that on the whole these are rather low-quality schools and that a better solution would be to offer these children 'first language support combined with good second language programmes' within mainstream schools.

What is Chinese?

Hong Kong has two official languages, English and Chinese, with 'Chinese' deliberately left undefined. What exactly does it refer to? For spoken language, it traditionally refers to Cantonese, and for writing, it refers to Modern Standard Chinese. However, each of these subsumes a range of practices. First, Cantonese exists both in a 'high' and a 'low' form. While 'high' Cantonese is used for public speeches, lectures, etc., 'low' Cantonese is used at home and with friends (Poon, 2010: 13). Spoken Cantonese has been made popular through television soaps and Cantopop music, and it needs to be noted that there also exists a written form of Hong Kong Cantonese, which is widely used in SMS, emails, blogs, Facebook, etc. (Poon, 2010: 23).

As for Modern Standard Chinese, two writing systems are used to represent it: traditional characters or simplified characters. Traditional characters are used in Hong Kong but simplified characters are increasingly appearing, due to the influence of mainland China, where the simplified characters were introduced in the middle of the 20th century. Moreover, Pinyin is the Romanization system used for transcribing Chinese characters into Latin script.

Since the 1997 changeover of sovereignty, the Hong Kong government has vigorously promoted Putonghua (Mandarin), which is the spoken form of Modern Standard Chinese and the national language of mainland China. As mentioned above, the official policy is for all Hong Kongers to become biliterate in Chinese and English, and trilingual in Cantonese, Putonghua and English. In fact, Putonghua became a compulsory subject in primary and secondary schools in 1998, and there are a number of pilot projects using Putonghua rather than Cantonese as the medium of instruction (Poon, 2010: 20). The government's aim is to introduce Putonghua as the medium of instruction for the Chinese language subject, and eventually as the medium of instruction for all school subjects (except English), as a result of which Cantonese would become just a home or community language (Poon, 2010: 58–59). Gradually, more and more schools are introducing Putonghua rather than Cantonese as their medium of instruction for the Chinese language subjects. As Tam (2011: 403) points out, there is at the moment 'a wide variety of PMI [Putonghua as medium of instruction] programme models, ranging from Putonghua being taught as a discrete independent subject to partial immersion programmes, i.e. selected classes are taught in Putonghua'.

One example is the primary school studied by Wang and Kirkpatrick (2013). In its endeavour to implement the new biliteracy and trilingualism policy, the school uses the three languages as media of instruction: Cantonese for maths, general studies, music, IT and Chinese literacy (in P1–P3, i.e. the first three years of primary education); Putonghua as the medium of instruction for the study of Putonghua and Chinese literacy (in P4–P6, i.e. the last three years of primary education); and English as the medium of instruction for English, physical education and visual arts. Wang and Kirkpatrick (2013: 102) add that 'currently, the school is trialling the use of Putonghua as the medium of instruction for Chinese literacy lessons in one of the three P1 classes'. Thus we note that, apart from the introduction of English as a medium of instruction for a small number of subjects already from P1 (the first year of primary education), there is also a gradual shift towards the increased use of Putonghua as the medium of instruction for the Chinese language subjects from P1 onwards.

It is interesting to note how the government's pedagogical justification for promoting Chinese has changed over the years: while in the past the promotion of Cantonese emphasized the importance of students being able to learn in their 'mother tongue', the present promotion of Putonghua moves away from mother tongue instruction and argues instead that the close link between Putonghua and Modern Standard Chinese makes it easier for students to acquire Chinese literacy. This is what makes Lin and Man (2009) assert that

it is the national unifying agenda through the imposition of the national language of Putonghua upon the schooling system that is hidden behind the official discourse of the pedagogical benefits of using Putonghua to improve students' written skills in Modern Standard Chinese. (Lin & Man, 2009: 84)

Bilingual education and medium of instruction in Hong Kong

According to Tsui (2007), the colonial period was marked by a policy of desinicization, while the postcolonial period is marked by the opposite process of resinicization. There may be some truth to this, but it needs to be added that the process of desinicization really only affected a small educated elite, who were given an English-medium education, whereas the masses continued to attend rather low-quality Chinese-medium schools. In this way, colonial language-in-education policy established the supremacy of English-medium education, by restricting it to the privileged few. The vast majority of students were forced to go through Chinese-medium education under British colonial rule, though this changed during the last few decades before the handover, as more and more English-medium secondary schools opened, partly under pressure from parents who wanted more access to English for their children. As a consequence, the new leaders of postcolonial Hong Kong felt that there was a need for resinicization of the masses through the reinstatement of mandatory Chinese-medium education, while the elites, as we will see, were allowed to continue with English-medium education. In this way, Chinese-medium education was imposed against the wishes of many parents.

The government's justification for this was that the sudden shift from Chinese-medium primary education to English-medium secondary education was very difficult for many students. As a result, these students resorted to survival strategies such as rote memorization, and their teachers relied upon English–Cantonese code-switching as a way of scaffolding their students' learning. Already the colonial government had looked upon such language mixing as a sign of falling standards and felt that there was a need for a clearer distinction between schools: each school should have only one medium of instruction, either English or Chinese (Lin, 2001: 142). This was the key idea behind the 1994 Medium of Instruction Grouping Assessment (MIGA) policy (Lin, 2001: 161). But as the policy was only advisory for schools, most of the schools that had been advised to switch to Chinese as their medium of instruction continued as English-medium schools but with an even higher degree of Cantonese–English language mixing (Lin & Man, 2009: 90).

Therefore, after the 1997 handover, the streaming policy was fully implemented and became mandatory in the first three years of secondary school, which also included the banning of Cantonese–English code-switching. One hundred and fourteen schools (initially 100, with 14 added after protests) were chosen as English-medium schools, while more than 400 schools became Chinese-medium schools. The former, all located in middle-class areas, were soon perceived as the elite schools; the latter, on the other hand, were looked down on as second rate (Lin, 2001: 162). Unfortunately, this amounted to a reinstatement of the colonial system of education, with a privileged elite allowed to attend English-medium schools, whereas the large majority of children were forced to attend lower-quality Chinese-medium schools.

The 1998 streaming policy thus reinstated mother tongue education in over 70% of public sector secondary schools (Lin, 2006: 293). This resolved the difficulty for many students of the sudden switch from Cantonese to English as the medium of instruction at the beginning of secondary education. But it created two other problems (Lin & Man, 2009: 67):

- lack of articulation between Chinese-medium secondary schools and English-medium university education;
- deepening social stratification.

According to Lin (2001: 160), it was an 'elitist and socially divisive' policy that she describes as 'elitism without meritocracy', which segregated students in terms of social class. The education system helped to construct and reproduce social stratification and inequality, widening the gap between English-educated cosmopolitans and non-English-speaking (or limited-English-speaking) lower-class subalterns (Lin, 2005: 51).

Thus, in Hong Kong, mother tongue education was imposed top-down, often against the wishes of parents – though we need to remember that 'only the spoken medium is mother tongue, while the written medium of schooling, Modern Standard Chinese, is in fact quite different from the students' mother tongue' (Lin & Man, 2009: 129). As already mentioned above, Pennycook (2002: 108) concludes that the common assumption that 'mother tongue or vernacular education is necessarily preferable to education in other languages' is brought into question by the Hong Kong experience. In fact, the value of the children's mother tongue was denigrated by forcing them into a second-rate Chinese-medium education and denying them access to English-medium education (Lin, 2005: 44).

What makes this even worse is that English-medium students actually seem to get better results than Chinese-medium students in A-level examinations and university admission tests. These findings are based on a longitudinal study conducted by Tsang (2008) and discussed in Li (2011):

In terms of meeting the minimal requirements for admission into local universities as measured by the student's A-level examination scores,

CMI [Chinese-medium instruction] students were worse by a wide margin. Interestingly, those CMI students who switched to English-medium instruction earlier (e.g. Form Four) tended to fare better than those who did so later (e.g. Form Six), with the group who received CMI instruction throughout (i.e. from Form One to Form Seven) having the lowest success rate … The findings led Tsang to conclude that, relative to gaining access to university education as one of the primary goals of secondary education, mother tongue education did not seem to be serving CMI students' best interests. (Li, 2011: 108)

Towards a flexible education system and bilingual pedagogies

Lin and Man argue that the dualistic, either-or streaming policy (either English-medium or Chinese-medium) is a form of 'monolingual reductionism … which is non-conducive to the development of biliterate and trilingual proficiencies among the school populations' (Lin & Man, 2009: 95; quoting So, 2000). They advocate a more flexible approach involving a more gradual change from Chinese-medium to English-medium education for all children, with gradually more and more subjects being taught through English, while some subjects continue to be taught through Chinese (Lin & Man, 2009: 67, 95).

In fact, the government has also moved in this direction of greater flexibility with its 'fine-tuning' policy implemented from 2010. Depending on the fulfilment of certain conditions, schools can nowadays opt for a continuum of medium-of-instruction policies, ranging from Chinese-medium at one end via Chinese and English as media of instruction in different subjects to English-medium at the other end (Poon, 2010: 42). The conditions that need to be fulfilled concern student ability (to learn through English), teacher capability (to teach in English) and the provision of support measures by the school (Poon, 2010: 41).

In this way, the English-medium and Chinese-medium labels are gradually disappearing, as schools have greater flexibility to offer both English and Chinese as media of instruction for different subjects according to students' needs and abilities. This greater autonomy of schools to choose their own medium of instruction is reminiscent of the South African situation (see Chapter 8), where it depends on two main factors:

- greater homogeneity vs heterogeneity of the school population (more homogeneous in rural schools, more heterogeneous in urban schools);
- pressure exerted by parents who want their children to have access to English as early as possible.

Whereas the first factor is much less relevant in Hong Kong, the second factor does apply. Indeed, in the new system, students can switch from Chinese-medium instruction (CMI) to EMI classes as soon as they reach the required level of proficiency in English, and many of them are highly motivated – and pushed by their parents – to make this effort, as 'being placed in EMI classes implies that these students will stand a higher chance of entering university and get a better job in future, and hopefully increase their social mobility' (Poon, 2013: 46).

At the same time, in Hong Kong's schools there is a need to rehabilitate bilingual strategies and code-switching. According to Lin and Man (2009: 136), it is essential to move beyond the purist ideology underlying the streaming policy towards bilingual pedagogies involving the strategic use of students' home language(s). As we have seen, there is a lot of code-switching both in Hong Kong society in general and in Hong Kong classrooms in particular. The latter is due at least partly to many students' limited knowledge of English. However, as we have also seen, because code-switching was looked upon negatively by policymakers and government officials, one rationale behind the 1998 streaming policy was to cut down on teachers' use of code-switching.

But teachers can use code-switching positively as a way of scaffolding their students' learning and making English-medium education more accessible and meaningful for all students, especially those with limited English resources (Lin, 2001: 155). According to Li (2008: 84), code-switching into Cantonese in lessons with English as the medium of instruction can help to 'clarify difficult concepts', 'introduce or consolidate students' bilingual lexicon' and 'build rapport by reducing social distance' between teacher and students. Lin (2006) gives the example of a science teacher whose use of code-switching is a way of building on students' linguistic and cultural resources to help them access the dominant discourse of science. She concludes that bilingual strategies such as code-switching can be fruitfully used in the particular sociocultural context of Hong Kong, as long as no unrealistic expectations are associated with it. Indeed, using code-switching to give students access to the global English discourses of science and technology will not make them fluent speakers of everyday English (Lin, 2006: 301). But what it can do is 'contribute to [a positive] transformation of [socially disadvantaged] students' habitus' (Lin, 1999: 411).

China

Diversity and unification

Just as in Hong Kong, there is an enormous and ever-increasing demand for English in mainland China. Official policy has responded to this demand by introducing English as a primary school subject from third grade. Before this reform, implemented on a gradual basis from 2001 onwards, English had on the whole only been taught at secondary level. As a result, nowadays the majority population, the Han Chinese, are expected to be bilingual in standard Chinese (Putonghua 'Common Language') and English, while the numerous minority groups are expected to be bilingual in their own minority language and standard Chinese.

However, as Lam and Wang (2008) show, the actual linguistic reality of China is far more complex than the official bilingual policy, with most people not only using standard Chinese and English but also a range of local or regional Chinese 'dialects' (*fangyan*) as well as minority languages. Many of the Chinese 'dialects' spoken by the Han Chinese are mutually unintelligible, a point that I will return to later in this chapter as it has important repercussions for education. As for the ethnic minorities (about 100 million people or over 8% of the total population of China), 56 groups are officially recognized and they speak over 100 languages, which mostly belong to the Sino-Tibetan, Altaic, Korean, Austric and Indo-European language families (Lam & Wang, 2008: 148; Tsung, 2009: 12).

Lam and Wang (2008) discuss in detail the circumstances of a number of Han Chinese and minority group members. Their vignettes of minority group members include, for instance, Mei whose home language is Yao (a minority language that she still uses for in-group communication). At school, she learnt Putonghua, but she also picked up the local Guilin 'dialect' used by most of her schoolmates. At later stages, she also learnt two foreign languages (English and Japanese). As for Ma, he used the Dong language at home and he also learnt the Zhuang language, two minority languages spoken in the area where he grew up. At school, he learnt both the Guiliu 'dialect' and Putonghua, as well as a number of foreign languages (mainly English). As for the Han Chinese group members that Lam and Wang interviewed, they used Putonghua, one or more local or regional 'dialects' and one or more foreign languages, though none of them had learnt any of the minority languages. On the whole, the minority group members tended to be even more multilingual than the Han Chinese group members, as all of them, apart from their home language(s), also learnt one of the Chinese 'dialects' as a kind of 'intermediary code' (Lam & Wang, 2008: 166) before learning Putonghua.

Yet, behind this remarkable linguistic diversity, there is also a strong ideology of homogeneity and uniformity focused on Putonghua, as Dong (2009) points out. Thus, not speaking Putonghua is sometimes identified with being poorly educated. As one of Dong's informants says, complaining about the fact that she could not understand a Chinese man who had recently migrated from the countryside to Beijing: 'What kind of education did he have if he couldn't even speak Putonghua?' (Dong, 2009: 117). Whereas the informant was a local Beijing woman, her male interlocutor was from Hubei province in the middle of China and could only speak his regional vernacular. Another of Dong's examples involves a discussion among primary schoolchildren in Beijing about the differences between rural and urban origins. At one point in the discussion, one of the migrant (or rural-origin) children says, 'Isn't it enough that we are all *Chinese?* Look, we all speak *Putonghua*' (Dong, 2009: 119; the italics reflect the speaker's emphasis on the words 'Chinese' and 'Putonghua'). Dong comments that the child is here overlaying her own (stigmatized) rural identity with a national identity – being Chinese – which is constructed around the use of Putonghua. This reveals the prevalence of the one nation–one language ideology even among 10-year-old children.

The construction of migrant language and identity as a 'problem'

Dong (2010) calls the process of construction and imposition of Putonghua as a national linguistic standard, 'the enregisterment of Putonghua in practice', with its symbolic dominance increasingly being accepted as natural and normative. One consequence of this is that rural or migrant languages and identities are perceived as a problem rather than a resource (Dong, 2011). The focus of Dong's (2011) study is rural–urban migration in China since the early 1980s. More than 150 million internal migrants have moved from the rural areas to metropolitan cities such as Beijing. In the process, their 'dialect' may well have changed from being a 'marker of comfortable, in-group identity' to a 'marker of rural, peripheral and stigmatized identity' in the metropolitan area (Dong, 2011: 55).

In the Beijing primary school where she carried out her ethnographic work, Dong found that teachers' categorizations of certain students as 'migrant' could have an impact upon their performance appraisals of these students. In an interview with Miss Zhang, the Chinese language teacher of Grade 1 and a native of Beijing, they talk about Hong, a student who, though she has grown up in Beijing and speaks with a Beijing accent, is still ascribed a migrant identity due to her origins. According to the teacher, Hong fails to distinguish between the two phonemes /n/ and /l/, and this is then generalized and seen as a feature typical of all 'dialect' speakers.

Dong (2011: 83) comments that in this way, variation between 'dialects' is erased and 'the languages of migrants are considered as homogeneous'. This is because they are seen from the normative perspective of Putonghua and hence all other varieties are negatively valued as being 'incorrect'. In the case of Miss Zhang's evaluation of Hong's speech, one small linguistic feature (the lack of a distinction between /n/ and /l/ sounds) becomes iconic of migrant identity, and leads to a negative assessment of Hong's school performance: she needs to speak 'better language' and to replace her 'mistakes' with the 'correct' language; she could be a 'better' student if she spoke the 'correct' language (Dong, 2011: 84). In this way, migrant students' repertoires are constructed as a problem rather than being built on as resources in their acquisition of Putonghua.

Dong insists that this construction of migrant language and identity as a problem is based on stereotypes rather than linguistic 'facts'. She notes that the lack of a distinction between /n/ and /l/ is often also present in the speech of local Beijing children of that age range (7–8 years), but here it usually goes unnoticed by teachers (Dong, 2011: 83). It is only when it occurs in the speech of a child categorized as 'migrant' that it becomes iconic in the teacher's eye of migrant language and identity, and is then perceived as negatively impacting upon the child's school performance.

Two forms of bilingual education

Nowadays, the Chinese education system is marked by two very different forms of bilingual education, though both involve the use of two media of instruction (Feng, 2007: 259):

- *Min-Han Jiantong* (mastery of minority language and the majority Chinese language) for ethnic minority groups, who can develop their own language, culture and identity, while at the same time learning Putonghua in order to ensure their participation in mainstream culture and strengthen their allegiance to the nation state. The ideal here is to develop bilingualism with bicultural identities, though the practice can be very different and can even at times amount to a form of 'concealed assimilation' (Feng, 2007: 271). These differences are due at least partly to the fact that schools can decide upon their own language policy and offer either minority language medium of instruction or Chinese medium of instruction streams for minority students, often depending upon such factors as the availability of teachers.
- *Zhuanye Waiyu Fuhexing Rencai* (in short, *Fuhexing Rencai*; all-round talents) for the majority Han group, who are expected to develop high levels of proficiency in both Chinese and an additional foreign language, namely, English. This is a form of additive bilingualism, but the difference from minority bilingualism is that the acquisition of English is supposed to be of a purely instrumental nature and should *not* foster

bicultural identities. On the contrary, the students should preserve their Chinese identity while acquiring specialized knowledge in one or more key academic areas as well as a high proficiency in the most important foreign language, English (in that sense, they will be 'all-round talents'). This use of bilingual Chinese–English education is a recent trend in Chinese society, and is due to the general dissatisfaction with the traditional way of teaching English as a foreign language, with its emphasis on discrete linguistic skills such as pronunciation, grammar and vocabulary. It is felt that the use of English as a medium of instruction for a number of non-linguistic subjects (especially mathematics and science) is a more promising way of achieving high competence in the language.

For minority group students, these two forms of bilingual education can be combined, so that they eventually become trilingual in their minority language, Putonghua and English. However, what makes this difficult for minority language students is that English is usually taught through the medium of Chinese (the students' second language) rather than their home minority language. This is due to such factors as the availability of teachers and textbooks: it would be preferable to use English-only (or English–minority language) textbooks and teaching materials and to employ teachers of English who can use both Chinese and the minority language for scaffolding purposes in the classroom, but such teachers and textbooks are not easily or widely available. Furthermore, testing usually includes a translation from English into Chinese, which, as Sunuodula and Feng (2011: 277) point out, could affect the minority students' 'learning outcome as measured by high-stake tests'.

A further linguistic complexity that is frequently overlooked in official policy discourses is that many Han Chinese students also use different home varieties, which are usually referred to as 'dialects'. In fact, these 'dialects' are often used not just in the home, but also in the early stages of education. This may mean that if minority students attend schools together with Han Chinese, they may learn, apart from their minority language (if it is offered by the school), first the local Chinese 'dialect', then Putonghua, and finally English (as we have seen in some of the vignettes mentioned in the section 'Diversity and unification').

In order to make education more accessible for minority language students, it has been suggested to cut out the still widespread use of Chinese 'dialects' in early education. Thus, Lam (2007) argues that

in communities where there is a high minority population, the use of Putonghua as a medium of instruction in the Chinese stream even at the primary level needs to be more strictly enforced or supported with well-trained teachers of Chinese. Then, if minority children choose to receive their basic education in Chinese, they do not have to undergo Double Submersion, that is, to learn through the medium of another regional Chinese dialect first before switching to Putonghua in secondary school or later. (Lam, 2007: 28)

While this is highly laudable in its concern for minority language students, there is, however, a somewhat disturbing underlying assumption, namely, that only 'languages' are worth preserving and 'dialects' can be eradicated (through 'enforcing' the use of Putonghua as a medium of instruction). The reason why this is particularly disturbing is that the distinction between 'languages' and 'dialects' is a politically motivated rather than a linguistic one. Hence, if minority students have a right to learn through their minority language as a medium of instruction at school, then Han Chinese students who speak a regional variety should also have the right to learn through this regional variety. In flexible multilingual education, all the linguistic varieties which are part of the children's repertoires, whether 'languages' or 'dialects', standardized or otherwise, need to be built on in education in a positive and additive way. This is of course not to deny that in some contexts – as in the Chinese context under discussion here – difficult choices need to be made (e.g. in the hiring of teachers) which can work in favour of the interests of one or the other group of students. In that sense, Lam is right to suggest that the weaker group in society – the minority group students – may be more in need of protection than the majority group.

Variation in minority language provision

While the Han majority group constitutes about 92% of China's population, the ethnic and linguistic minorities comprise about 8%; many of the latter have shifted from a minority language to Chinese, but there are still estimated to be over 60 million speakers of a minority language as their first or home language (Feng, 2005: 530). They mostly live in the western areas of China, including autonomous regions such as Tibet, Xinjiang and Inner Mongolia, as well as autonomous counties and prefectures such as Yunnan, Qinghai and Guizhou (Zhou, 2005: 108). At the national level, the language-in-education policy prescribes the use of Putonghua as the medium of instruction but allows for minority languages to be used as a supplementary medium. At the local level, there is huge variation in how the national policy is implemented, and what role and status is accorded to minority languages in education. According to Zhou (2005: 109), local policies vary from tolerance via permission to promotion policies. Examples of promotion policies are Tibet, which stipulates the use of Tibetan as the main medium of instruction and Chinese as the secondary medium, and Inner Mongolia, which stipulates the use of Mongol as the main medium of instruction and Chinese as the secondary one. Similarly, in Yanbian Korean Autonomous Prefecture, in the northeastern province of Jilin, Korean is used as the main medium of instruction in almost all minority schools (Ding & Yu, 2013: 459). Such promotion policies are mostly found in areas where the minority language is highly valued in society, for political or economic reasons, as in Yanbian, where Korean as a minority language has a high instrumental value, mostly because Korean–Chinese bilinguals can often get good jobs in South Korea. In other parts of China, it is more common to find permission or tolerance policies. Permission policies rely on the hierarchy of languages as defined in the national policy, typically prescribing the use of Chinese as the main medium and the minority language as the secondary medium. As for tolerance policies, they fail to explicitly mention the role to be played by minority languages in education and hence 'may do little more than tolerate minority language literacy and commit no financial or institutional support to it' (Zhou, 2005: 118).

Obviously, the three forms of promotion, permission and tolerance policies are not clear-cut categories but rather exist on a continuum. Ding and Yu (2013) discuss an example of a mixed permission–promotion type of policy in relation to the Yi minority language, which is spoken by about 7.7 million people. Their study focuses on bilingual education as it is implemented in minority schools in Liangshan, an autonomous prefecture in south-west Sichuan province. Two types of minority schools are available: first, schools using the minority language as the medium of instruction; and secondly, schools using Chinese as the medium of instruction. In the former schools, Chinese is often only taught as a subject, and in the latter, the minority language is often only taught as a subject. This presents a 'dilemma' (Ding & Yu, 2013) for minority group parents: if they enrol their child in a school using the minority language as the medium of instruction, she or he may not acquire a high enough competence in Chinese in order to successfully pass high-stakes tests at the higher levels of education; and if they enrol their child in a school using Chinese as the medium of instruction, then he or she may not develop a high enough competence in the minority language, which could lead to the eventual demise of this language. Such a scenario is increasingly likely for many minority languages, as more and more children attend Chinese-medium schools, or even mainstream schools where the minority language is not even offered as a subject, for the simple reason that Chinese is more important than the minority language for educational and professional success.

A way forward here might be for schools to offer more flexible dual language or partial immersion types of bi-/multilingual education programmes, with about half of the subjects taught through the minority language and the other half through Chinese. Interestingly, this type of programme is commonly offered in Chinese–English bilingual education, with about half of the subjects taught through Chinese and the other half through English, but it is still relatively rare in minority language–Chinese bilingual education. However, as we will see in the following section, this is in the process of changing, at least in some parts of China.

From mother tongue to bilingual education programmes

In Chapter 3, we saw how Māori-medium education programmes have tended to shift towards more balanced, additive bilingual programmes, endeavouring to develop students' bilingualism and biliteracy in both Māori and English. A similar trend towards flexible bilingual education programmes is noticeable in China, especially in northern China. In the 1980s, mother tongue education programmes, which used the minority language as the medium of instruction and taught Putonghua and written Chinese as a subject, were widespread in such areas as the Inner Mongolian Autonomous Region and the Xinjiang Uyghur Autonomous Region. These programmes frequently reflected the political aim of resisting what was widely perceived as 'Chinese linguistic assimilation' (Tsung, 2009: 112). Students who graduated from these programmes tended to be highly proficient in the minority language (e.g. the Mongolian language in the case of the Inner Mongolian Autonomous Region), but there was also a drawback, as explained by Tsung (2009: 113):

> these graduates had inadequate Chinese language skills and were deprived of the skills needed to succeed in the wider Inner Mongolian society which is dominated by Chinese. Consequently some Mongols sharply criticized such schemes as crippling the younger generation.

From the 1990s onwards, as China entered a period of economic growth, Chinese came to be perceived more and more as the language of social mobility. As a result, many parents enrolled their children in Chinese-medium schools and the mother tongue education programmes experienced a sharp decline in student intake. Additionally, a rapidly increasing number of students and their parents also wanted access to English, the other language of social mobility in China, which, however, was often not taught in the mother tongue education programmes.

The mother tongue education programmes have had to adapt to these changing conditions and demands, and there has been, especially since 2000, a shift to more Chinese language education in the form of either bilingual education programmes or school mergers. In bilingual education programmes, the minority language is used as the medium of instruction in the initial stages of education; but at higher levels, more and more subjects are taught through Chinese. In this way, they often resemble transitional bilingual education models, transitioning students from the minority language to the dominant language in society. The consequence of such programmes can easily be the gradual disappearance and loss of the minority language. The other policy involves the merging of schools, with the explicit aim of bringing together ethnic minority students with ethnic Chinese (Han) students in order to foster intercultural awareness and social integration. But there is frequently a gap between policy and practice, in that ethnic minority students, though attending the same schools as the Han students, are often separated from them through being placed in different streams or classes.

Despite these unresolved issues, academics such as Tsung (2009) are optimistic about the possibility of constructing a trilingual society in such areas of northern China as the Inner Mongolian and the Xinjiang Uyghur Autonomous Regions, and she concludes as follows:

> Due to social and economic changes, [the] language policy of changing the mother tongue to a bilingual education will likely lead to monolingualism being replaced by bilingualism. If this present policy of bilingualism is to be further enriched to the level of tri-lingualism, then schools must be given the necessary resources to fulfill their mission. In sum, the ideal situation is a tri-lingual society where [the regional language (Uyghur, Mongol, …)] is taken to be the language of solidarity, Chinese the language of power, and English as a language for globalization. (Tsung, 2009: 156)

Lessons to be Learnt From the Hong Kong and China Experience

In this concluding section, I briefly summarize the main points that can be learnt from the Hong Kong and China experience:

- in Hong Kong, the 1998 streaming policy forcing large numbers of students to attend mother tongue education (with Chinese as the medium of instruction) constructed and reproduced social stratification and inequality;

- the unpopularity of this system throws doubt upon the common assumption that mother tongue education is automatically and necessarily preferable to education in other languages (Pennycook, 2002);
- the government's gradual move away from mother tongue education (in Cantonese) and towards the promotion of Putonghua seems to be motivated more by political than pedagogical concerns;
- on the other hand, the government's 2010 'fine-tuning' policy is a step in the right direction, in that it gives schools greater flexibility to choose Chinese and English as media of instruction for different subjects according to students' needs and abilities;
- concomitantly, applied linguists have called for more flexible bilingual pedagogies including the strategic use of classroom code-switching as a way of scaffolding students' learning;
- in China, majority group students are expected to develop proficiency in both Chinese (Putonghua) and English; many also speak local or regional varieties commonly referred to as 'dialects' which, however, are increasingly marginalized through the emphasis on Putonghua;
- minority language education often operates on an either-or logic: while large numbers of schools used to offer mother tongue – i.e. minority language – education, with Chinese taught as a subject, many have now switched to transitional bilingual education programmes, with students being transitioned from the minority language to Chinese, or even Chinese-medium education, where the minority language is only taught as a subject;
- a way forward would be to introduce more flexible dual language or partial immersion education programmes, operating with a both-and logic and additionally also providing high-quality access to English.

7 Singapore

Singapore is a multi-ethnic and multilingual state, where the government has invested heavily in the creation of a sense of national unity and social cohesion. In this chapter, I explore how the language-in-education policy balance set up by the Singapore government over the last few decades is in the process of being broken up by the forces of globalization, and how it is not just the global role of English but also that of Mandarin which are the catalysts for change.

When Singapore gained independence from British colonialism in 1965, it was initially a member of the Malaysian Federation. This explains why the national language of Singapore is Malay, though it now recognizes four co-official languages: Malay, Mandarin, Tamil and English. The population is divided into three main ethnic groups, the biggest of which is the Chinese group (78%), followed by the Malay (14%) and Indian groups (7%) (Lin & Man, 2009: 105). To each ethnic group, an official mother tongue is assigned:

Ethnic group	Official mother tongue
Chinese	Mandarin Chinese
Malay	Malay
Indian	Tamil

In Singapore's official policy, the child is simply assigned the father's ethnicity, and the corresponding mother tongue, whether or not this language is actually used by the child's family as a home language. This policy essentializes both ethnicity and language use, whereas the reality is far more complex than the official representation of it (Bokhorst-Heng, 1999); thus, concerning language use, many Chinese Singaporeans are speakers of other Chinese languages such as Cantonese, Hokkien, Teochew, etc.; many Malay Singaporeans are speakers of Javanese, Boyanese, etc.; and many Indian Singaporeans are speakers of Hindi, Gujerati, Punjabi, Urdu, Bengali, etc.

During the colonial period, vernacular-medium education in Chinese, Malay or Tamil was the most common form of education, while English-medium education was reserved for a small elite. After independence, more and more parents enrolled their children in English-medium schools, and there were fewer and fewer students in the Chinese-, Malay- or Tamil-medium schools. As a result, from 1987, the government introduced a state-wide system of bilingual education, with English taught as the first language (L1) and the official mother tongue as the second language (L2). Thus, for instance, Chinese Singaporeans go to Chinese schools where they are taught first English and then Mandarin (usually referred to as Putonghua in China). This system of education is frequently described as 'English plus mother tongue bilingualism'.

English is seen primarily as the global language of business and science, but at the same time also as a carrier of decadent Western values. Therefore, the officially assigned mother tongues play an important role as repositories of traditional Asian values. However, as already pointed out, one major obstacle faced by the government in the realization of its language-in-education policy aims has been the fact that many Singaporeans speak other languages than the official mother tongues as their home languages. It is for this reason that the government launched a language policy campaign addressed to the Chinese Singaporeans, who constitute by far the largest ethnic group in Singapore, namely, the Speak Mandarin campaign. The Chinese Singaporeans who were speakers of other Chinese varieties or languages were encouraged to switch over to Mandarin. However, language policies seldom turn out exactly the way that policymakers expect them to do. In this case, large numbers of Chinese Singaporeans actually switched from their variety of Chinese to a variety of English, often in order to better prepare their children for the school system, in which English (as the L1) plays a more important role than Mandarin (the L2).

The result has been the development of a Singaporean variety of English known as Singlish (or Singaporean English). Singlish has spread so much that it has become, in Rubdy's (2001: 347, 352) words, an 'icon of national identity', a 'language of solidarity, identity and pride' and 'the glue that binds Singaporeans'. However, as Rubdy points out, this does not fit into the government's ideal of economic development, which is based on the use of standard English as the global lingua franca of international trade. Hence, they have attempted to stigmatize Singlish as 'English corrupted by Singaporeans' (Rubdy, 2001: 348) and have launched a new campaign aiming to promote standard English and to eradicate Singlish: the Speak Good English movement.

While the government relentlessly pursues its language policy goals, though – as we have seen – not always with the intended success, global economic developments can easily upset the precarious language policy balance that has been achieved. The most important of these developments has undoubtedly been the rise of mainland China as an economic power. As a result, Mandarin has acquired more instrumental value because of Singapore's extensive trade links with China. Mandarin has thus become more important than the other official mother tongues, Malay and Tamil. This has upset the delicate balance between the three official mother tongues, which were supposed to be equally important as the bearers of Asian cultural values and identities. Thus, not only has Singlish taken over, at least partly, this role of a marker of Singaporean identity, but moreover Mandarin is breaking through its traditional role as the official mother tongue and acquiring new instrumental value alongside English (see Wee, 2008). Because of these shifts in the roles and values of the different languages in Singapore, many non-Chinese parents are now demanding the right for their children to learn Mandarin at school. (For the moment, the Malay ethnic group have to send their children to a school where they learn English as their L1 and Malay as their L2, and Indian ethnic children learn English as their L1 and usually Tamil as their L2; and Mandarin, if it is taught at all, is only available as a third language.) All this obviously undermines the government's language planning and upsets the delicate balance that it had endeavoured to construct between English and the official mother tongues. It could mean that, even while there is no doubt that Singapore will remain multilingual, its educational system might evolve in the long term into a largely bilingual English–Mandarin one (see below).

The Declining Roles of Malay and Tamil

Just as English is displacing Chinese as a home language, it is also displacing Tamil and, to a lesser extent, Malay. It is often said that the reason why Malay is more resistant to the shift to English is that the Malay community is closely knit and united by a common religion, namely, Islam. But even in the domain of religion, an increasing presence of English can be observed:

> Another trend that is becoming more noticeable in the Malay community is that Islamic religious teaching is being taught in the English language as more children are more comfortable in English than in Malay. English is also being used during Friday prayers at the mosques, although not frequently … Even the religious-educated speakers prefer to speak either Arabic or English, rather than Arabic and Malay. (Aidil Subhan, 2007: 168–169)

While language shift seems to be happening especially among highly educated young adults (Cavallero & Serwe, 2010), there is also an increasing rate of language change: the Malay language in Singapore is still widely used as a home language but it is changing through contact with other languages, especially English, which is deplored by some people, including academics. Here, for instance, is Aidil Subhan (2007) discussing the contemporary use of Malay in the media:

> From the data available, it is heartening to note that thus far the quantity of output, such as the daily newspapers, is increasing. Nevertheless, the standard of reporting in the print media and the level of Malay used in the electronic media leaves much to be desired. Numerous mistakes in spelling and pronunciation, including a mixture of English and Malay, is a daily happening. (Aidil Subhan, 2007: 171)

In the Indian community, too, there is a concern with 'pure' Tamil. Schools used to teach 'pure' literary Tamil, which can be radically divergent from the colloquial varieties that children use at home – though this policy has recently been changed, as we will see. Thus, a concern with linguistic purity is quite common in the schools serving the different communities in Singapore: schools teach Beijing Mandarin (Putonghua), standard Malay and standard English, while vernacular varieties are usually denigrated. However, the situation was more extreme in the Indian community, not only because Literary Tamil is quite different from the vernacular varieties, but even more so because young people tended to see little or no value in learning Literary Tamil. It was just another school subject that they had to pass, but it had no instrumental value in Singaporean society and was hardly ever used outside school. No wonder then that the language-in-education policy was not very successful for Indian students. Schiffman (2007), writing prior to the policy change, puts it as follows:

> This policy is anti-Tamil because it denigrates the home variety, which is the actual 'mother tongue' of the Tamil community, and attempts to replace it with a variety never used for authentic communication by Tamils anywhere. (Schiffman, 2007: 212)

In this way, the policy failed to build on the children's home linguistic resources, and the highly problematic underlying assumption was that the colloquial variety 'can be (and, in fact, *should* be) ignored' in the teaching of Literary Tamil (Schiffman, 2007: 218). This is very similar to the equally problematic assumptions that the eradication of Singlish can help to improve students' proficiency in standard English, and that the eradication of Chinese 'dialects' can help with their acquisition of standard Mandarin/ Putonghua (see below).

All these factors help us to understand why the language shift to English has been very strong in the Indian community. Schiffman (2007: 212) concludes that 'the Tamil language in Singapore, spoken by about 60% of the Indian population, which itself represents about 7% of Singapore's population, is in a very precarious position'. Indeed, since 2005, the Indian community is the only community in which English is used more as the primary home language than the official 'mother tongue' (i.e. Tamil), with 39% (up from 32.3% in 1990) reporting the use of English and only 38.8% (down from 43.2%) reporting the use of Tamil as the primary language spoken at home. By comparison, the figures for the Malay and Chinese communities are 47.2% reporting the use of Mandarin and 28.7% reporting the use of English as the home language in the Chinese community, and 86.8% reporting the use of Malay and 13% reporting the use of English as the home language in the Malay community (Vaish *et al.*, 2010: 160).

Fortunately, the policy of using Literary Tamil as the medium of instruction in the schools serving the Indian community has recently been changed. In an attempt to reverse or at least slow down the shift from Tamil to English, the government introduced the teaching of Standard Colloquial Tamil in 2007. Nevertheless, the shift from Tamil to English still continues and is even accelerated by the fact that the Indian community in Singapore is very heterogeneous with speakers not only of Tamil but also of many other Indian languages such as Hindi, Punjabi, Bengali, Urdu, etc. (with these languages also taught in some schools). As a result, the intraethnic language is often English rather than Tamil, especially among younger people. As for religious activities, this is not a domain conducive to Tamil language maintenance either; such activities tend to be carried out in Sanskrit, with explanations given in Tamil, English or another language.

The Eradication of Chinese 'Dialects'

As we have already noted in the discussion of language-in-education policy in China, it often seems as if only 'languages' are worth preserving, whereas 'dialects' can be eradicated. Yet, the so-called 'dialects' of Chinese are to a large extent mutually unintelligible and cannot be looked upon as 'dialects' for purely linguistic reasons. It is true that they share the same written form as Mandarin or Putonghua, the standard variety of Chinese. But the main reason why they are perceived as 'dialects' is that, once China had chosen Putonghua as its standard variety, all the other languages which happened to be spoken in the country were downgraded to the status of non-standard 'dialects'.

Hence, it is rather disturbing that much of the linguistic human rights literature is concerned with interlanguage rather than intralanguage discrimination. In other words, it only focuses on the defence of standard varieties (or 'languages') and largely ignores non-standard varieties (or 'dialects'). As a result, the Singapore experience is frequently (though by no means always) looked upon as an example of highly successful language policy and planning (see e.g. Lo Bianco, 2007: 5). Yet, we cannot forget that the imposition of Mandarin has involved the (attempted) eradication of the main Chinese 'dialects' used in Singapore (including Cantonese, Hokkien and Teochew). Mandarin has now become the primary home language (along with English) of the Chinese Singaporeans, and the education system teaches English and Mandarin, with the latter considered as the community's sole official mother tongue.

However, this does not mean that the 'dialects' have completely disappeared. They are still used in specific contexts, such as electoral campaigns. According to Lim (2009),

> in the lead-up to the general elections in 2001 and 2006, for example, ministers, including the then Prime Minister, gave election rally speeches in not only the official languages (English, Mandarin, etc.) but also in Hokkien, Teochew and Cantonese, in order to reach out to older Chinese Singaporeans and better connect with their voters. (Lim, 2009: 65)

The same need to connect with all Singaporeans was evident during the severe acute respiratory syndrome (SARS) pandemic in 2003, when, exceptionally, the radio and television stations were permitted to broadcast health warnings in 'dialect' so as to ensure that the messages would reach everybody. More specifically, Hokkien has traditionally been used as a lingua franca within the army, 'where young men of extremely varied socio-economic backgrounds are forced to work and interact together, serving especially well for neutralizing class differences so as to get along with fellow soldiers and simply get things done' (Lim, 2009: 64). But the most resilient Chinese 'dialect' is probably Cantonese for the following two reasons among others: first, there was an influx of Cantonese-speaking migrants from Hong Kong in the 1980s and 1990s (Lim, 2010: 34) and, secondly, Cantonese has high cultural prestige in Singapore because of the popularity of Cantopop music and Cantonese cinema (Lim, 2010: 44). Sometimes, the 'dialects' also survive in more symbolic ways: for instance, as discussed by Bokhorst-Heng and Lee (2007), many Chinese Singaporean parents have resisted the government's call to give their children Mandarin names and continue to use dialect ones. Bokhorst-Heng and Lee explain this resistance by arguing that here the limits of the government campaign were reached: while the Chinese Singaporeans clearly saw the economic advantage of using

Mandarin rather than dialect, there was no instrumental value attached to the change of names; moreover, such a change of names was looked upon as a break with family ties and personal ancestry.

Singlish (Singaporean English)

Singlish and identity

Singlish is perceived as a non-standard variety (or 'dialect') of English, but it is important to realize that it is not a monolithic entity. On the contrary, there is a linguistic continuum with varieties ranging from Standard Singapore English to Colloquial Singapore English (usually referred to as Singlish), with many speakers switching between these varieties depending on who they talk to and in which context. Some of the distinguishing features of Singlish can be seen from the following examples, the first of which is taken from Alsagoff (2007: 31) and the second from Fong (2004: 98):

(1) Here got too many durian, ah.
     (There are too many durians here.)
(2) Prabhudeva kena cheat in the movie lah.
     (Prabhudeva was cheated in the movie.)

They include in Example 1 the null subject construction *got* instead of the existential construction *there are*, the lack of plural marking on the noun *durian* and the discourse particle *ah*. Example 2 illustrates the *kena* passive construction, with the main verb often used in the infinitive form, and another discourse particle, namely, *lah*, which 'indicates speaker's mood/ attitude and appeals to addressee to accommodate the mood/attitude' (Wee, 2004: 125). According to Deterding (2007: 66), *lah* is 'perhaps the one word that is most emblematic of Singapore English', and he suggests that the source of *lah* – as well as other discourse particles – may be various similar particles in other languages that are widely used in Singapore, including Hokkien, Cantonese and Malay (Deterding, 2007: 71).

Singlish is widespread in Singapore, but it is valued in very different ways by the Singapore government and by its speakers. The government started the Speak Good English movement in 2000, with the aim of getting Singaporeans to use standard English for purely instrumental reasons. Standard English, they argue, is needed for international business and science in this globalized world. As for Singlish, it is looked upon as bad English, and the government would like to eradicate it. However, it has not been very successful in its attempts, partly because it failed to realise that one can promote standard English without having to eradicate Singlish and partly because it underestimated the strength of the link between Singlish and Singaporean identity for many citizens.

Indeed, an increasing number of Singaporeans are using Singlish as their home language or one of their home languages. Though it is a working-class variety, it has a lot of 'covert prestige' as the language of solidarity that binds Singaporeans together. Unlike the overt prestige of standard, national and official languages, linguistic varieties such as Singlish can have a high value attributed to them within a particular in-group for expressing that in-group's cultural identity. But Singlish has outgrown its association with a particular in-group and has come to be perceived as uniquely Singaporean and as a key marker of Singaporean identity in general. As a result, code-switching between Singlish and more standard varieties of English is frequently used for all sorts of effects by members of all social classes.

There is thus an increasing gap between the official language policy and the lived experience of a large number of people in Singapore who identify with Singlish, or with both Singlish and a local language. In this way, Singaporeans have appropriated English – in the sense of making it their own, using it for their own ends and needs – and they identify not so much with standard English but rather with their own local, nativized variety. Nor does this necessarily mean the loss of other languages; on the contrary, Singlish usually coexists with both local languages and with the more standard varieties of English.

Language ideologies and ideological contradictions

A number of language ideologies have marked the linguistic development of Singapore since its independence in 1965. At that time, the main lingua francas were Hokkien and Bazaar Malay (colloquial, non-standard Malay). As already mentioned, Hokkien is still used as a lingua franca in the army, though nowadays alongside English. Mandarin was the home language of hardly any of the original Chinese immigrants to Singapore; it was promoted for mainly social and political reasons, as well as cultural ones (namely, its association with ancient Chinese culture). In this way, the government's linguistic engineering marked a shift from (what was perceived as) non-standard bilingualism in Hokkien and Bazaar Malay to (what is perceived as) a more standard bilingualism in English and Mandarin. The ongoing fight against Singlish fits into this ideology of the importance of the standard (see Lin & Man, 2009).

Furthermore, the government espouses a Darwinian ideology of languages in competition, at least as far as Singlish and standard English are concerned. While English and the official mother tongue are promoted as complementary, the relationship between Singlish and standard English is looked upon as conflictual. Hence the attempt to eradicate Singlish, as the possibility of 'peaceful' coexistence is discounted. Yet, from a sociolinguistic point of view, the emergence of a nativized variety of English alongside the standard taught at school would be seen as a normal development when a language takes hold in a population and enters into contact with other languages present in the linguistic ecology (Stroud & Wee, 2010: 197). Moreover, from a sociolinguistic perspective, Singlish and standard English should not be looked upon as two wholly separate varieties but a linguistic continuum along which speakers shift according to the degree of formality of the situation they are in. Accordingly, Wee (2010) insists that Singlish is a 'non-extensive social language' and that code-switching between Singlish and more standard varieties of English is commonplace. This implies that no (spoken or written) text is fully and only in Singlish, but rather that speakers/writers use more or less Singlish, and one consequence of the use of more Singlish is that the text tends to be perceived as having a comic effect.

Wee (2010) also points to an ideological contradiction between the government's official position on (the need to eradicate) Singlish and its own practices. Thus, for example, the government itself commissioned a rap song against SARS by Phua Chu Kang, which is – at least partly – in Singlish. Phua Chu Kang (played by actor Gurmit Singh) is the protagonist of a highly popular sitcom on Singaporean television, who became famous for the way he spoke Singlish but, after a complaint by the government, was sent to remedial English classes (as part of the programme) and gradually metamorphosed into a speaker of standard English in subsequent episodes. In the case of the SARS rap song, the government argued that it decided to use Singlish exceptionally because it was essential to reach the whole population, including the less educated, in its campaign to stop the spread of the 2003 SARS pandemic (i.e. the same argument that was also made in relation to the use of 'dialect', as already noted above).

This throws an interesting light on the role of Singlish in Singapore. It also confirms Wee's point that texts are not wholly in Singlish but tend to mix Singlish and standard English, as can be seen from the following extract from the SARS rap song (or SAR-vivor Rap):

Some say leh, some say lah
Spread kaya, but don't spread SARS!
...

Don't be a hero and continue working
Wait the whole company kena quarantine!
(kaya – charm, something that attracts people's attention or admiration,
also: coconut sauce; kena – undergo, experience, often used as a passive
marker; both derived from Malay; quoted from Wee, 2010: 107–108)

Singlish is also used by the government 'to create a bond of solidarity amidst
a Singaporean diaspora' (Wee, 2010: 100). Thus, when Singapore Day, a gov-
ernment-sponsored event, was celebrated in London in April 2009, 'the event
made occasional use of Singlish … interspersed with more Standard English
constructions' (Wee, 2010: 108). Wee points out that, unlike the SAR-vivor
Rap, the Singapore Day event was addressed to an educated audience of highly
skilled Singaporeans working abroad, and that these 'occasional switches
into Singlish can help establish a sense of shared "Singaporean-ness"' (Wee,
2010: 110). Singlish is also used by the Singapore Tourist Board on its website, where it is described as Singaporeans' 'own brand' of English, 'fondly'
referred to as Singlish, which is very different from the government's usual
portrayal of Singlish as valueless (Wee, 2011: 82).

Singlish as a resource in education

Building on students' actual linguistic repertoires would mean seeing
Singlish as a resource rather than an impediment (Rubdy, 2007). In fact,
many classroom studies in Singapore have found widespread code-switching
between Singlish and standard English (e.g. Alsagoff, 2010: 121–126; Lim,
2009: 60; Stroud & Wee, 2007: 46–47). The official line, however, is that
the use of Singlish in classrooms leads to interference problems. But this is
contradicted by sociolinguistic research such as that of Siegel (1999, 2010),
which has shown that the vernacular can be harnessed as a resource to help
students acquire the standard variety in a better way. It can act as a bridge
or scaffold to lead students towards a deeper understanding of academic
subject matter, by linking it with students' own lifeworld knowledge and
experience (Rubdy, 2007: 320–321).

Vaish (2013), too, argues that the use of Singlish in classrooms would allow
for more exploratory talk on the students' part and increase opportunities for
meaningful learning. She describes classroom learning as a dialogic process
in which students make academic, standard language varieties their own by
fusing them with their own vernacular varieties. She concludes as follows:

Pedagogy in which the teacher relinquishes control of classroom talk
to the student should be emphasized in teacher training in Singapore

even if this means the entry of non-standard languages in the English classroom. At the same time the teacher can re-cast the students' words into Standard English to sensitize children toward differences in register. (Vaish, 2013: 540)

Stroud and Wee (2006: 304–305) describe this pedagogical strategy as 'double-crossing', where the teacher 'cross[es] over into the student's peer oriented ways of speaking, with the specific intention of inducing the student to cross back (hence, the double-crossing) into ways of speaking that are more typically associated with the target language'. Another pedagogical strategy is to make students aware of the differences between the vernacular and the standard (Rubdy, 2007: 321).

On the other hand, however, it is important for the teacher not to simply encourage students' use of mixed language, as this could reproduce their social disadvantage. Stroud and Wee (2012) express this warning as follows:

if we are at all concerned about the fact that students do enter schools from different kinds of backgrounds, and that this can detrimentally influence their ability to succeed in the formal school environment, we cannot simply romanticize such language mixing. We have to acknowledge that while there is nothing inherently bad or wrong with mixing, it can become socially disadvantageous if it means that speakers are unable to (in other contexts) interact without having to resort to such mixing. (Stroud & Wee, 2012: 106)

Hence, teachers – as well as sociolinguists – need to move beyond a mere celebration of translanguaging and ensure that their students become aware of the differences between their mixed language and the standard variety, thus leading them to develop high proficiency in the standard, which is required for their educational and later professional success.

Stroud and Wee substantiate this important point with reference to a number of case studies of Singaporean adolescents, including Fandi, an ethnic Malay whose home languages include Malay and English, and Ping, an ethnic Chinese whose main home language is Mandarin with code-switching into English. Actually, Ping's parents use Hokkien to communicate with each other, but they speak in Mandarin to their children, thus aligning the home languages with the official language policy and the dominant linguistic market (Bourdieu, 1991) in Singapore. Both Fandi and Ping use codeswitching and translanguaging so much that both of them seem unable to fully interact in either English or, respectively, Malay and Mandarin. Stroud and Wee (2012) insist that they are not taking a 'deficit' perspective here, but that

> different linguistic repertoires are accorded different values in different markets (Bourdieu 1991) and here, we have to be realistic and acknowledge that the (socially acquired) inability to fully interact in a single language, especially English, does put Ping and Fandi at a social disadvantage in Singapore society, since it has potentially serious consequences for the social trajectories of adolescents like them. (Stroud & Wee, 2012: 103)

Indeed, Ping and Fandi's repertoires consist primarily of a mixed English–Mandarin or Malay code, which is accorded a low value in the dominant linguistic market of Singaporean society, including the educational system. Both face difficulties at school with English, and Stroud and Wee (2012) show how they rely on a number of avoidance strategies as a way of coping with, or compensating for, these difficulties. Here is an example of such an avoidance strategy in connection with making presentations at school:

> In Ping's case, the strategy is to avoid events where she may have to *ad lib*. Ping's self-image as someone who is (supposed to be) good in English does not allow her to completely avoid public speaking. Events where she reads to the entire school allow her to sustain this self-image. In Fandi's case, no such self-image exists and his strategy is to avoid as far as possible all forms of public speaking. Where this is not possible, Fandi then relies on the hope that even if you do not speak well, provided the audience is made up of personal friends, he is less likely to be judged harshly. (Stroud & Wee, 2012: 114)

Ping and Fandi also have difficulties at school with their respective 'mother tongue', Mandarin and Malay, and Stroud and Wee (2012: 117) point out that both teenagers do not have a sufficiently strong mastery of either English or their 'mother tongue' in order to 'interact and articulate fully in just one language alone'. They therefore conclude that Ping's and Fandi's

> code-switches are more likely the result of gaps in [their] vocabulary rather than the strategic manipulation of codes to achieve interpersonal goals. This is a potentially serious problem because Singapore's bilingual policy is based on the belief that 'properly' bilingual individuals are those in complete control of two separate sets of monolingual proficiencies.

The mixing of elements is construed as a form of linguistic contamination, and the linguistic repertoires of individuals like Ping [and Fandi] will be judged as linguistic deficiencies. (Stroud & Wee, 2012: 117)

And, of course, it just remains to be added that Singapore is by no means the only country whose language-in-education policy values bi- and multilingualism in the form of two or more mutually exclusive monolingualisms!

Increasing acceptability of Singlish

The government's concerns about the unintelligibility of Singlish are largely unfounded. As this particular variety of English becomes better known internationally, it will also gain in acceptability and intelligibility. A case in point is the lexical item *kiasu* (from Hokkien, 'being afraid to lose out'), of which Gupta (2010) charts the movement from Singlish to standard English. Starting off as army slang, it soon became part of the colloquial vocabulary of Singlish. In the next step, it was used by a member of the Singaporean parliament and, as a result, became widespread in media discourses, first in Singapore and then in other countries including the UK. The final step was that it was included in the *Oxford English Dictionary*. Lim (2009: 67) uses this example in order to back up her argument that 'the more exposure the rest of the world has to a variety like Singlish – through scholarly work, film and media, etc. – the more the variety will become increasingly intelligible and possibly increase in positive attitudes'. Moreover, the fact that this is already happening is illustrated by the success of the locally produced film 'Singapore Dreaming' with its high Singlish content, which has won a number of major international awards, including the Montblanc Screenwriters Award at the 2006 San Sebastian International Film Festival, the Audience Award for Narrative Feature at the 2007 Asian-American International Film Festival in New York and the Best Asian/Middle Eastern Film Award at the 2007 Tokyo International Film Festival (Wee, 2013: 115–116).

Importantly, the development of positive attitudes towards Singlish would also help students such as Ping and Fandi, in that they would no longer be looked upon by others nor would they look upon themselves as linguistically deficient. On the contrary, their variety would be positively valued, like Swiss German and Cypriot Greek (see Chapter 2), and built on in an additive way by teachers in order to make them aware of the differences between their variety and the standard variety, and to lead them towards better mastery of the standard.

'Mother Tongue' Between Official Discourse and Linguistic Reality

We have already seen how the official 'mother tongue' does not always correspond to the linguistic reality. As a result, the government has put pressure on families to bring their linguistic behaviour in line with the requirements of the educational system. In other words, the government's message to parents is along the following lines: if they belong for instance to the Chinese ethnic group and if at home they use one of the Chinese 'dialects' such as Hokkien, they should make an effort to switch to Mandarin, which would make it easier for their children to achieve educational success – since Mandarin, and not Hokkien, plays an important role in the Singaporean school system. Dixon (2009: 127) comments on this policy in the following terms: 'Singapore's solution to the problem of a difference between home language and school language is to change families' home languages, rather than provide schooling in the students' original home language'. Scholars such as Lin and Man (2009: 110) have criticized this approach as a form of 'high-handed, iron-cage-like, linguistic engineering' by the state, whose 'political and economic goals take priority over all other goals (e.g. maintaining heritage literacies, maintaining the mother tongues of the communities and intergenerational linguistic and sociocultural continuities)'.

However, we have also seen that policies do not always have the intended effects. One unintended effect of the government's policy was that many Chinese families switched to English as their home language, since after all English plays an even more important role in education than Mandarin. The parents thought that, if the aim is to help their children, then English might be an even better choice for a home language than Mandarin. We have also seen how this has led to the emergence of a specifically Singaporean variety of English known as Singlish.

In this way, there is now a sizeable group of the population that has English as their home language, or one of their home languages. This group consists of two major parts:

- mostly Chinese families who have switched to English as a result of the government's pressure to abandon the Chinese 'dialects';
- the Eurasians and Europeans who live and work in Singapore and whose home language is or includes English.

These shifts in home languages threaten to undermine the government's official mother tongue policy. According to the policy, English cannot be a 'mother tongue', since this would give an unfair advantage to the members of this particular group and since bilingualism in English and an official mother tongue is required of everybody. This means that the children of Eurasian parents have to take a mother tongue subject at school in order to meet the L2 requirements of the education system, even though this is a foreign language to them. Despite complaints about this situation by the admittedly small Eurasian community, the government has refused to budge on the issue. Wee (2002) lists four main reasons why English as a mother tongue is not acceptable to the government:

- English is seen as a 'neutral', purely pragmatic or instrumental language, the lingua franca for interethnic and international communication, and hence it cannot be tied to a particular ethnic community.
- English is seen as a vehicle for decadent Western values, as opposed to the mother tongues, which are supposed to act as a 'cultural ballast' (Wee, 2002: 291). If English were the mother tongue of a particular ethnic community such as the Eurasians, then either that community 'would have to be seen as being ultimately Westernized or the possibility that English can be a vehicle for more traditionally Asian values must be allowed' (Wee, 2002: 291). Both of these options would seem to be unacceptable to the government, as the first one would be incompatible with the goal of building a sense of (Asian) national unity and the second one would undermine the traditional role attributed to the mother tongues in the official language policy.
- Allowing English as a mother tongue might open up a 'Pandora's box' (Wee, 2002: 291), as more and more Singaporeans with English as (one of) their home language(s) might want to claim it as their mother tongue.
- Chinese Singaporeans are already to some extent divided between more English-educated and more Chinese-educated ones. If the former were allowed to have English as their mother tongue, this would 'cement the division' (Wee, 2002: 292) of the Chinese community, which again would undermine the government's endeavour to construct a sense of national unity.

However, the consequence of these ongoing shifts in home languages for the education system is that nowadays, as far as the Chinese ethnic group is concerned, over 60% of Primary 1 students use – or rather reported using – English predominantly as their home language (Li et al., 2012: 533). As a result, in these classrooms there is a wide range and diversity of abilities in the Chinese language. It is because of this new situation that the government has had to introduce a lower-level 'B' syllabus in Mandarin, with a modular

curriculum emphasizing oral communicative skills and the use of information and communication technology (ICT), as opposed to the traditional
curriculum with its focus on writing and character memorization (Li *et al.*,
2012: 534). There are now different streams in both primary and secondary
schools, with the official mother tongue (Mandarin) taught as an L2 rather
than an L1 for many of the students who have English as their home language and for whom Mandarin is indeed a foreign language (Stroud & Wee,
2012: 195). A further consequence of this is that the government has also
had to lower the Chinese language requirements for admission to university
(Lin & Man, 2009: 108). Because of this weakening link between Mandarin
(the official mother tongue) and identity, as well as the new identity-linked
values of English/Singlish, it is becoming increasingly difficult for the government to sustain the model of the three official mother tongues.

Increasing Diversity and Future Developments

Linguistic and cultural diversity is increasing in Singapore as a result of
the continuing high level of in-migration, with foreign workers now making
up 36% of Singapore's population (Rubdy & McKay, 2013: 157). In the 21st
century, there has been a new wave of immigration, mostly from mainland China and India. While the latter group tends to be highly skilled and
English speaking, the former includes many mothers accompanying their
children who study in Singaporean schools and who commonly speak only
Mandarin and no English (Lim, 2009: 63). They are locally known as *peidu*
(Mandarin 'accompany study') mamas. As they frequently work in shops,
Lim notes that nowadays one hears complaints from Singaporeans about
having to deal with sales staff who do not understand English. There is even
a Facebook site called 'I am Singaporean and tired of service staff who can
only speak Mandarin' (Lim, 2009: 63), which suggests that here, just as in
the USA and many other places in the world, language is used as a proxy for
what is largely an anti-immigration sentiment (cf. Chapter 5 on the English-
only movement). It is this recent migration pattern that has contributed to
the spread of Putonghua/Mandarin in contemporary Singapore.

These developments have prompted scholars to come up with two possible yet different scenarios for the sociolinguistic future of Singapore. The
first scenario builds on two recent trends: the rapid spread of Putonghua/
Mandarin, as discussed above, and the possible consequences of the Speak
Good English movement, with the government telling people to stop using
Singlish. If the Chinese community feels that in their home language use
they should move away from Singlish, they might use more Mandarin
instead. In turn, this could lead to an increasing social divide between

a cosmopolitan elite using mostly standard English, and the majority of the Chinese community ('the heartlanders') using mostly or only a local variety of Mandarin (Rubdy, 2001: 352).

The use of such a local variety of Mandarin could also lead to a clash with the need for the standard variety (Putonghua) as taught in mainland China (Wee, 2008: 39). There could be a deepening conflict between the identity values of local Mandarin and the high instrumental value of the standard, and the question of which variety of Mandarin should be used could become a burning issue (Wee, 2008: 40). Indeed, as with English and Singlish, the government may soon feel the need to launch a Speak *Good* Mandarin movement!

An alternative scenario for the future could be the emergence of English monolingualism in Singapore (Stroud & Wee, 2012: 193). This is confirmed by Lin and Man's (2009: 132) analysis that the Singaporean education system works against the students' heritage languages, as witnessed by the falling standards in Mandarin: 'English monolingualism rather than bilingualism seems to be fostered'. At most, a weak form of bilingualism is aimed at, with high standards in English but often not very high ones in the official mother tongue. We need to recall that the Singaporean education system is not a form of mother tongue education. Indeed, at the time when Singapore adopted English as the primary medium of instruction in school, it was an L2 for most of its citizens. As Pakir (2008: 196) explains, 'the Singapore experience shows that a second language (L2) can successfully be used as a medium of instruction for the general population'. It is just that nowadays, due to the switch to English in many Singaporean homes, the system has become more L1 based.

However, in light of the rapidly increasing linguistic and cultural diversity in contemporary Singapore, a monolingual English system of education might be an 'aberration', in the words of Makoni *et al.* (2010: 11). Even more importantly, there is a need for Singapore to move away from an increasingly untenable link between (Asian) 'mother tongue' and identity, and towards greater choice and flexibility in future language-in-education policies, with all students having access to English as well as learning another language of their choice (Stroud & Wee, 2012: 214; Wee, 2013: 120–121). According to Wee and Bokhorst-Heng (2005), a more 'open' bilingual policy is needed in which students can choose to learn, in addition to English,

whichever language they want for any number of reasons: either because they consider this other language interesting, they see it as part of their heritage, or simply because they think it is economically useful. The state may then still want to encourage Singaporean citizens to learn their various mother tongues, but this would no longer be part of an official policy which would be mandatory in the schools. Instead, Singaporeans would be able to exercise their own choice in deciding what language they consider to be their mother tongue. (Wee & Bokhorst-Heng, 2005: 176–177)

In practice, of course, we know what the other language with high instrumental value in Singaporean society is, and so the education system might well evolve into a bilingual English–Mandarin one, not just for the ethnic Chinese students but for the whole school population.

Lessons to be Learnt From the Singapore Experience

In this concluding section, I briefly summarize the main points that can be learnt from the Singaporean experience:

- because it is important to build on students' home linguistic resources, the vernacular variety (Singlish) should be used in classrooms to help students acquire the standard variety in a better way;
- Singlish can act as a scaffold or bridge between academic subject matter and students' own lifeworld experience;
- it is important for teachers to have a positive attitude towards the vernacular and to make students aware of the differences between the vernacular and the standard;
- however, simply advocating or encouraging students' translanguaging is an irresponsible strategy on the teacher's part that can reproduce students' social disadvantage (Stroud & Wee, 2012);
- Singapore's experience shows that an L2 (in this case, English) can be successfully used as a medium of instruction for the whole school population, which contradicts some of the claims made by mother tongue education advocates;
- in light of the increasing diversity of Singaporean society, the best education system for Singapore might be a flexible bilingual system in which students learn English and another language of their choice (with additional languages offered as electives).

8 South Africa

After the Anglo-Boer War (1899–1902), the defeated Afrikaners became British citizens and South Africa a 'dominion' of the British Empire (like Canada and Australia). The majority of whites were Afrikaans speaking, so that this extraterritorial variety of Dutch (rather than English) became the language frequently associated with white supremacy. This was particularly the case after 1948, when the National Party gained power and the white Afrikaner nationalists began setting up the apartheid system (the whites formed about 20% of the total population). Some of the major events in the history of anti-apartheid resistance include the following: in 1960, the anti-pass law campaigns gathered momentum and led to brutal government retaliation culminating in the Sharpeville massacre, where police shot 69 demonstrators and injured many others; in 1976, during the Soweto rising, schoolchildren protesting against the imposition of Afrikaans in schools were massacred; the following year, Steve Biko, an activist of the Black Consciousness movement and a hero of anti-apartheid resistance, died in custody from police brutality. The other great hero, Nelson Mandela, was released in 1990 after 27 years of imprisonment. This important event heralded the end of the apartheid system and the gradual transition from a racist to a democratic political regime. Indeed, in the elections of April 1994, an African National Congress (ANC) government was elected and Mandela became its president. Under Mandela, South Africa developed – or was supposed to develop – into a multi-ethnic 'rainbow nation'.

Just as in colonial Singapore and Hong Kong, vernacular or mother tongue education had been used for the purpose of social domination in South Africa during the period of apartheid. In 1953, the apartheid government introduced the Bantu Education Act, which enforced compulsory mother tongue education for all blacks and blocked their access to English. This was rightly seen by the black population as an attempt by the apartheid government to imprison them within a second-rate education and to ensure that black schoolchildren would not reach a high command of English. Among the black population, this has led to negative attitudes towards the indigenous African languages, as well as negative attitudes towards Afrikaans as the language of the oppressors. On the other hand, many South Africans now demand access to English and, through English, to better educational and employment opportunities.

After the transition from apartheid to democracy, Nelson Mandela's government voted a new constitution which recognizes 11 official languages: English, Afrikaans, isiZulu, isiXhosa, Sesotho, Sepedi (or Sesotho sa Leboa, Northern Sotho), Setswana, Xitsonga, siSwati, Tshivenda and isiNdebele. The government has endeavoured to revitalize the indigenous African languages by promoting them as media of instruction, so that education is often bi- or trilingual with the African 'mother tongue' as the first language (L1), English as the second language (L2) and Afrikaans as the third language (L3). However, as we will see, the revalorization of indigenous languages has been fraught with problems.

The relative failure of official language policy is due primarily to people's perception of English as the key to upward social mobility. In fact, nowadays, more and more black South Africans are bilingual in both English and an African language such as Zulu or Xhosa. Others use mixed codes such as Tsotsitaal or Isicamtho, which incorporate linguistic material from indigenous languages as well as English and Afrikaans, as informal means of wider communication, especially in urban communities. Therefore, mother tongue education or dual language programmes in English and an African language can be hard to implement in such highly multilingual urban areas, for the simple reason that most children have complex linguistic repertoires and it can be hard or even impossible to identify each child's L1.

Fortunately, in the new democratic South Africa, the education system has been flexible; as Probyn (2005) puts it,

> in metropolitan areas such as around Johannesburg in the centre of the country, African schools reflect the mix of indigenous home languages in their communities and so have tended to introduce English medium instruction even earlier, from Grade 1, to accommodate the wide range of home languages in the classroom. (Probyn, 2005: 157)

At the same time, Probyn insists that this is not a matter of replacing African languages with English; on the contrary, most parents value both their indigenous home languages and English, and they want their children to study all of them at school. Teachers, too, frequently rely on code-switching between English and the indigenous languages (see e.g. Setati *et al.*, 2002). Therefore, I argue in this chapter that the best system of education for South Africa might be a flexible system of additive multilingual education, building on the whole of children's complex repertoires and giving them access to both English and indigenous languages, including urban vernaculars.

South Africa and the Legacy of Apartheid

As referenced in the previous section, the apartheid government of South Africa introduced the Bantu Education Act in 1953, which instituted mother tongue education in African languages. This policy was consistent with the recommendations of the 1953 UNESCO report advocating mother tongue education, but its purpose was clearly separatist and discriminatory (Probyn, 2005: 154), as it was fuelled by an ideology of white supremacy and a fear of linguistic and cultural heterogeneity. Chick (2001) links this fear to the Herderian ideology of European nation states and interprets the policy of apartheid South Africa as an extreme version of it. He comments upon the Nationalist government's introduction of mother tongue instruction for indigenous language speakers in the following terms:

> Since mother tongue instruction is usually associated with multilingual policies, it is important to note that rather than a break with the ideology of European nation-states this policy reflects an extreme version of it. Rather than opening up space for historically marginalized languages, it was a key strategy in the grand apartheid goal of final exclusion of speakers of such languages i.e. their location in separate, linguistically and culturally homogeneous 'nation-states' or Bantustans. (Chick, 2001: 31)

Because of this disturbing link of mother tongue education with the racist policies of the apartheid system, it is now more important than ever to respect people's linguistic choices, whether they choose to switch from indigenous varieties to urban vernaculars, or desire for their children an English-medium education, from which they themselves had been debarred under the apartheid system. Mother tongue education may continue to imprison them within fixed, reified, essentialized ethnic identities. Their choice to use the new urban languages, on the other hand, would seem to constitute a much more empowering option, as it indexes 'the coming together of different ethnic groups held separate by apartheid policy' (Brutt-Griffler, 2006: 46).

Bourne (2007) summarizes the situation as follows:

> Colonial education policy in Africa tended towards vernacular education for the native population, where only the children of the elite bought themselves into an English education. The apartheid years in South Africa strengthened the resistance to education in languages other than English, again seen as a way of denying access to employment opportunities and higher education.

Today, despite a supportive national policy towards mother tongue education, the majority of South African parents struggle to enrol their children in English medium schools to avoid their placement in other language streams which are seen as being second class. It seems clear that it is not only that English is seen as providing social mobility, but that the motivations of those offering separate language streams are questioned: people still simply do not believe that the schools are committed to raising standards and ensuring high levels of academic success for their children. Separate language streams are viewed in post-apartheid South Africa, with some justification, as an attempt by the economic elite to exclude and marginalise some sections of society, to the benefit of their own children. (Bourne, 2007: 143–144)

What Bourne implicitly raises here is the key issue of researcher reflexivity: as researchers, do we (or to what extent do we) collude – unwittingly or not – with the political and economic elites? Indeed, it has been too easy for researchers to take up a position of superiority and to look upon South African parents who prefer their children to be educated through English rather than an indigenous African language as 'victims of "false consciousness"' (Orman, 2008: 163) or as 'afflicted' by an 'attitudinal malaise' or 'syndrome' (Alexander, 2006: 242).

The Demise of Afrikaans in Democratic South Africa?

Afrikaans is predominantly thought of as a white or European language closely related to Dutch, though many of its speakers prefer to look upon it as an indigenous South African language. It is the language originally used by the Dutch colonizers, but mixed over time through contact with many other local languages; it is mostly spoken by whites and 'Coloureds' (people of mixed race). It exists in a number of varieties, with a major distinction between standard Afrikaans, as used by many white Afrikaners, and the non-standard varieties, heavily mixed with English, used by many Coloured people. While the latter varieties are often referred to derogatively as *Kaaps* or *kombuistaal* (kitchen language), they can have covert prestige and play the role of a language of solidarity especially among young people in the Coloured communities (Deumert, 2005: 116). On the other hand, standard Afrikaans is frequently looked upon as the 'pure' variety, which developed in line with the apartheid government's obsession with purity. During the apartheid period, it was the symbol of Afrikaner identity and, because of this historical legacy, it is still nowadays often perceived as the language of oppression by many black and Coloured people. Thus, for instance, many blacks still associate it with such tragic events as the Soweto student uprising, when the apartheid government attempted to impose Afrikaans as a medium of instruction in African secondary schools.

During the years of the apartheid system, Afrikaans developed into the most powerful language in society, alongside English. It has been fully standardized, has a vibrant literature of its own and was the primary language in all official domains. However, in democratic South Africa, Afrikaans has lost this dominant position. In a way, it is a 'victim of its own successes', as Giliomee (2003: 26) puts it. For example, to focus on just one domain of use, it has lost its primary role in the education system. The new democratic government has put pressure on previously Afrikaans-medium schools to offer parallel courses with English as the medium of instruction, as a way of opening up these courses to black students. It is because of such developments that scholars have started to raise questions about the 'steady decline of Afrikaans as an academic language' and the 'increasing marginalization of Afrikaans and perhaps even its eclipse as a public language' (Giliomee, 2003: 23, 24). In some popular and media discourses, Afrikaans, from being the dominant language, has been reinvented as an endangered minority language in need of protection on a par with all other indigenous South African languages.

Yet, it needs to be stressed that Afrikaans is still used extensively as one of the lingua francas of contemporary South Africa and that it is the primary home language of an economically powerful group in society. On the whole, it continues to be used in family transmission, though it is also the case that many Coloured speakers have switched or are switching from Afrikaans to English. Kamwangamalu (2001) comments on the changing sociolinguistic situation of Afrikaans in the following way:

> Therefore, although as a result of the demise of apartheid, Afrikaans no longer receives special treatment from the state and has been reduced to one of the eleven languages in the country's official linguistic heritage, the language is not likely to come under any threat of attrition, in spite of the territory it has lost and is likely to lose to its historical rival, English, in the higher domains, such as the government and administration, the media, the army, the court, to list but a few. (Kamwangamalu, 2001: 425)

In this difficult situation, many Afrikaans language activists and experts have now come out in defence of *both* Afrikaans *and* African languages, relying upon a discourse of linguistic human rights and attempting to form an alliance in the fight against English language hegemony. Some academics such as Alexander (2001: 9) even see Afrikaans language activism, with its historical experience of successfully resisting the encroachment of English, as potentially playing 'a key role in establishing democracy in South Africa if it shares its assets and privileges with the other native languages' (quoted in Orman, 2008: 153). However, Orman (2008) points out two problems with this: first, there is the continuing 'suspicion that the language of minority rights and linguistic pluralism is merely being appropriated in order to mask more sinister political intentions' (Orman, 2008: 117). Secondly, Orman (2008) rightly adds that

> some degree of caution and historical situatedness would therefore seem to be advisable when seeking to draw inspiration for the post-apartheid national integration project from the social processes which facilitated the development of Afrikaans. One would do well to consider whether a highly emotional, virulently xenophobic movement such as that which accompanied the rise of Afrikaans does not fall some way short of serving as the ideal model of linguistic development for the marginalized languages of South Africa. (Orman, 2008: 154)

What Might be the Best Language-in-Education Policy for Coloured Students?

It has been argued (e.g. Braam, 2004) that since many members of the Coloured communities are shifting from Afrikaans to English, it would be important to introduce mother tongue-based bilingual education (with Afrikaans as the assumed 'mother tongue') for their children, both to help them achieve greater educational success and at the same time to stop or slow down the demise of Afrikaans. This argument is certainly valid at least for students from Coloured families who have not yet switched to English, but what has not been sufficiently discussed is the variety of Afrikaans that they will be taught at school. Will they be taught standard Afrikaans, the language of the white Afrikaners, or their own vernacular varieties? If the former option were to be chosen, this would mean that the students would have to learn almost a new foreign language. It is only in the case of the latter option that schools would actually build on students' own home resources. Moreover, as noted above, the vernacular varieties of Afrikaans tend to be heavily mixed with English, so that it would probably make sense to offer these students a flexible bilingual education programme in both (vernacular) Afrikaans and English.

In the publication already referenced above, Braam (2004) discusses a research project carried out in a suburban primary school in the Western Cape, which formerly used Afrikaans as its medium of instruction but is now switching more and more to English. It is attended by large numbers of Coloured students, most of whom use a vernacular variety of Afrikaans, which 'marks [the community] as a distinct underclass on a regional and national level' (Braam, 2004: 44). Braam (2004: 40) insists on the importance of 'integrat[ing] their particular dialect into their learning experience as a means to promote strong identity linkages with their learning environment'. Yet, the question of language variation is insufficiently addressed; while Braam (2004: 30) quotes a teacher saying that 'children speak a dialect in the community, "so even if we use Afrikaans terms when teaching, it does not facilitate learning"', this key issue is not further discussed in his paper. Moreover, considering that Braam (2004: 23) himself acknowledges that the home languages of many of the students' families include both Afrikaans and English, it might have been preferable to advocate, not Afrikaans-based bilingual education, but rather flexible bilingual education in both vernacular Afrikaans and English. The reason why Braam (2004: 6) advocates the former is that the 'underlying objective' of his research is 'to raise the status of Afrikaans' in contemporary South African society; if, on the other hand, his primary objective had been to improve these disadvantaged students' opportunities of educational success, it would have made better sense to advocate a bilingual education programme building on their home resources in *both* English and vernacular Afrikaans (cf. Banda [2010] for a similar argument).

Nativization of English in South Africa

Just like Afrikaans, English exists in a number of varieties in South Africa, ranging from standard South African English to South African Indian English (the variety used by people who migrated from the Indian subcontinent to South Africa) and Black South African English (BSAE). The distinctive syntactic characteristics of BSAE include the following:

the extension of progressive forms to stative verbs (*The team I **am having** now is a strong one*); the use of a to-infinitive complement after make (*What **makes** them **to stop** that product?*); subject-auxiliary inversion in embedded questions (*Unfortunately we do not know where **is she** at the* *moment*); the use of resumptive pronouns in relative clauses (*That is the man who Bongani saw **him***); and frequent use of copy pronouns (*The parents, **they** supposed to pay ten rands*). (Chick & Wade, 1997: 278; bold in original)

Chick and Wade (1997) construct a scenario for the future development of English in South Africa, arguing that BSAE may see its status raised, as more and more of its speakers gain access to influential and powerful positions in society. They mention in particular 'the increasing number of BSAE-speaking announcers and presenters on radio and television, positions that until quite recently were restricted to speakers of standard South African English' (Chick & Wade, 1997: 280). As a result of these social changes, there could be at least a partial restandardization of South African English in the direction of BSAE. BSAE could acquire both more instrumental and more integrative (identity-linked) values in society, unlike standard South African English, which is too closely associated with a small group of middle-class whites. This could also give speakers of BSAE more of a sense of ownership of the language, with BSAE gradually becoming iconic of South African identity, like Singlish in Singapore, but with more social prestige attached to it. Chick and Wade (1997) conclude on an optimistic note:

> Since restandardization would involve expanding the range of English varieties that are considered appropriate in domains of power, it could result in a wider range of people entering such domains and being able to participate effectively in them. (Chick & Wade, 1997: 282)

That their predictions have largely turned out to be right is confirmed for instance by Mesthrie and Upton (2013: 2), who describe BSAE as 'the variety that has prospered the most since 1994, being a major variety to be heard in the media, in parliament, at public gatherings and so forth'. At the same time, it is worth emphasizing that other scholars do not see BSAE as a homogeneous variety due to its highly fluid and variable nature.

Harmonizing Nguni and Sotho: An Unsuccessful Way of Implementing a Multilingual Language Policy

After discussing the roles of Afrikaans and English in contemporary South African society, in this section I turn to the so-called 'indigenous' or 'African' languages, though this labelling is quite problematic, not just because of the colonial loading of these terms but also because even

English – as we have seen in the previous section – may be in the process of becoming an indigenous language in South Africa. Like Afrikaans and English, these languages obviously also exist in a number of varieties, ranging from standard to vernacular. Furthermore, most of these languages exist on two linguistic continua, the Nguni and the Sotho continua, such that languages and varieties leak into each other, with no clear boundaries between them.

The South African constitution nominally recognizes nine of these languages: isiZulu, isiXhosa, Sepedi, Setswana, Sesotho, Xitsonga, siSwati, Tshivenda and isiNdebele. Because they do not play very important roles in the official domains, the question has been discussed whether and how it is possible to raise their status. One idea in this connection is that the nine African languages recognized in the constitution constitute perhaps too high a number and that, if there were a smaller number of languages, it might be easier to promote their use in official domains. As a result, Alexander (1992, 2000) has come up with the proposal to harmonize the Nguni and Sotho language clusters. The Nguni languages comprise isiZulu, isiXhosa, siSwati and isiNdebele, and the Sotho languages include Sepedi, Setswana and Sesotho. Within each cluster, the different languages are to a large extent mutually intelligible. Hence, it might be feasible to create overarching written Nguni and Sotho standards for use in official domains and in education, which could exist alongside the spoken and informal varieties. In this way, the number of official languages could be reduced to four: English, Afrikaans, the Nguni standard and the Sotho standard, leaving Tsonga and Venda, which are not mutually intelligible with other varieties, but which could be recognized as official regional languages in the northern parts of South Africa where they are used (Orman, 2008: 160).

However, the reactions to Alexander's proposal were very negative or even hostile. It was seen as an attempt to eradicate the South African languages (isiZulu, isiXhosa, siSwati, isiNdebele, Sepedi, Setswana, Sesotho), and the people who criticized Alexander relied upon a discourse of linguistic human rights in order to defend these languages. But perhaps the main reason why Alexander's proposal did not lead anywhere was that it was not in line with most people's language use and attitudes, at least at that time. Indeed, it advocated the creation of artificial (Nguni and Sotho) standards to be built on other artificial standards (standard Zulu, standard Xhosa, etc.) and then to be imposed upon people. As Orman (2008: 160) puts it, 'democratic aspirations are clearly at odds with any suggestion of standardized forms of Nguni and Sotho being foisted upon an unsuspecting and unwelcoming population by state decree'. Especially in education, it would be preferable to build the language of schooling directly upon the linguistic varieties actually used by people, rather than the standard varieties (of Zulu, Xhosa, etc.) which frequently seem more like a foreign language to them. This is a key point that will be developed in the remainder of this chapter, which focuses upon the education system in post-apartheid South Africa, and the roles of English, Afrikaans and the African languages in it.

Media of Instruction in the Education System of Democratic South Africa

As a result of the 1997 Language-in-Education policy, schools previously reserved for white (or Indian or Coloured) students are now desegregated and racially mixed. However, many of these schools charge high fees and thus are only accessible to middle-class African students. Rural and township schools, which were previously reserved for African students, have seen very little change, in that they continue to be underfunded and also to have a huge majority of poor African students. In this way, as Probyn (2005: 156) notes, racial divisions have been replaced by social class divisions.

Many rural schools practise a form of mother tongue education with a switch to English as the medium of instruction after three or four years, whereas many urban schools, because they have students with many different home languages, often use English as their medium of instruction right from the beginning. As for the elite and high-fee schools previously reserved for white students, many of them have switched from Afrikaans to English as their medium of instruction, and some have also introduced African languages as school subjects. However, this is by no means a general rule, especially at secondary level; thus, Deumert (2010: 10) notes that in 2009, 45.5% of the secondary schools in Cape Town did not offer Xhosa (or another African language) either as a medium of instruction or even as a subject. Finally, in higher education, universities usually use English as the medium of instruction. At former Afrikaans universities, there is sometimes a choice between English or Afrikaans as the medium of instruction. On the other hand, African languages are usually only offered as a subject.

The picture we get of the medium of instruction in the education system of democratic South Africa is thus a heterogeneous one, as heterogeneous as the country's population. According to the constitution, children have a right to learn in (the official variety of) their 'mother tongue' and schools must fulfil this right 'where this is reasonably practicable' (Kamwangamalu, 2001: 410). In this way, schools can 'determine their own language policy in consultation with parents and the school community' (Ncoko *et al.*, 2000: 226). As we have seen, while some (especially urban) schools offer

English immersion from first grade onwards, other (especially rural) schools start with a form of mother tongue education in (the official variety of) an African language and switch to English after a number of years. The sudden transition often causes great difficulties for many students, when English changes from being a subject to being the medium of instruction, and all or most subjects are taught through it. As a result, a more gradual shift from African language to English as the medium of instruction has become an increasingly popular option with schools, students and parents (Lin & Man, 2009: 51).

Mother Tongue Education or Flexible Multilingual Education?

The debate about mother tongue education has been particularly virulent in relation to a number of African countries. Why should such countries as South Africa use English, a colonial language, as the medium of instruction in their educational system? Is it not time for Africans to 'decolonize their minds', as Ngugi wa Thiong'o (1986) famously put it? There is an urgent need to valorize the indigenous African languages, and this could be achieved by using them as media of instruction. Being educated in their own language would also offer millions of schoolchildren better chances of educational success, whereas the present system mostly aims at the social reproduction of a small English-speaking elite.

These are cogent and persuasive arguments and therefore need to be taken seriously. They have led to educational reforms in many African countries, which are now trying out some forms of mother tongue education. They are advocated by large numbers of well-meaning scholars, who are genuinely concerned about improving educational opportunities for all. Yet, at the same time, they are highly problematic because they erase an important part of the linguistic reality in these countries. The main culprit encouraging such erasure is the mother tongue ideology (the belief that everybody has one and only one mother tongue), which informs these proposals. In the sections that follow, I attempt to portray the linguistic reality of South Africa in its full complexity and draw the conclusion that flexible multilingual education might be preferable to mother tongue education.

Deconstructing the indigenous vs colonial language distinction

The first thing to note is that, like many binary oppositions, the distinction between indigenous and colonial languages does not hold. Scholars such as Makoni *et al.* (2007) argue that the so-called 'indigenous mother tongues' are as much European or colonial constructions as the European languages. Rather than being authentic products of indigenous cultures, languages such as Setswana (in South Africa), Shona (in Zimbabwe) and many others are directly linked with the European colonial project, and their standard varieties were constructed by European missionaries and the colonial administrations. In fact, de Klerk (2002) points out that the nine African languages chosen as official languages of South Africa were those that had been standardized in this way and had been taught as part of the apartheid government's Bantu education programme; he therefore comments that 'through an ironic twist, linguistic human rights in the South African constitution enshrined the ethnolinguistic mapping of the country' as it had been constructed under the apartheid system (de Klerk, 2002: 39). Makoni *et al.* (2007) explain this in the following way:

> These written languages – produced as much by colonial agency as by South African, and bearing at times little resemblance to the spoken language of the region's peoples – became, in effect, mother tongues in search of speakers. (Makoni *et al.*, 2007: 40)

Yet, it is these artificially constructed mother tongues that have become (or should become) the basis of primary education, according to the proponents of mother tongue education.

A widening gap between 'school' and 'street' varieties

Cook (2009) has carried out an ethnographic study of language use in Tlhabane and Phokeng in North West province of South Africa. In the government schools, standard Setswana is taught as the mother tongue and English as a foreign language. Yet, most schoolchildren's home language is not standard Setswana but Street Setswana. Standard Setswana (also called 'pure' or 'school' Setswana) is the variety 'invented' by European missionaries during the period of colonialism, while Street Setswana is a more hybrid urban vernacular that incorporates lexical material from English, Afrikaans, Zulu and Tsotsitaal (Cook, 2009: 98). The school ideology is that only standard Setswana should be promoted and valued as being iconic of Tswana ethnicity. Hence, first grade is taught with standard Setswana as the medium of instruction; English is a subject from first grade + Afrikaans usually from third grade. By fourth grade, most subjects are taught through English as the medium of instruction, while Setswana remains a mandatory subject throughout primary and secondary education (Cook, 2009: 102).

The consequence is that during the first few years of schooling, the children often cannot follow the education which is supposed to be in their mother tongue. Cook found that, in practice, teachers frequently code-switched into Street Setswana or English during the lessons, when students did not get the point in standard Setswana. She notes that students often understand English better than standard Setswana:

Not only are many students more familiar with certain English terms than with their standard Setswana equivalents, but they are more comfortable with English in general than standard Setswana. (Cook, 2009: 110)

It is not surprising, therefore, that the school emphasis on standard Setswana discourages many students and strengthens their preference for English, which they look upon as the language of opportunities and power.

The situation described by Cook is by no means unique. Numerous other studies have shown that this is a trend that is happening throughout African classrooms. For instance, Makoni *et al.* (2010: 3) state that 'students who have Zulu attributed to them as a mother tongue based on their ethnicity liken learning in Zulu to learning in a foreign language', and Murray (2002: 441) argues that the fact that English is an important part of the linguistic repertoire of many urban children explains their frequent claim that they 'find it easier to study English as a subject than their home language'. There is thus an increasing gap in mother tongue education between the standard indigenous varieties used as school languages and the home languages spoken by most of the schoolchildren. For more and more children, the mother tongue taught in the classroom has less and less to do with their own linguistic repertoires. This is an urgent problem that needs to be addressed by mother tongue programmes in many African countries.

The spread of urban vernaculars

This problem affecting mother tongue education has been exacerbated by such factors as accelerated migration to urban centres, which has furthered the shift from the rural indigenous varieties to pan-ethnic urban vernaculars. Throughout Africa, the widespread use of urban languages such as Wolof in Senegal, Nouchi in Côte d'Ivoire, Lingala in the Democratic Republic of the Congo and Isicamtho, Tsotsitaal, Pretoria Sotho or Street Setswana in South Africa, both reflects and constructs new post-ethnic urban identities (McLaughlin, 2009: 13).

All these languages are hybrid in the sense that they incorporate material from a number of other languages. This is no different from the way in which a language such as English, for instance, has, over the centuries, incorporated huge amounts of linguistic material from French and other languages. However, because of their hybridity, the new urban languages tend to be looked down upon within most educational systems. As a result, the contradictory nature of mother tongue education consists in the fact that the true mother tongues of many children are ignored or rejected, while the children continue to be taught in indigenous mother tongues that are actually foreign to them. Yet, it is the new urban languages that 'more directly express the cultural legacy that is supposed to be preserved', rather than the 'colonially imposed "standard indigenous languages"' (Makoni *et al.*, 2007: 35).

It is important to note that the situation of the standard varieties of African languages is very different from that of standard European languages. As Probyn (2008: 219) puts it, 'Ironically, the standard varieties are associated with rural areas and so are less prestigious than urban varieties'. Slabbert and Finlayson (2002) explain this as follows:

> the non-pure/non-standard varieties of the African languages are spoken by the more affluent, modernized urban individuals and thus represent the aspirational values associated with the European standard varieties. (Slabbert & Finlayson, 2002: 242)

This in turn allows us to understand Banda's (2000: 61) assertion that 'the urban varieties can be used to make African languages popular', especially with urban black students.

Mother tongue education and ethnolinguistic essentialism

We have seen that the problem with mother tongue education is that official policies are often based on an essentializing link with language inheritance rather than on the children's actual language expertise; Tswanas, for instance, are simply assumed to have standard Setswana as their mother tongue. The negative consequence of such essentialist categorizing is that, if the children master a non-standard variety (Street Setswana) instead of the standard variety, then their linguistic competencies may be stigmatized in the classroom and they may be looked upon as deficient or even 'semilingual' (unable to speak any language proficiently).

Therefore, the question of 'which variety of the mother tongue should be used as the medium of instruction' arises. And here, some researchers answer very clearly that it is the urban vernaculars that are 'more appropriate for use in education than the standard varieties' (Makoni *et al.*, 2010: 13).

They thus take up the opposite stance to that advocated by many proponents of mother tongue education. But they go even further when they
argue that, since most of these children are multilingual, 'the use of a single
standard language in a classroom setting is an aberration' (Makoni et al.,
2010: 11). Other researchers concur: thus, for instance, Banda (2000: 52)
asks, 'What, then, is the utility of the "mother tongue" concept given the
multilingual reality?' and Murray (2002) summarizes the issue as follows:

> In recent debates the whole notion of a single home language or mother
> tongue has been challenged, and it has been suggested that for many
> urban children English is very much part of the home repertoire.
> (Murray, 2002: 441)

In this way, these researchers have pulled the rug from under mother
tongue education, by questioning the very assumption that mother tongue
education is based on. They question in what sense children with multilingual repertoires can be said to have a particular 'mother tongue' and argue
that for these children it may be preferable to offer flexible multilingual programmes rather than education through one medium of instruction only,
whether English or an indigenous language, as many South African schools
are still wont to do.

Are Indigenous African Languages Endangered?

An argument often put forward in favour of mother tongue education
in an indigenous language is that this is necessary in order to save the indigenous language from being 'killed' by a global language such as English. Let
us take Xhosa as an example of an indigenous language which is sometimes
perceived as being endangered. However, once we study the language situation in the Western Cape area, we quickly realize that this is not a simple
situation of an indigenous language being endangered by English. In fact,
what is going on is much more complex.

The first thing that strikes the researcher is an ever-increasing split
between urban and rural Xhosa. According to Dyers (2009: 260), the rural
variety of Xhosa is the standard or school variety which is often perceived
as the 'deeper' or 'purer' variety. It is widely used in literary texts and other
cultural forms. Hence, it can be seen in a very positive light, but at the same
time it can also be looked upon as backwards because of its association
with rural areas. On the other hand, urban Xhosa is the spoken or 'light'
variety, which involves more code-mixing with English and Afrikaans. It
is often celebrated in popular culture (television soaps, pop music; it is also

increasingly used in community newspapers). Just like rural Xhosa, it can be seen in two very different ways: as an index of urban identity, it can be seen in a very positive light, but at the same time it can also be looked down upon as mere 'slang'.

Dowling (2011: 348–349) points out that, because of this wide divide between rural and urban Xhosa, many young people in Cape Town often find English easier than standard Xhosa. Because they are exposed to more print in English, many English words are more accessible to them than the standard Xhosa equivalents. Nevertheless, Xhosa is still the dominant language in the township communities, whereas English – and Afrikaans, which is also widely used in the Western Cape – dominate in such public spaces as the workplace, shopping areas and public transport (Dowling, 2011: 351).

This suggests that Xhosa is not in fact an endangered language; on the contrary, the number of Xhosa speakers in the Cape Town area is increasing because of the high immigration rate from the rural Eastern Cape. However, the Xhosa of these new residents is strongly influenced by the urban varieties of Xhosa widely used within the townships. Nor are the rural Eastern Cape areas unaffected, since the urban vernaculars are brought to these areas by visiting city dwellers (Dyers, 2009: 266). Hence, what we have here is a typical situation of language contact and language change. Xhosa is in the process of changing under the influence of other languages, in particular English and Afrikaans. Many township inhabitants are widening their repertoire to include not only urban varieties of Xhosa but increasingly also English and Afrikaans, which, in turn, affects the variety of Xhosa that they speak (Dyers, 2009: 267; see also Deumert, 2013).

We now understand that what some mother tongue education proponents are concerned about is not Xhosa in general, but much more specifically one particular variety of Xhosa, namely, rural or standard Xhosa, which seems to be the only one they consider worth preserving (cf. following section). For them, standard Xhosa is indexical of a particular Xhosa culture, which is in danger of disappearing, although this argument about authentic Xhosa culture has been convincingly deconstructed by such scholars as Makoni, Brutt-Griffler and Mashiri, as we have seen above. In the end, then, these mother tongue education proponents are not attempting to preserve Xhosa, but rather to prevent it from changing. However, every sociolinguist is aware that language contact inevitably induces language change. Hence, the mother tongue education proponents are fighting a losing battle in the name of some imagined ideal of a 'pure' and 'authentic' Xhosa language and culture.

To make a historical parallel, it is as if they were trying to prevent English from changing under the influence of French during the Middle

Ages. They would probably have liked to preserve Old English in its pristine form and prevent it from mutating into Middle English and on into Modern English (whose varieties are far more code-mixed with French than Old English varieties). They might have looked upon Middle English varieties as 'debased' varieties and advocated the use of 'pure' Old English in education. Similarly, in South Africa, they tend to look down upon the urban vernaculars and insist upon the use of only the standard, rural variety at school. In this way, they are Don Quixote-like figures fighting against the inevitability of language change. But the most worrying thing is that in this process they frequently forget about what should be their foremost concern, namely, what is best for the children?

Towards Flexible Multilingual Pedagogies

Typically, in many South African schools, English is taught with a lot of code-switching into indigenous languages such as Xhosa. Teachers use code-switching as a teaching strategy in order to scaffold their students' learning, or to encourage exploratory talk in the classroom (Setati et al., 2002: 135). Moreover, according to Probyn (2009: 130), teachers code-switch not only for cognitive but also affective reasons (for classroom management, making jokes, etc.). Some mother tongue education advocates, on the other hand, object to teachers' use of code-switching and prefer 'language separation' pedagogic approaches. Thus, for instance, Bloch et al. (2010) comment as follows on teachers' code-switching practices:

> We observed [a particular teacher] using English mathematics textbooks, though she tried to talk in Xhosa to the children. However, her language emerged as code-mixing rather than the systematic use of one or the other language … It will take some effort and time for teachers to stop using code-mixing as it has become common practice with many. The need to code-mix will only fade once all significant aspects of teaching are delivered as a matter of course in Xhosa. (Bloch et al., 2010: 102)

Bloch et al. disapprove of the use of mixed language in classrooms, emphasizing the role of standard Xhosa and promoting the teaching of Xhosa and English as two wholly separate languages.

However, what these proponents of mother tongue education seem to forget is that many South African children nowadays are multilingual, and therefore it is important for the school system to build on the whole of their repertoires as far as possible. As Busch (2010: 283) puts it, implementing a mother tongue education programme would be tantamount to 'monolingualization', that is 'reduc[ing] the heteroglossia of individual speakers either to monolingualism or to a dichotomy between "mother tongue" and "target language"'. In such a programme, children would be perceived in exclusive terms as (for instance) *either* 'Xhosa speakers' *or* 'English speakers'. Busch (2010: 293) talks about the 'damage inflicted by categorization according to the ascribed mother tongues', and comments on the 'monolingual habitus' of mother tongue education, which 'functions as an "engine" that reduces the complexity of students' everyday lives' (Busch, 2010: 290).

For many of the South African children whose case was considered in this chapter, a flexible bi-/multilingual programme would probably be best. Depending on the nature of the children's communicative repertoires, it will be necessary to look for local solutions, but in many contexts it might make sense to set up bilingual programmes in both English and an African language (often one of the new urban languages), which would form the best possible bridge with the students' actual home linguistic resources. It needs to be pointed out that because of the highly variable and heterogeneous nature of the new urban varieties, the question of how to use them in education is not easy to answer. As a first step, they could at least be used as an additional, largely spoken medium of instruction, alongside English, in the initial stages of education; and this could act as a bridge towards the later acquisition of a more standardized variety of the language. An approach such as the Corsican paradigm of *polynomie* could be usefully applied here (see Chapter 2; see also the section 'Difficulties in Implementing Flexible Multilingual Education' in Chapter 11).

At the same time, when arguing for flexible multilingual education, we should be careful not to reject mother tongue education *en bloc*. In many situations, it will be the best way of ensuring children's educational success. But it cannot simply be proclaimed as the ideal system of education, as some sociolinguists are wont to do. On the contrary, as we have shown in this chapter, it depends on each context, and in heterogeneous and multilingual contexts, it is often the case that more flexible dual-medium and bi-/multiliteracy approaches will be more promising ways of building on children's complex repertoires.

Lessons to be Learnt from the South African Experience

In this concluding section, I briefly summarize the main points that can be learnt from the South African experience:

- the historical dimension cannot be ignored if we want to understand present-day trends and attitudes;
- Bantu education under the apartheid system consisted of an extreme form of mother tongue education; hence, any attempt to impose mother tongue education in African languages is likely to be resisted by both students and parents;
- South Africa has moved from the highly fixed and restrictive system of Bantu education to a much more flexible bi-/multilingual system;
- contemporary South African society is marked by the rapid spread of urban vernaculars, which are increasingly different from the standard varieties of African languages taught at school;
- an even greater degree of flexibility is needed in response to these sociolinguistic changes; in particular, the use of both urban vernaculars and English as media of instruction would open up greater access to educational opportunities for many children (especially children in urban areas with multilingual repertoires);
- the use of flexible multilingual pedagogies (bridging and scaffolding strategies, code-switching, etc.) allows teachers to build on the whole of these children's repertoires.

9 Luxembourg

With a population of 502,100 and a geographical size of 2,586 km², the Grand Duchy of Luxembourg is situated between Belgium, France and Germany and is one of the six founding member states of the European Union (EU). Luxembourg is home to the highest proportion of resident foreigners in the EU (43.1%), the majority of whom are passport holders of other EU member states. With 15.9% of the total population, Portuguese passport holders currently make up the largest number of resident foreigners, followed by French (5.9%), Italian (3.6%), Belgian (3.3%), other EU (8.3%) and non-EU (6%) residents. The number of resident foreigners climbed steadily after World War II and increased dramatically from the 1970s onwards (Weber & Horner, 2012b: 4).

Since the late 1960s, Luxembourg's niche for international banking and special tax schemes has propelled economic prosperity. Together with the resident foreigners, 149,000 *frontaliers* (cross-border commuters) make up a large proportion of the workforce in the Grand Duchy. Their presence is linked to the small geographical size of Luxembourg as well as EU regulations facilitating free movement of the EU workforce. Nearly 80% of the *frontaliers* come from France and Belgium and are (primarily) French speaking, over 20% come from Germany and are (primarily) German speaking (Weber & Horner, 2012b: 4; Wille *et al.*, 2012).

The language situation in Luxembourg is frequently referred to as 'triglossic' in reference to the three languages recognized by the 1984 language law: Luxembourgish, French and German. The distinction between spoken and written language has been pivotal to understanding long-standing norms and patterns of language use in Luxembourg, with most spoken communication among the native-born taking place in Luxembourgish and written functions carried out primarily in standard French or German. Luxembourgish language varieties are Germanic and are similar to Moselle Franconian varieties (likewise Germanic) spoken in adjacent parts of Germany, Belgium and France. For this reason, basic literacy skills are taught via standard German in state schools. French is introduced as a subject in the second year of primary school, becoming a full subject in the third year and gradually replacing German as the main medium of instruction at secondary level, particularly in the prestigious *lycées classiques*. Based on the Education Act of 1843, practices in state schools have perpetuated elite bilingualism, or the valorization of standard German and French (Davis, 1994). Nowadays, however, French is spoken as a (supplemental) home language – as opposed to a (mere) school language – by a larger segment of the population than ever before, mostly due to its widespread use by *frontaliers* and resident foreigners. The late 1970s and early 1980s was a period marked by a high immigration rate especially from Portugal, in consequence of an agreement concerning the recruitment of 'guest workers' signed by the Luxembourgish and Portuguese governments. It was during this period that pressure and support for the development of Luxembourgish grew; moreover, in 1984, a language law was passed, which for the first time officially recognized Luxembourgish as the national language and, in theory, as an administrative language. However, this legislation simultaneously reinforced the sociolinguistic *status quo* by designating French and German as legal, judicial and administrative languages, precisely the state of affairs prior to the ratification of the law even if it was previously *de facto* rather than *de jure* policy. The ratification of the 1984 law signals a shift towards explicit language policy, thus imparting on Luxembourgish a higher position in the hierarchy of languages (Horner & Weber, 2008: 106f). Luxembourgish is declared the 'national language' in Article 1, while the expression 'official language' is studiously avoided in the text of the law. This wording provides a springboard for language ideological debates which frequently revolve around the status and use of Luxembourgish. Language-in-education debates, on the other hand, tend to focus on the 'trilingual ideal' (Horner & Weber, 2008: 87), that is, the mastery of the standard, written varieties of German and French together with the presupposed (consistent) use of spoken Luxembourgish.

Luxembourgish: Constructing an Endangered Language

If a 'dialect' is constructed as a 'language' and if it is a small language, spoken by a limited number of people, then *ipso facto* it also tends to be regarded as an endangered language. In other words, a linguistic variety almost paradoxically comes to be perceived as being endangered through having its status upgraded to that of a 'language'. A good example of this is Luxembourgish, which has been upgraded from a 'dialect' of German to the 'national language' of Luxembourg, as enshrined in the 1984 language law.

Luxembourgish is a 'small' language, relatively speaking, in the sense that it is spoken by an estimated few hundred thousand people. However, it must be stressed that Luxembourgish cannot be regarded as a minority language, if this concept is used 'not to draw attention to numerical size of particular groups, but to refer to situational differences in power, rights and privileges' (Pavlenko & Blackledge, 2004: 4). This distinction – a small language but not a minority language – points to the non-prototypicality of the Luxembourgish language situation. Members of linguistic minorities in Luxembourg speak languages such as Portuguese and Italian, which are official languages of other EU member states and are bound up with norms linked to linguistic standardization. As for the dominant languages in Luxembourg (Luxembourgish, German and French), all three are officially recognized in the language law of 1984. But it is the first of these, which in the law is referred to as the national language of Luxembourgers, that is the focus of explicitly framed standardization efforts and related debates. In the context of these debates, critical issues of power and inequalities have been increasingly blurred, and it is therefore essential to distinguish between languages and their speakers. When the focus is on speakers, it is clear that people who speak Luxembourgish as a home language are in no way oppressed for this reason. On the contrary, it is speakers of Portuguese and other languages who are sometimes discriminated against because the language-in-education policy of the state largely erases their linguistic needs and forces them to go through a German-language literacy program. On the other hand, when the focus is on languages, as it often is in language ideological debates in Luxembourg, Luxembourgish is presented as an endangered language that is in need not only of standardization but also of protection and preservation (Horner & Weber, 2010).

In relation to the high level of in-migration during the last few decades, there are fears that Luxembourgish might die out and that 'Luxembourgers' might become a minority in 'their own country' in the not too distant future. In this way, a wide-ranging discourse of endangerment has spread, concerning not just the survival of the language but also of the nation itself (cf. Duchêne & Heller, 2007). As far as the language is concerned, suggestions to ensure its survival include the following:

- inserting a language clause into the constitution;
- promoting Luxembourgish to the level of an EU working language;
- introducing it into the educational system as a full subject and/or as the medium of basic literacy.

Inserting a language clause into the constitution is a demand that was formulated a number of years ago by *Actioun Lëtzebuergesch*, the association founded in 1971 to promote the use of Luxembourgish. As for the recognition of Luxembourgish as an EU working language, this has been fuelled by the 2004 entry of Malta into the EU, with as a consequence the addition of another small language, Maltese, to the list of EU working languages. While French is the EU working language for Luxembourg, the government is now considering entering into negotiations to have Luxembourgish also acknowledged at EU level as a lesser-used but officially recognized language. Such recognition would allow Luxembourgish citizens to write to the EU in their 'mother tongue' if so desired. Similar rights have already been granted to Catalan, Basque and Galician speakers in Spain, and to Welsh speakers in the UK. The final point concerns the role of Luxembourgish in the educational domain, which will be discussed in the following section.

Constructing Luxembourgish as the 'Language of Integration'

In juxtaposition to the roles of German and French, the role of Luxembourgish in the school system is limited and somewhat controversial. Officially, Luxembourgish is 'banned' as a medium of instruction in most contexts of primary and secondary education, but it is nevertheless used unofficially by many teachers to explain difficult points to their students (Davis, 1994: 98–104; Weber, 2009: 100–103). As a formal school subject, however, its role is quite limited: it is taught for one hour per week throughout the six years of primary school and in the first year of secondary school.

There is a growing momentum to increase the currently permitted amount of instruction of Luxembourgish as a subject within the curriculum. The push for more Luxembourgish in schools is an interesting development from a number of perspectives. In practical terms, expanding the role of Luxembourgish in schools cannot happen immediately because the language has not fully undergone the processes of standardization and is not used as a means of written communication in the full range of domains by most speakers. As a result, adequate pedagogical materials are only beginning to be developed. Although Luxembourgish is being used more and more as a written language, and issues of standardization are becoming more visible and subject to debate (Horner, 2005), the functional compartmentalization of languages in the Luxembourgish school system has not (yet) been fundamentally shaken up. This distribution of languages, with Luxembourgish being used mostly for spoken interaction and French and German mostly as written languages, could be seen – in the words of Jaffe (2007: 75) – as 'doing both pragmatic and symbolic scaffolding': not only does it scaffold the children's learning (explaining difficult points in Luxembourgish) but it also projects a particular ideological model of the ideal Luxembourger (speaking

Luxembourgish and learning standard German and French as additional languages, mostly for the purposes of writing).

The push for more Luxembourgish has primarily targeted the area of preschool education, which consists of one optional year of *précoce* (for children
aged three) and two obligatory years of *préscolaire* (from age four upwards).
In the Luxembourgish Ministry of Education document *L'Education précoce* (dated 2000), it is assumed that children who do not already speak
Luxembourgish will acquire it through 'natural' interaction with other
pupils and teachers. Such increased use of Luxembourgish has been hailed as
a solution to the perceived problem of social heterogeneity and as a way of
achieving the vaguely formulated goals of 'integration' and 'social cohesion'
(see Horner, 2009a). It is hoped that the teaching and use of Luxembourgish
during the three years of preschool will help these children to 'integrate'
and prepare them for the German-language literacy programme of primary
school:

> *Education précoce* groups will include both Luxembourgish children and
> children who have learnt another L1. It is clear that the aim of *Education
> précoce* and *préscolaire* is to get children to acquire a good mastery of
> the Luxembourgish language, for this is considered, within our school
> system, as a powerful stepping-stone towards the later acquisition of
> German, the language of literacy in primary school. (Quoted in Horner
> & Weber, 2010: 186)

This text emphasizes the learning and promotion of Luxembourgish,
which is simply assumed to be the (one and only) mother tongue of all
'Luxembourgish children'. At the same time, the close linguistic relatedness
of Luxembourgish and German is used to justify the maintenance of the
German-language literacy program. In this way, the text attempts to maintain a somewhat precarious balance between monolingual identification
with the mother tongue and trilingual identification with the three languages used in the educational system: Luxembourgish, German and French
(though French is not explicitly mentioned here, the official text is actually
written in French). Horner (2004, 2007b) has shown how the cultural model
of Luxembourgish national identity allows for an oscillation between these
two poles: identification with Luxembourgish versus identification with the
trilingual ideal. Her detailed analyses illustrate how official, international,
as well as educational discourses often tend towards the latter option,
whereas internal and popular discourses are frequently informed by the former. However, the recent emphasis on Luxembourgish as the 'language of
integration', which – as we have just seen – is even beginning to colonize the

educational domain, has shifted the balance in favour of the 'monolingual identification with Luxembourgish' model (see Horner, 2009b). In these discourses, 'linguistic integration' only refers to knowledge of Luxembourgish, and (for instance) residents of Portuguese origin who have learnt French are not seen as having taken a first step towards integration.

The Eradication of French from Preschool

The new emphasis on Luxembourgish is reflected in most language-in-education policies from the 1990s onwards – though within the framework of the traditional trilingualism of Luxembourgish education. Thus, for instance, in the Ministry of Education document *Pour une école d'intégration* (For a School of Integration; dated 1998), it is acknowledged that French is frequently used as a lingua franca in schools:

> In the schools with a high percentage of foreign children, the language of communication between the children outside the classroom is often French. In the classroom, it can happen that the teacher is forced to use French so that the children can understand him/her … The large numbers of foreign children in some schools are one of the main factors impeding integration. The phenomenon of 'linguistic immersion' does not work, or works in the opposite direction: Luxembourgish children communicate in French with their non-Luxembourgish friends. (Quoted in Weber & Horner, 2010: 251)

The widespread presence of French in the classrooms of the 1990s is seen as a problem, an impediment to 'integration': instead of migrant students learning Luxembourgish through contact with Luxembourgish-speaking peers, it is the latter who learn French through contact with the former. One might have thought that, from the perspective of educational 'integration', this would be seen as a welcome development; after all, success within the trilingual Luxembourgish school system, at least at the higher levels, depends much more on a mastery of French than of Luxembourgish. Yet, what prevails in the ministry discourse is a nationalist ideology that looks on the Luxembourgish language as the sole icon of Luxembourgishness. In this ideology, French is seen as a threat and hence needs to be eradicated, at least from preschool education. In order to achieve this, the authors of the ministry document, as we will see, present an argument in favour of mother tongue education. The document is informed by the discourse of ethnolinguistic essentialism: Luxembourgish is seen as the one and only mother tongue of Luxembourgish children and Portuguese as the one and only mother tongue of luso-descendant children – even though in reality many of the children in both groups are bi- or multilingual. In this way, the official language-in-education policy does not build on the whole of the children's home linguistic resources; instead, it simplifies the children's complex multilingual use of language and reduces it to monolingualism (in the 'mother tongue').

In the case of luso-descendant children, preschool education thus aims at developing only their competence in Luxembourgish (while at the same time respecting their assumed 'mother tongue', i.e. Portuguese), as a result of which many of them fail to develop their knowledge of French, which they then learn in its standard version as a foreign language from Year 2 of primary school onwards. This policy, based on the mother tongue ideology, also involves bringing in Portuguese 'mother tongue' assistants, which might seem to be a progressive measure but which is explicitly justified here as allowing preschool teachers to cut out French and focus on Luxembourgish:

a Portuguese assistant works together with the Luxembourgish teacher in the classroom for three hours per week.
This measure has a number of very positive effects: ...
– the Luxembourgish teacher is no longer forced to use French so that the children can understand her; as a consequence, the foreign children can concentrate on the learning of Luxembourgish, the only language spoken by the teacher, while at the same time keeping in touch with their heritage language. (Quoted in Weber & Horner, 2010: 252)

Behind the essentialist discourse about respect for the 'mother tongue', the aim here is ultimately assimilationist: the children are taught to speak Luxembourgish and later they learn standard German and French mostly for writing purposes – which, as has been suggested above, corresponds to the traditional 'trilingual ideal' of Luxembourgish society and education. In other words, societal assimilation is here considered to be more important than successful 'integration' into the school system (in the sense of providing students with the best possible chances of educational success). Indeed, if the primary concern were success within the school system, then the children's home resources in vernacular French would be valued and built on in preschool education as a preparation for primary and secondary education. As has already been suggested, the rationale behind this assimilationist policy is a typical instantiation of the discourse of endangerment: a fear of Luxembourgish dying out, of Luxembourgers becoming a minority and of Luxembourg becoming a monolingual francophone country, due to the continuing high level of in-migration mostly from 'romanophone' countries. Finally, it needs to be emphasized that this assimilationist discourse is also a hegemonic and ultimately disempowering one in its effects upon the pupils who speak Portuguese and other Romance languages: it is about fashioning second-class Luxembourgers, since many of these children struggle with the compulsory German-language literacy programme of primary school and as a consequence end up in the lower streams of the technical lycees and are denied access to higher-status jobs (see the section 'A Difficult Situation for Migrant Students', p. 155). In other words, the children are subjected to a double process of simultaneous normalization and marginalization.

German as Medium of Instruction: From Mother Tongue Education to L2 Immersion

As a result of the official language-in-education policy, Luxembourgish has increasingly become the main language used in preschool education. Then, in the first year of primary school, all children go through a German-language literacy programme, whether their home language(s) include Luxembourgish (a Germanic language) or non-Germanic languages such as French, Portuguese, Italian, Spanish, Cape Verdean Creole, etc. French is introduced in the second year of primary school and becomes a full subject from the third year onwards. Most other subjects continue to be taught through the medium of German throughout primary school (with the exception of sports, music and arts, where Luxembourgish is specified as the medium of instruction). Speakers of Portuguese and Italian can opt for a two-hour per week course taught in their 'mother tongue' throughout the six years of primary school (the so-called *cours intégrés*, integrated courses). Otherwise, Portuguese and Italian do not play a role in the Luxembourgish school system, except for upper secondary school students specializing in languages and literatures, who can choose Spanish, Italian or Portuguese as their *quatrième langue vivante* (fourth modern language). English, too, is only taught in secondary school, as the third modern language (after German and French; Luxembourgish is not included in the count here).

There is some terminological confusion about whether and to what extent these languages are 'foreign' languages. This is due to such factors as the important role traditionally played by French in Luxembourg and the close linguistic relationship between German and Luxembourgish. Indeed, Luxembourgish used to be considered as a dialect of German (usually referred to in the 19th century as 'our German' or 'Luxembourgish German') and has only recently been promoted to the level of 'national language of the Luxembourgers' (as stated in the 1984 language law). But, as we have already seen, the language law also recognizes French and German as legislative and/or administrative languages. In today's official discourses, while the mother tongue of Luxembourgers is usually assumed to be Luxembourgish, one also finds references to the Luxembourgish–German–French trilingualism as their 'true' mother tongue (e.g. Berg & Weis, 2005: 33; for the historical antecedents of this view, see Horner, 2007b). Luxembourgish is mostly used as a language of spoken interaction and plays only a limited role within the educational system. The main languages taught are German and French, but they are taught neither as mother tongues nor as foreign languages but with a more mixed methodology as 'second languages' (L2s). Depending on the audience to which they are addressed, official and academic discourses either refer to German as the first foreign language learned from the age of 6, French as the second foreign language learned from the age of 7 and English as the third foreign language learned from the age of 13 or, alternatively, we find English referred to as the first (truly) foreign language (as in Berg & Weis, 2005: 76; Willems & Milmeister, 2006: 84). In Fehlen (2009), both versions are present simultaneously, seemingly without an awareness on the author's part of their contradictory nature: on page 48, English is described as the *erste wirkliche Fremdsprache* (first truly foreign language), whereas on page 50, French is described as the *zweite Fremdsprache* (second foreign language) after German.

The Berg and Weis report, officially prepared for the Ministry of Education, is a good illustration of the ideological motivations behind these contradictions. German and French alternate between being referred to as 'the usual languages of the country' (Berg & Weis, 2005: 23) and 'the languages of the Other' (Berg & Weis, 2005: 33). As for Luxembourgish, the authors worry that having Luxembourgish as the only mother tongue of Luxembourgers could lead to xenophobia, with Luxembourgish potentially becoming *une langue d'exclusion, permettant aux autochtones de se cloisonner* (a language of exclusion, allowing the autochthones to cut themselves off; Berg & Weis, 2005: 45). They therefore add somewhat hesitantly that *peut-être le multilinguisme est la langue maternelle cachée de beaucoup de Luxembourgeois* (maybe multilingualism is the hidden mother tongue of many Luxembourgers; Berg & Weis, 2005: 33), for such an identification with three languages (Luxembourgish, German and French) would not only highlight Luxembourgers' high level of linguistic capital but also guarantee their open-minded attitude and their *acceptation de la diversité linguistique* (acceptance of linguistic diversity; Berg & Weis, 2005: 47).

Thus, we have a choice between three different representations of foreign language provision in the Luxembourgish school system (focusing on *langues vivantes* 'modern languages' to the exclusion of Latin):

(a) English as the first foreign language and Spanish, Italian or (rarely) Portuguese taught in a highly restricted way in the upper levels of the *lycée classique;*
(b) if French is also a foreign language: French as the first foreign language, English the second one and Spanish/Italian/Portuguese as the third one;
(c) if German is also considered as a foreign language: German as the first foreign language, French the second one, English the third one and Spanish/Italian/Portuguese as the fourth one.

This final version would make Luxembourg a European model for language learning and teaching, in the sense that almost everybody going through the school system learns three foreign languages and a small group of students even learn four. It was also this version that was drawn upon as a way of explaining away Luxembourg's bad results in the 2001 Programme for International Student Assessment (PISA) tests: one reason for the low results, it was alleged, was that Luxembourgish students could not answer the questions in their 'mother tongue' but had to do it in an L2 or foreign language (German or French; see Horner, 2007a). Finally, this version throws an interesting light upon the relativity of the concepts that inform much sociolinguistic research on mother tongue education: if German were perceived as the 'mother tongue' of the majority of schoolchildren (as it was in the 19th and part of the 20th centuries), then Luxembourgish schools would be seen as offering a form of mother tongue education; if, on the other hand, German were perceived as a separate language from Luxembourgish (as it commonly is nowadays), then the school system would be seen as offering a form of immersion education in a second or foreign language.

The Roles of English and of the 'Immigrant' Languages

The model of Luxembourgish–German–French trilingualism perpetuated by the school system is strictly circumscribed. The only changes in the last few decades have been the inroads made on the one hand by 'immigrant' languages (Italian and Portuguese) and on the other hand, increasingly by English, the global language. In this section, I look at the role of these languages within the Luxembourgish educational system, first focusing on English and then considering the roles of Portuguese and Italian.

English is taught from the second year of secondary school onwards, except for students who study Latin and thus only start learning English in the third year of *lycée classique*. By the end of their secondary school studies, students are expected to reach the level of the Cambridge Advanced Examination (University of Cambridge Local Examinations Syndicate [UCLES] – Certificate in Advanced English), though this is now being redefined in terms of the *Common European Framework of Reference* (CEFR) levels B1 and B2. Over the years, English has gradually strengthened its position within the educational system, though by competing with and to some extent displacing Latin rather than German or French, the languages which are firmly entrenched from primary school upwards (see Horner, 2007a: 143). As the Ministry of Education document *Réajustement de l'enseignement des langues* (Readjustment of Language Teaching; dated 2007) acknowledges, English is still in a way the *parent pauvre* (poor relative) of French and German in the educational system. The Council of Europe, too, in their 2005 report on language learning and teaching in Luxembourg, suggests that students should already start to learn English in the first year of secondary school, and that some content and language integrated (CLIL)-type learning should be introduced in English. In other words, some non-linguistic subjects should be taught through the medium of English at the higher levels of secondary education. This would also be of great practical benefit for the students, as it has become increasingly clear that English and French are the most important languages facilitating access to the Luxembourgish labour market (except for civil servant positions, where the traditional trilingual competence in Luxembourgish, German and French is still usually required; see Klein, 2007).

As for the languages of the main transnational communities, their 'concrete inclusion [within the Luxembourgish school system] remains minimal' (de Korne, 2012). Portuguese and Italian may be used a little in the initial stages of education to help children who speak them in the home, both in the form of mother tongue assistants in preschool education and *cours intégrés* (integrated courses) in primary school. Moreover, in the upper grades of *lycée classique*, Italian, Spanish or (rarely) Portuguese can be chosen by students in the language section as their 'fourth modern language'. But all in all, they are treated as *sous-langues* (sublanguages, valueless languages) – a term used in a recent report on language teaching in Luxembourg compiled for the Ministry of Education (Berg & Weis, 2005: 45).

At secondary level, the lusophone and other romanophone students can enrol in a *filière francophone* (francophone stream) with French instead of

German as the medium of instruction, more and more of which are offered within the vocational *lycées techniques*. An option offered within the classical lycees is the *classe ALLET (allemand langue étrangère*, German as a foreign language), where students who are weak in German attend two extra lessons of German per week, with German as a foreign language teaching methodology, during the first three years of secondary school; then in the fourth year, these students are expected to have reached a level of German which will allow them to continue in the mainstream classroom. A problem with the ALLET programme is that these classes are built on a deficit model: instead of building on these students' strengths, the students are looked upon as deficient in their knowledge of German and hence in need of extra tuition.

Moreover, the programmes for learning Italian, Spanish or Portuguese as a fourth modern language are aimed at the elite *lycée classique* students and not (or not specifically) at students with these languages among their home linguistic resources. Hence, there is no attempt to build on any of the students' previous knowledge of these languages. On the contrary, in the official programme for the Italian course, it is stated that

> To bring to life the teaching of this fourth language (*further removed from our audiovisual environment* than French, German and English) and to make it more effective, use will be made of the new technologies of information and communication. Indeed, these methods will not only allow the pupils to work in a more autonomous and creative way but will moreover put them in direct contact with Italian adolescents (via the internet for instance). (Quoted in Weber, 2010: 9; italics added)

In this way, the Italian community in Luxembourg is rendered invisible. As for the Portuguese community, it is by far the largest migrant community in Luxembourg. Yet, Portuguese is so seldom offered as a fourth modern language in the *lycées classiques* that I have been unable to trace even a programme for the Portuguese course. It is simply absent from the list of available subjects in the official *Horaires et Programmes* (Timetables and Programmes) published by the Ministry of Education.

Trilingual Education and Linguistic Diversity

Much of the multilingual teaching in Luxembourgish schools is of the CLIL type, where an L2 is used as a vehicle to teach non-linguistic content matter. As we have seen, German is the main medium of instruction in primary education. At secondary level, there is a distinction – as already noted above – between the elite *lycées classiques* and the more vocational *lycées techniques*. In the *lycées classiques*, most subjects continue to be taught with German as the medium of instruction but change over half way through to French as the medium of instruction. Only mathematics switches from German to French as the medium of instruction immediately after the end of primary school and is taught through the medium of French throughout the seven years of secondary education. In the *lycées techniques*, German is the language of instruction for all non-linguistic subjects, though a wide range of streams with French as the medium of instruction has been added over the years. Although Luxembourg has a long experience of CLIL-type teaching, essential pedagogical questions are only now beginning to be addressed under the influence of recent research on CLIL in European countries: in particular, the need for language teachers and subject teachers to work collaboratively, as well as the need for tailored teaching materials, since textbooks produced abroad in the foreign language may often be linguistically too complex for the students. Indeed, this is a problem that has beset the teaching of mathematics through French from the first year of the *lycée classique* onwards.

Concerning CLIL more generally, Budach *et al.* (2008: 38) point out that it constitutes an elite form of bilingual education in the sense that it mostly involves the global European languages such as English or French. Hence, it is not surprising that it is strongly promoted by the EU, as it fits into the ideological EU framework of 'plurilingualism' with its emphasis on European languages. The EU's commitment to (European) language diversity is a central component of the project of European unification, as can be seen from its motto 'unity in diversity'. In the words of Kraus (2008: 8), 'Europe's constitutional discourse establishes a close link between the affirmation of common civic ties and the protection of diversity'. As a result, in most European language-in-education policy documents there is much emphasis on the need to respect linguistic and cultural diversity. A related emphasis is the need for national education systems to provide for the teaching of a wide range of languages. This influence can also be felt in recent language-in-education policy documents in Luxembourg, which stress the need for a policy of diversification of the languages taught at school. Here is a representative extract from the Ministry of Education report, *Readjustment of Language Teaching* (dated 2007):

The schools will be encouraged to embrace linguistic diversification by offering their students, especially in the upper grades [of the classical lycees], the possibility of learning languages which are not part of their curriculum, as an option and within an extracurricular framework. The following languages could benefit from such an initiative: Italian,

Spanish, Portuguese, Russian, Dutch, Greek, but also perhaps other languages such as Arabic and Chinese. (Quoted in Weber & Horner, 2010: 247)

While this more diversified approach to language teaching may be highly laudable in theory, in practice its effects will be minimal. Indeed, it does not offer an alternative to the large number of romanophone and luso-descendant children who are forced to go through the German-language literacy programme, as a result of which many of them are denied access to the elite *lycées classiques* and end up instead in the lower streams of the *lycées techniques*. Consequently, most of these students will not be able to avail themselves of the wider range of languages on offer, since these will only be taught in the upper grades of the *lycées classiques*.

The situation in trilingual Luxembourg is thus similar in certain respects to that in (officially) monolingual EU member states such as France, as discussed in Chapter 4 (see also Hélot & Young, 2005). Here, too, the European discourse of diversity has left its mark on recent language-in-education policy documents but again only in theory. In practice, according to Hélot and Young, immigrant languages continue to be largely ignored and the dominant culture is one of monoglossia and homogeneism. The same applies in Luxembourg, with the exception that here migrants are expected to assimilate into the fixed trilingual framework of Luxembourgish, German and French. Thus, in both countries, diversity is envisaged 'as a root of problems that need to be remedied' (Hélot & Young, 2005: 245).

A Difficult Situation for Migrant Students

The language-in-education policies discussed in this chapter have had important implications for the increasing number of romanophone students in Luxembourgish schools, especially from the 1990s onwards. A first contradiction is that they encounter more Luxembourgish especially at preschool level, where it is constructed as the language of integration, whereas outside school more and more French is used by increasing numbers of people in Luxembourgish society. This has created a fracture between educational policy and actual language practices, in that Luxembourgish is constructed as the sole language of integration in schools, while many migrant children live in areas where French is a widely used lingua franca.

Secondly, students are frequently given intensive instruction in German, sometimes at the cost of English, even though the latter is one subject where many of them could have excelled. Because of low grades in German, they often end up in the lower streams of the technical lycees, where English is only taught at a fairly rudimentary level. They are thus deprived of an important job qualification on both the Luxembourgish and the European employment market. In this way, there is an increasing disjuncture between the employment market (where French and English are the most important languages) and language-in-education policy (where German is the language of basic literacy). This is not unlike situations in other multilingual areas of Europe such as Catalonia, where migrant students are taught in Catalan, constructed by schools as the language of integration, while many of them live in predominantly Spanish-speaking areas; moreover, they are sometimes given extra instruction in Catalan and/or Castilian Spanish during the time that the local students learn a foreign language such as English (see Chapter 10).

Along with increasing globalization and migration, one important catalyst for what has happened in Luxembourg, Catalonia and many other multilingual parts of Europe was the EU policy on regional minority languages. Like Catalonia, Luxembourg managed to take advantage of EU support for the promotion of lesser-used European 'mother tongues' within educational systems. Luxembourgish in its new guise as the 'language of integration' took preschool education by force and pushed out French, which had been widely used before, simply because of the presence of large numbers of romanophone pupils in classrooms (Horner & Weber, 2010). But otherwise, the fixed trilingual system of education has remained unchanged, with Luxembourgish mostly in preschool, German as the language of basic literacy and the main medium of instruction in primary school, and French being taught as a subject at primary level.

The Luxembourg situation also confirms something that was already discussed in Chapter 7 on Singapore, namely, that the celebration by some researchers of translanguaging in itself is highly problematic. Indeed, translanguaging practices are widely used by teachers within the Luxembourgish school system, which might seem to make it a good instantiation of heteroglossic multilingual education (as argued in García, 2009: 267–269). However, the translanguaging is largely restricted to shifts into Luxembourgish (see the section on 'Constructing Luxembourgish as the "Language of Integration"', p. 145), and hence fails to open up new multilingual spaces for the many migrants students with Romance languages (Portuguese, French, etc.) as their home languages; for these students, it merely constitutes an 'added challenge', as Lasagabaster (2009) puts it euphemistically (with reference to the similar situation in some of the Autonomous Communities of Spain – see Chapter 10).

It should be clear that, for instance, a French-language literacy option or a flexible biliteracy programme in French and German would potentially allow these students to progress more rapidly and give them a better chance of acquiring higher levels of proficiency in the school languages (including in particular greater access to English). This could either be a parallel-medium programme (one French-language literacy stream and a parallel German-language literacy stream), with students from both streams being brought together as much as possible and learning from each other, or a dual-medium (German and French biliteracy) programme, with students who are more proficient in one language playing the role of experts and helping those students who are more proficient in the other language. About 50% of the subjects could be taught with German as the medium of instruction and the other 50% through French, whereas in the present system almost all subjects are taught with German as the medium of instruction throughout primary school. Such a flexible bilingual school project has recently been proposed by a group of teachers in Luxembourg city, but they have been criticized for not sufficiently taking into account the role of Luxembourgish as the language of integration. In a recent publication (Pettinger & Heggen, 2012), the teachers have responded to this criticism by arguing that educational success in the Luxembourgish school system still depends to a large extent on one's mastery of standard German and French:

> It is true that the use of Luxembourgish is a factor of integration but educational success is even more so! The latter allows not only cultural but also economic integration, both of which are indispensable for true social integration ... Hence, it is logical that, as long as German and French are the languages of success or failure, priority must be given to mastery of these two languages. (Pettinger & Heggen, 2012: 43; my translation from the original French)

Nonetheless, the criticisms of the teachers' proposal suggest that it might be worthwhile to think about extending the proposal in the direction of a more flexible multilingual (rather than 'bilingual') project that is not just focused on the teaching and learning of standard French and German but encompasses a wider range of languages including in particular Luxembourgish, Portuguese and English. In this way, projects such as this could lead to a critical rethinking of the whole language learning and teaching regime of the Luxembourgish education system.

So far, however, such more flexible bi-/multilingual school projects have not been implemented by the Ministry of Education. Indeed, the latest Education Act of 2009 offers no such opening in matters of language, only a small opening in the area of teaching methodology (see Horner & Weber, 2013). It introduces competence-based learning, along with standardized tests in the third year of primary school (average age eight, with the same test in the same language to be taken by all students). At the same time, preschool and primary education merge into *l'école fondamentale* (fundamental or basic school), organized in cycles instead of school-years, without, however, changing the specific regime of language teaching and learning in the system. One of the keywords of the new system is differentiation, in the sense that it allows for the possibility of grouping pupils of different ages according to their levels within each cycle.

This system is unlikely to work for a heterogeneous school population of on average 42% 'foreign' children in the Luxembourgish primary schools, with some schools actually having more than 50% romanophone pupils in their classrooms. Yet, questions concerning the language of basic literacy and the medium of instruction in primary school were not key issues of debate during the discussions leading up to the ratification of the new Education Act. Nor was the danger of internal segregation or ghettoization (under the name of 'differentiation'), with many children of migrant background potentially ending up in the lower streams, seriously considered.

At the same time, the opportunities offered by the new system should not be ignored: the competence-based approach could bring in much needed flexibility, in the sense that only the levels to be reached in the various subjects would need to be fixed and different routes could be allowed for in order to reach these ends. Within such a system, it would be easier to give teachers greater autonomy; for instance, a teacher who teaches large numbers of romanophone pupils might decide to adopt a French-language literacy programme and to teach German as a foreign language, as long as all the pupils reach the required level in both German and French after a certain number of years. However, it is doubtful whether the new law allows for this kind of flexibility.

Lessons to be Learnt from the Luxembourg Experience

In this concluding section, I briefly summarize the main points that can be learnt from the Luxembourg experience:

- the Luxembourgish language is a small language that is frequently perceived as being endangered (even though it is still widely used in family transmission); one way of defending it has been to construct it as the language of integration, especially in preschool education;

- in the name of mother tongue education, French has been eradicated from preschool and the focus has been put instead on the assumed 'mother tongues', in particular Luxembourgish and, nominally at least, Portuguese;
- a further twist on the whole concept of mother tongue education is revealed by the historical shift in the perception of languages in Luxembourg: in the 19th century, Luxembourgish was perceived as a 'dialect' of German and hence the school system was seen as offering a mother tongue education programme in standard German, whereas nowadays Luxembourgish is perceived as a language in its own right and hence the (same) system has been reinterpreted as offering L2 immersion;
- romanophone students are often given extra instruction in German and, as an indirect consequence, may be denied access to (a high proficiency in) English, through being oriented towards lower-quality streams where little or no English is taught;
- a more flexible system providing these students with greater access to French and English would potentially offer them better educational and professional opportunities.

10 Three Autonomous Communities of Spain: Catalonia, the Basque Country and Galicia

Catalan, Basque and Galician are official regional languages in, respectively, Catalonia, the Basque Country and Galicia, and the communities have become increasingly bilingual in Catalan/Basque/Galician and Spanish. After the linguistic repression during the dictatorship of General Franco (1939–1975), Catalan, Basque and Galician have been progressively rehabilitated as national symbols of their respective communitiy.

There are major socio-economic differences between the three communities. Catalonia is a highly developed and economically successful community that attracted numerous 'internal' migrants, mostly from the south of Spain, in the 1950s, 1960s and 1970s. Many of these Spanish-speaking workers settled in urban areas of Catalonia, so that even nowadays Spanish rather than Catalan is the most widely used language in, for instance, the working-class areas of Barcelona. As a result, Catalan is often perceived as being more directly associated with the educated and powerful middle class.

Basque and Galician, on the other hand, exist in a very different sociolinguistic environment. They are mostly used in poor, rural areas, whereas the urban middle classes have often switched over to Spanish. As a consequence, the language revitalization movements have led to disagreements about the standard in both communities: urban middle-class children now learn Standard Basque (*Euskara Batua*) or Standard Galician (*Galego normativo*) at school, and frequently look down upon the more mixed varieties used by native speakers in the poor, rural areas (see also the discussion in Chapter 2).

Another difference is that Catalan has by far the largest number of speakers: about 11 million. Catalan or varieties close to Catalan are spoken not only in Catalonia but also in the Balearic Islands, the Valencia area, parts of Aragon, Andorra (where it is the official language of the state), parts of southern France and Alghero, Sardinia (Wright, 2004: 209).

However, as Wright (2004: 209) points out, these different groups have sometimes been 'unwilling to be satellites to a centre [i.e. Barcelona] that they do not recognize as their own'. Just as the Catalonians have always rejected any categorization of Catalan as a 'mere dialect' of Castilian Spanish, these groups do not want their languages to be categorized as 'dialects' of Catalan (Wright, 2004: 210).

Catalonia

Catalonia and migration

Starting in the 1920s and increasing dramatically from the 1960s onwards, internal migration has seen many workers move from the south of Spain (first from Murcia and later from Andalusia) to the Barcelona area in search of employment. In this way, Catalonia has a largely non-native working class, amounting to almost half of the population, who speak mostly Castilian Spanish. Because these internal migrants often lived together in suburban areas on the periphery of Barcelona and were thus residentially segregated from Catalan speakers, the use of Castilian Spanish has been maintained for a long time. At the same time, their children, who go through Catalan-medium education, are now fluent in both Catalan and Spanish, as well as other languages such as English.

Another reason why Spanish is widely used in Catalonia is that there are many migrants from Latin America, who often moved into the areas where Spanish already predominated. In particular, there is a large community of Argentineans, who started arriving in the 1960s and 1970s. They were mostly political refugees from the Argentinean dictatorship of that time. They were often middle class and highly qualified, and many of them perceived themselves as 'downgraded' in the host society (Garzón, 2011: 43). Few of them learned Catalan, because they saw no direct need of it as they were speakers of Spanish. Their children, on the other hand, have gone through the Catalonian school system and as a result have become bilingual in Catalan and Spanish. Nowadays, the community sees multilingualism in Catalan, Spanish and English as increasingly important for both educational and professional success.

In the 1990s, internal migration slowed down significantly, as Spain and in particular Catalonia went through a period of political stability and economic growth. International migration from Latin America, on the other hand, continued, not only from Argentina but also from many other Latin American countries such as Colombia, Ecuador, Peru and, most recently, Bolivia and Venezuela. Moreover, the flourishing economy attracted migrants from all over the world. Together these migrants now constitute about 15% of the population of Catalonia. As a result, many children have entered the Catalonian school system with no or very little knowledge of either Catalan or Spanish, thus confronting the educational authorities with a new challenge.

The largest group of migrants in 21st-century Catalonia are the Moroccans, who constituted 26.6% of all migrants in 2006 (Hernández-Carr, 2011: 96). While the first wave of Moroccans arrived in the 1960s and 1970s, migration from Morocco has mushroomed since the mid-1990s. The primary reason for this migration is economic, with many migrants having low levels of education. Their home languages include Tamazigh (Berber) and/or (colloquial) Arabic. The Moroccan community in Catalonia suffers from negative stereotyping and widespread prejudices against Muslim people. The male members of this community mostly learn Spanish at work, as they tend to work in the construction sector alongside Spanish-speaking internal migrants (at least up to 2007, the start of the current economic crisis). The female members, on the other hand, frequently stay at home and pick up whichever language is used in their immediate neighbourhoods, which is usually Catalan in rural areas and Spanish in Barcelona or other urban areas. Their children learn both Catalan and Spanish at school, and at home they usually continue to speak in Berber or Arabic with their parents, often mixed with Catalan and Spanish. The members of this community frequently experience a lack of upward social mobility, increasingly in these times of economic crisis, due to a wide range of factors including lack of legal status, discrimination at work or insufficient proficiency in English (which nowadays is increasingly required for professional success in addition to Catalan and Spanish).

Who is Catalan?

With such a large number of migrants, both internal and international, and many of them Spanish speaking, it is not surprising that the question of 'who is Catalan?' is a frequently debated one. There is no clear and simple answer to this question, with the boundary drawn in discourses often fluctuating between more inclusive and more exclusive definitions. The inclusive position of civic nationalism, often found in official government discourses, is that everybody who lives and works in Catalonia is Catalan. But other, more exclusive positions of ethnic nationalism can also frequently be found, not just in popular but even in academic discourses. They range from the position that only those who have native or native-like proficiency in the Catalan language are Catalan to the position that only those with deep roots in Catalonia are Catalan.

The last mentioned position is taken for instance at the end of Strubell's (1999) paper, where he argues that the Catalan language and the Catalan people are threatened by what he calls a 'demographic issue':

> Since the 1930s the fecundity rate of Catalans has been close to or even below replacement levels ... During the 1950s and 1960s, as so often happens, the first generation of immigrants had a much higher number of children per couple. Today the present fecundity rate is well below the replacement level, even when we look at the whole of the population. This will make Catalan extremely fragile in terms of its ability to integrate newcomers successfully. (Strubell, 1999: 34–35)

For this reason, Strubell is taken to task by Haselbach (1999). Haselbach argues that Strubell shifts in his paper from a social constructivist understanding of Catalan-ness (as whoever speaks Catalan) to an essentialist one pitching 'rooted' Catalans against migrants in a struggle for survival: 'Strubell's argument is contradictory: he starts with a linguistic concern, and he ends with worries about *Volk und Raum'* (people and space/territory; Haselbach, 1999: 57). Ultimately, according to Haselbach (1999), this is an issue of power:

> The real point of nationalist politics is ... to actively construct an identity group, a social constellation with insiders and outsiders. The question of who is in and who is out, is not a problem of descent, but a question of economic chances, careers, jobs; it is the starting point of further political ambitions, for control, for resources, for territory. The differentiation of in-group and out-group is thus a question of current power and actual interest. (Haselbach, 1999: 59)

A difficult situation for migrant students

In Catalonia in the 1980s, the 'catalanization' of state education was implemented as part of the political programme of linguistic normalization (bringing the language back to its 'normal' state). However, Pujolar (2010) points out that, just as in Luxembourg, official discourse changed in response to the accelerated migration of the 1990s: it shifted its emphasis from Catalan as a national symbol to Catalan as a means of social cohesion and integration.

As a result, many migrant students are now put in reception or 'integration' classes where Catalan (rather than Spanish) is the language of instruction. Corona *et al.* (2008) argue that this clashes with many of these students' experience of Spanish being widely used as a lingua franca in their out-of-school lives. Corona *et al.* analyse the textbooks in use in these reception programmes and show that they frequently portray Catalan as the key to social participation and belonging. But in the lived reality of the students themselves, it is often Spanish rather than Catalan that is 'the language which opens up doors to friendships' (Corona *et al.*, 2008: 137). They thus experience a fracture similar to the one that exists in Luxembourg between educational policy and individuals' actual language practices: they learn Catalan at school but outside school they mostly use Spanish, just as in Luxembourg where many migrant children learn Luxembourgish in pre-school but often use French outside school.

Therefore, Pujolar (2010: 235) talks about a split between two types of integration: 'educational integration' that is supposed to take place through Catalan, and a 'more informal social integration' that tends to happen through Spanish. He also notes 'the absence of an explicit formulation of the role of Spanish in the design of the principles and policies of integration' (Pujolar, 2010: 240). Interestingly, in Luxembourg there is a similar absence of an explicit formulation of the role of French in the integration policy. The resulting situation does not really open up new multilingual spaces for the migrant students, mainly because the language regime of the education system is a fixed rather than a flexible one. The migrant students are like square pegs that have to fit into round holes. Their own home languages are largely ignored, and instead they are expected to assimilate into the fixed trilingualism of first Catalan, then Castilian Spanish and, third, usually English as a foreign language. What makes it even worse for the migrant students is that they are sometimes forced to take intensive Catalan or Spanish courses during the time that autochthonous students learn English as their third language (L3). In this way, it can happen that the migrant students are debarred from taking English, though this is the one subject where many of them could excel. According to Escobar Urmeneta and Unamuno (2008: 246), this is an 'unofficial but apparently common practice'. Again, this is parallel to the situation in Luxembourg, where many migrant students in the lower streams of the technical lycees miss out almost completely on the opportunity of learning English.

How successful are the reception classes?

Newman *et al.* (2013) have carried out an ethnographic study of reception classes for newcomer students, interviewing mostly Spanish-speaking Latin American students who attend these classes. The reception classes are meant to help migrant students to 'integrate' into the educational system, primarily by teaching them Catalan and bringing them up to the level where they can fully join the mainstream class. However, the researchers found that often these classes are not very successful and instead function more like an obstacle in the students' way or even a form of discrimination. This is the case especially in schools using the 'pullout' model, where students are taken out of the mainstream class for several hours per day for intensive Catalan language instruction. This is similar to the system in Arizona, for instance, with its four-hour English Language Development block (see the discussion in Chapter 5), and in both cases the model – with its exclusive focus upon teaching discrete language skills – has not been very effective.

As a result, more and more schools in Catalonia are now introducing more progressive and more effective models, based on Content and Language Integrated Learning (CLIL) methodologies. These new reception classes are much more successful in terms of students' academic results, and they also lead to students having more positive attitudes towards Catalan, looking upon it more as a resource rather than as an obstacle in their educational career. Here, for instance, is what Rulfo, one of the students interviewed by Newman *et al.* (2013), said about the Catalan-medium courses in his content-based reception class:

> In a way it's good [that classes are given in Catalan] because that way you learn to understand them and to speak it. And words you don't know, that you don't understand, well, you can ask the teacher and that way you learn little by little. (Newman *et al.*, 2013: 206)

For students such as Rulfo, Catalan is not only the formal medium of instruction at school but it has also become a language of everyday communication that he uses spontaneously in his interactions both with other newcomers and with autochthonous students (see also Trenchs-Parera & Patiño-Santos, 2013).

The tension between choice and compulsion

The Spanish constitution defines the duty to learn Castilian Spanish, while Catalonia's Statute of Autonomy defines the duty to learn the official regional language of Catalonia, namely, Catalan. As a result, language-in-education policy in Catalonia since the 1990s has been marked by the compulsory study of both Catalan and Spanish, with the former as the main medium of instruction. In this way, a single model of Catalan immersion has gradually been imposed throughout preschool, primary and secondary education. According to May (2001: 249), this position was reinforced in the 1998 Catalan Linguistic Policy Act, thus constituting a 'movement away from a more gradualist, "politics of persuasion" approach to one much closer to the Québec model of legislative enforcement à la Bill 101' (see the discussion in Chapter 3).

This means that the huge majority of students in Catalonia's primary schools study through Catalan as the medium of instruction, while learning Spanish as a subject – though at higher levels of primary education and in secondary education, both Catalan and Spanish tend to be used as media of instruction. Moreover, most students learn English as their L3, first as a subject and later often also as an additional medium of instruction. The most important recent change in this connection is that, whereas English used to be taught from sixth grade, it is now usually already taught from first grade (i.e. from age 6 onwards).

Thus, the Catalonian educational system is gradually opening up to include an increasing number of media of instruction, adding Spanish and/or English to the primary medium, Catalan. But at the earliest levels, Catalan is used as the sole medium of instruction, with the other languages – Spanish and usually English – being taught as subjects. The justification for this is that bilingual education programmes with both Catalan and Spanish as media of instruction from the beginning 'have tended to reproduce the unbalanced linguistic situation that exists out of school' (Vila i Moreno, 2010: 149). Vila i Moreno (2010) continues as follows:

> It is only by making (very) extensive use of Catalan – in fact, as the predominant means of communication within schools – that schools manage to bilingualize all the student population. (Vila i Moreno, 2010: 149)

Interestingly, this is the same argument that has been used in Quebec as a way of justifying the imposition of French-only education (see Chapter 3). Hence, it could be concluded that the primary concern of Catalonian language-in-education policy is not flexible bi- or multilingual education but Catalan-medium education. In other words, the main focus is on one particular language, namely, Catalan, rather than on students' needs.

This implies that Catalonian education still functions very much within the monolingual mindset, which is often concerned with protecting the 'purity' of Catalan and is opposed to such sociolinguistic phenomena as language variation, change and diversity. For instance, Strubell (2001: 277–278) warns that, because many speakers of Catalan are second language (L2) speakers, often with Spanish as their first language and Catalan as their L2, the 'degradation of the language' and a 'decline in the quality of Catalan is unavoidable – in lexicon, phonetics, grammar – on account of interference from Spanish'. As a way of showing how widespread such concerns are, Wright (2004: 208) mentions that there is in Catalonia an official terminology source 'to supply neologisms, halt borrowings and maintain the "purity" of the language', as well as a telephone service 'to answer doubts about official Catalan usage'.

As a consequence, it may well be the case that many teachers and policymakers harbour negative attitudes towards the language use of migrants, who have to learn two closely related languages – Catalan and Spanish – within a relatively short period of time and hence are likely to code-switch extensively between the two. As we have seen, many of them learn Catalan as the school language, whereas they use mostly Spanish in their out-of-school environment. We reach the conclusion that what may be a good policy for the revitalization of the Catalan language can potentially have detrimental effects on the educational careers of a particular group of students within Catalonian society. If, as we have consistently done in this book, put children before languages, then it is urgent to revise the Catalan-medium language-in-education policy and to move towards a more flexible and equitable multilingual policy which takes into account these students' linguistic resources in a positive way and also provides them with high-quality access to English.

The recent debates and court cases in Catalonia about Catalan vs Spanish as the medium of instruction in schools seem to point in the direction of a need for greater flexibility. However, the court cases against Catalan-only policies were brought by pro-Spanish organizations, using the discourse of linguistic human rights and the associated neo-liberal discourse of giving parents the right to choose. They were thus concerned with the rights of the dominant group in Spanish society as a whole, whereas, as far as I have seen, no voices have been raised in defence of the most vulnerable groups in society, the migrant students, whose home languages largely continue to be ignored by the school system, both in Catalonia and in Spain as a whole.

From Norma to *la Queta*

The attitudes towards the Catalan language described in the previous section may, however, be changing in contemporary Catalonian society, in line with the shift in emphasis that Pujolar (2010) traces from Catalan as a national symbol to Catalan as a means of social cohesion and integration or, in Woolard's (2008) terminology, from the perception of Catalan as a 'language of authenticity' to a 'language of anonymity'. In the 1980s, the 'normal' practice was to keep a clear boundary between Catalan and Spanish.

Catalan was mostly seen as an in-group language, indexical of an authentic ethnolinguistic identity. In the Barcelona of that time, there was a language ideological debate – which has remained largely unresolved – between the advocates of 'Catalan light' and 'Catalan heavy' (Woolard, 1999); while the former wanted standard Catalan to be based on the varieties commonly used in Barcelona, including any Spanish elements in them, the latter looked down upon such varieties as being too mixed with Spanish and argued for a 'pure' Catalan maximally distant from Spanish. The point is of course that Catalan and Spanish are closely related languages and hence numerous 'bivalent' elements can be found in Catalan. By 'bivalent', Woolard (1999: 6–7) means linguistic elements that have simultaneous membership in two linguistic systems, in other words, elements that could 'belong' to both Catalan and Spanish.

Woolard (1999) analyses the virtuoso performances of professional comedians in Barcelona in the 1980s, who deliberately mixed languages and played with bivalent words and phrases. A comedian named Eugenio, in particular, was well known for introducing most of his jokes in the following way: *El saben aquel...* (Do you know the one...), where *el* is clearly Catalan, *aquel* clearly Spanish, but *saben* is bivalent. Eugenio's bivalent linguistic practices challenged the normative language habits of that time, which insisted on a strict separation between Catalan and Spanish. Thus, his strategic use of bivalent elements had political and ideological significance, though it could be interpreted in different ways by his audience, depending on whether they were of Catalan or Castilian background. Woolard (1999) comments as follows:

> This is a double-edged satire, a purist mockery of castilianized Catalan and a puncturing of Catalan pretensions to linguistic hegemony. The ironizing voice is ambiguous and the comedy is bivalent, simultaneously heard differently by different segments of the audience. (Woolard, 1999: 22–23)

According to Woolard (1999, 2008), such linguistic practices have become less ideologically significant in contemporary Catalonian society, as a new generation of Catalan speakers makes their presence felt. They are non-native speakers of Catalan, who have learnt it at school and use both Catalan and Spanish, thus reflecting their often more hybrid identities as both Catalan and Castilian (and possibly others, such as Latin American). As a result, Catalan is increasingly becoming an 'anonymous' or ethnically unmarked language (Pujolar & Gonzàlez, 2013). Code-switching between Catalan and Spanish may also have become more frequent (Woolard, 1999:

21), leading to the development of new mixed varieties. An example of such a hybrid code used by Catalan–Spanish bilingual youths of Latin American origin in Barcelona is described in Corona *et al.* (2013).

In her discussion of these changing linguistic practices and attitudes, Woolard (2008) compares and contrasts two official advertising campaigns for the promotion of Catalan. In the first catalanization campaign of 1983, the protagonist was a cartoon character of a 10-year-old girl named Norma, who advised and admonished people on their linguistic practices. As the protagonist's name already indicates, there was a strong focus on norms and purism (i.e. how to avoid Castilianisms; see also Woolard, 1986: 101). In 2005, a new and very different catalanization campaign was launched under the name *Dóna corda al català* (Wind up Catalan). This time, the protagonist was a set of chattering teeth called *la Queta* (short for *la Boqueta* 'little mouth'). Significantly *la Queta* was speaking and singing in markedly non-native Catalan, making mistakes and urging people to use Catalan without feeling ashamed, even if they are not fully fluent in it. The campaign was targeted at young people, telling them that Catalan is not (just) a language imposed by school but a living language that can also be used in transgressive ways – as exemplified for instance by *la Queta*'s use of insults in Catalan. The aim is to establish Catalan as the normal, unmarked language of everyday life, an 'anonymous' language that can be used by everybody living in Catalonia.

In this way, as Woolard (2008) notes, the *la Queta* campaign can be seen not only as transcending the ideology of authenticity but also the ideology of anonymity, which usually remains fixed upon the use of the standard language. Here, on the other hand, young people are encouraged not to worry about making mistakes, as the important thing is to use the language, even in transgressive ways. However, Woolard also notes that this progressive campaign was poorly received in Catalonia, which shows that language attitudes are rather slow to change. Nonetheless, Woolard (2008: 320) concludes on an optimistic note that the campaign 'may be a harbinger of deeper discursive and ideological changes to come in Catalonia'.

The Basque Country

Choice of medium of instruction in the schools of the Basque Country

Like Catalan, Basque is one of the official regional languages of Spain, and is spoken in two autonomous regions of Spain, the Basque Autonomous Community (BAC) and Navarre, as well as in the adjacent *Pyrénées Atlantiques* part of France. This section focuses on the BAC, which comprises the three provinces of Araba, Bizkaia and Gipuzkoa. Since 1982, there have been three types of schools in the BAC, usually referred to as Model A, B and D schools (there is no letter 'C' in Basque):

- Model A schools: Spanish as the medium of instruction and Basque as the L2 or foreign language.
- Model B schools: both Basque and Spanish as media of instruction.
- Model D schools: Basque as the medium of instruction and Spanish as the L2.

Just as in Luxembourg and Catalonia, recent sociolinguistic changes in the Basque Country include increased migration as well as the growing importance of English as the global language, with the consequent pressure exerted by parents upon schools to use more English. In the face of these developments, public debate about education has become increasingly polarized between the two ideological positions of fixity and flexibility: supporters of the former position advocate retrenchment and consolidation of Basque as the endangered minority language, with more Basque in all schools for all students; the others advocate a more flexible move towards bilingual (Basque–Spanish) or multilingual (Basque–Spanish–English) education.

There are some signs that the flexibility position has already begun to influence schools. According to Cenoz (2008), the boundaries between Model A, B and D schools are becoming blurred and schools are adapting to the changing student population, with more schools also using English as a medium of instruction (alongside Basque and Spanish). Cenoz (2008) argues that nowadays there is a continuum of schools from less multilingual to more multilingual ones:

Some schools have only one language of instruction (Basque or Spanish) and can be placed towards the less multilingual end of the continuum on this variable. Other schools have two languages of instruction: Basque and English, Basque and Spanish, Spanish and English and others three languages of instruction (usually Basque, Spanish and a foreign language which is English in most cases). (Cenoz, 2008: 26)

An example of 'more multilingual' schools are the Ikastolas or Basque-medium schools, which nowadays also use Spanish and English as media of instruction, and which teach English already from the age of four. It would thus seem that, unlike Luxembourg and Catalonia, the BAC is moving in the direction of a more flexible education system which endeavours to respond to the children's linguistic needs and, above all, which takes into account the importance for all the children of learning English as the global language.

An unintended consequence of the successful policy of revitalization

Basque-medium education and Model D schools have been highly successful and popular not only with Basque-speaking but also Spanish-speaking parents, many of whom enrol their children in these schools. One consequence of this is that migrant students, who frequently attend Spanish-medium or Model A schools, find themselves segregated at least to some extent. In other words, a form of ghettoization of these students has occurred as an unintended consequence of the successful policy of Basque revitalization (Cenoz, 2009: 79).

However, as we have seen in the previous section, this is happening at a time when the distinctions between Model A, B and D schools are in the process of breaking up, with English pushing in strongly as a third or additional medium of instruction. The use of English as a medium of instruction can be quite attractive for many migrant students, who may have English as (one of) their home language(s) or in any case find it easier to compete in English with local students. Thus, we see again that access (to the dominant languages in society plus English) is more important than choice (between Model A, B and D schools). In this way, it is to be hoped that the Basque education system is moving in the right direction of a flexible multilingual system, aiming to develop in students differentiated levels of competence in Basque, Spanish and English. Such a flexible language-in-education policy may also eventually lead to a wider definition of Basqueness that includes not only native speakers but also L2 learners of Basque (Echeverria, 2010) – just the opposite of fixed and restrictive policies that tend to polarize communities (see also the discussion in Chapter 3).

The construction of a standard: *Euskara Batua* (Unified Basque)

Urla (2012) tells the story of how a unified standard, *Euskara Batua*, was constructed. As in so many other cases (see Chapter 2), the development of standard Basque led to heated debates. A major controversy concerned the inclusion of the letter 'h' in the standardized orthography of *Euskara Batua*, which was perceived as a 'northern' feature and associated with French Basques. As a result, the new standard also came to be associated with a particular political position, namely, that of a 'newer generation of leftist nationalists' (Urla, 2012: 85) favouring a unification of French and Spanish Basques and independence for the whole of the Basque-speaking area:

> Batua's opponents argued that linguistic barbarisms were being committed simply to promote an 'extremist' vision of Basque nationalism. Among the most pernicious manifestations of this 'intransigence and fanaticism' in the view of opponents was the letter 'H'. (Urla, 2012: 85)

In this way, the presence vs absence of the letter 'h' became iconic of opposed political stances and developed into a major 'point of contention between radical and conservative nationalists' (Urla, 2012: 99).

By the 1990s, Batua had gradually been accepted as the standard and was widely used in the media, in education and other public institutions. The vernacular varieties of Basque were often devalued, and pressure was put on people to switch to the standard instead. As Batua was in the process of being institutionalized, it also acquired new associations with educational norms and mainstream values, and it became less and less a sign of radicalism. In turn, this led to a revalorization of the vernacular varieties of Basque in the late 1990s, with the vernacular being increasingly used – often alongside the standard – for 'local appeal and identity' (Urla, 2012: 105). As Urla (2012: 107) puts it, for Basque youth the vernacular gradually became a way 'to signal a kind of identification with "realness", authenticity, and populism in relation to a progressively institutionalized Basque political culture'.

Especially in her studies of radical youth culture and free radio stations, Urla traces this shift taking place in the ideological connotations of Basque, with vernacular Basque now signalling 'antiauthoritarianism and populist identity' (Urla, 2012: 178). She analyses the verbal performances of the free radio station programmers as exemplars of linguistic creativity bringing together playful uses of the language with highly colloquial speech styles. These young people used 'particular features of vernacular to craft a deliberately unpolished, irreverent, and "in your face" broadcasting voice in Basque' (Urla, 2012: 172). For them, vernacular was a means of 'distancing themselves from conventional morality and state institutions' and of 'carving out a voice for themselves in the shifting political and linguistic landscape that was taking shape after Basque autonomy' (Urla, 2012: 179).

There are important implications in this for education. As we have seen, there is at the moment a fairly wide gap between the standard taught at school and the vernacular varieties used in out-of-school contexts including in particular youth culture. As a result, young people from non-Basque-speaking homes, who only learnt Basque as taught at school, sometimes prefer to use Spanish rather than Basque outside school, simply because they do not know vernacular Basque (Echeverria, 2003: 367). Therefore, Echeverria (2003) insists that it would be crucial to include the vernacular in the teaching of Basque at school:

> RLS [Reversing Language Shift] efforts would have more success in ideologizing young people on behalf of the heritage language if they were to provide them with a variety of the minority language conducive to fun or 'hip' communicative purposes. (Echeverria, 2003: 368)

Echeverria also emphasizes the importance of integrating popular cultural forms into schools and classrooms. For instance, many Basque music, dance and other cultural classes are only offered to native speakers at Basque-medium schools. Yet, it would be important to also involve learners of Basque in such classes, as in this way they would gain access to new social networks comprising Basque-speaking peers.

Shifting priorities: The 2009 report of the Advisory Council on Basque

In its 2009 report 'Bases for Language Policy at the Start of the 21st century: Toward a Renewed Social Accord', the Advisory Council on Basque, a committee that includes, among others, writers, academics and representatives of cultural associations, sets out a vision for the future of Basque language revitalization. It was written in a difficult time of increased ETA (*Euskadi Ta Askatasuna* 'Basque Homeland and Freedom') terrorist activity and repression of many forms of Basque cultural activism by the central Spanish state, as well as increasing accusations of linguistic fanaticism and discrimination of Spanish-speaking residents levelled at the Basque language movement (cf. the section on Catalan for a brief discussion of a similar backlash taking place in Catalonia).

In response to such criticisms, the report explicitly acknowledges Spanish as one of the languages of the Basque Country and insists that the primary aim of the language movement is *not* 'to "save" Basque like a museum object, but to produce a harmonious bilingual society' (Urla, 2012: 210). It moves away from the 'familiar tropes of linguistic nationalism' (Urla, 2012: 218) such as the return to a Basque-speaking nation or Basque monolingualism, and embraces a 'societal-wide bilingualism that will allow citizens to live in the language in which they are most comfortable' (Urla, 2012: 208). It thus works towards a wider definition of Basqueness that includes both native speakers and L2 learners of Basque with a wide range of competences from basic knowledge to advanced fluency (cf. Echeverria, 2010). It is worth quoting Urla (2012) at some length here:

> The 2009 Advisory Council Report, unanimously endorsed by all its members, indicates significant shifts in some of the most basic premises of linguistic nationalism that once shaped language revitalization. The once inseparable association between ethnicity, patriotism and speaking/knowing Basque has been set aside. The binary view of the linguistic universe and the aspiration of exact equivalency between Basque and Spanish are being displaced in favour of more flexibility and a pluralistic understanding of the linguistic landscape. (Urla, 2012: 209–210)

By navigating a middle way between the earlier and more fixed type of linguistic nationalism (often focused on Basque monolingualism) and the at times repressive attitudes and policies of Spain's ruling *Partido Popular/* Popular Party (often focused on Spanish monolingualism), the Advisory Council advocates instead an inclusive, pluralistic and bi-/multilingual vision for the linguistic future of the Basque Country. It is to be hoped that this vision will also come to inform the educational system, thus opening up greater implementational spaces for multilingual practices and providing the best possible educational opportunities not just for Basque- and Spanish-speaking schoolchildren but also for the many migrant students using different home languages. In order to achieve such educational equity and social justice, the system needs to provide all students with high-quality access to Basque, Spanish and English, and to build on all the students' home linguistic resources, including vernacular varieties of Basque (cf. previous section).

Galicia

The development of standard Galician

Galicia is an Autonomous Community situated in north-western Spain. The Galician language is a Romance language situated on a linguistic continuum between Spanish and Portuguese varieties, and consequently has been looked upon at various times as a dialect of either Spanish or Portuguese. Like Basque, and unlike Catalan, it is mostly used in poor, rural areas, and was, therefore, for a long time associated with poverty and lack of education. As a result of the movement of revitalization, a new variety of Galician is nowadays taught at school, and is frequently used by young middle-class people in urban areas, alongside the traditional, rural varieties.

On the whole, Spanish continues to predominate in Galician society, and Galician is used in symbolic rather than instrumental or communicative ways in urban areas. But in rural areas, Galician continues to be the everyday language of many inhabitants. There is widespread bilingualism in Galician and Spanish in the community, as almost everybody has at least a receptive competence in Galician due to the high degree of mutual intelligibility between the two (Ramallo, 2007).

There have been a number of societal conflicts linked to the development of standard Galician. A widespread debate concerning spelling norms, which broke out in the 1970s and continued for several decades, is usually referred to as the 'normative wars' (O'Rourke, 2011: 73). There were two conflicting positions: on the one hand, the *independendistas* (pro-independence) or *isolacionistas* (isolationists) view Galician as an independent language and aim to keep it separate from Spanish and Portuguese. In this way, they want to ensure that Galician is perceived as a separate language and not as a dialect of either Spanish or Portuguese. On the other hand, the *lusistas* (pro-Portuguese) or *reintegracionistas* (reintegrationists) point to the historical links between Galician and Portuguese, and hence want to realign Galician with Portuguese. They view Galician as a variety of Portuguese, which has changed and diverged from Portuguese as a result of long-standing contact with Spanish. Some reintegrationists even go as far as advocating not only linguistic but also political reunification with Portugal. However, most of them simply focus on the linguistic dimension and advocate 'the "reintegration" of Portuguese orthography in Galician' (O'Rourke, 2011: 73). This ideological conflict was resolved to a large extent in 2003, with the publication of changes to the prescribed form of standard Galician, in which 'consideration was taken of certain reintegrationist proposals regarding orthography' (O'Rourke, 2011: 73).

Another conflict is ongoing between the traditional speakers of Galician (*falante tradicional*), whose varieties are sometimes looked down upon because they are mixed with Spanish, and the new speakers (*neofalante*), whose standard or school variety is frequently perceived as artificial. As in the Basque Country and so many other indigenous language communities, there is thus a deepening divide between the traditional varieties, used mostly in rural areas by older and lower-class speakers, and the new standard, used primarily in urban areas by young, educated, middle-class speakers.

Choice of medium of instruction in Galician schools

The revitalization of Galician started in 1983 with the law of Galician Normalization, which allowed a choice between Galician and Spanish as the medium of instruction in the two initial years of education. After this, Spanish normally took over as the medium of instruction, though it was stated that Galician should be used as the medium of instruction for at least one non-language subject, as well as being a mandatory subject throughout primary and secondary education. However, actual classroom practice often depended on individual teachers' linguistic preferences or abilities (O'Rourke, 2011: 87). The official ideology was one of 'harmonious bilingualism', with both Galician and Spanish perceived as indexical of the community's identity, though this was contested by nationalists who feared that the official policies would lead to the demise of the Galician language (O'Rourke, 2011: 82).

From 2005 to 2009, there was a new regional coalition government of the Socialists with the Galician Nationalist Party. In 2007, they implemented a decree for the teaching of Galician that stipulated that a minimum of 50% of school subjects were to be taught through Galician as the medium of instruction (O'Rourke, 2011: 88). Similar to what is happening in Catalonia, the decree was attacked by a pro-Spanish organization called *Galicia Bilingüe*, using a discourse of linguistic human rights and insisting on parents' right to choose. In 2009, the centre-right Popular Party regained power, whose leader had promised, if elected, to abolish the controversial decree (O'Rourke, 2011: 89). In 2010, the regional government voted a new decree stipulating the following measures among others:

* in preschool education (up to the age of seven), parents can choose either Galician or Spanish as the medium of instruction for their children;
* the aim of primary and secondary education is to develop multilingualism in students, with one third of the subjects to be taught through Galician, one third through Spanish and one third through English;
* students can use the language of their choice in the classroom.

This means that nowadays most primary and secondary schools use both Galician and Spanish (as well as English) as media of instruction, but in preschool education Spanish is more widespread than Galician, since the medium of instruction depends on the parents' decision and on the children's home language, which is usually Spanish at least in urban areas (O'Rourke & Ramallo, 2011). The government argues that the multilingual policy reflects the economic, political, social and linguistic reality of the region, whereas any attempt to 'establish monolingualism in Spanish or in Galician would not' (Beswick, 2007: 249). However, for the Bilingual Galicia organization, the new decree does not go far enough in matters of choice and parents' rights, while for the nationalist movements, it goes too far and will inevitably lead to the demise of Galician. Thus, the debate in society is ongoing, and legal appeals have been made against the decree by a number of organizations. At the same time, scholars worry that the continuing social conflict between Bilingual Galicia and the nationalist movement could 'be working against the language' (O'Rourke, 2011: 90).

The dominance of a 'culture of monoglossia'

Del Valle (2000) argues that both the regional government's discourses advocating harmonious bilingualism in Spanish and Galician and the counter-discourses of the nationalists demanding affirmative action for Galician are grounded in the same assumption, namely, what he calls 'the linguistic culture of monoglossia' (del Valle, 2000: 118). Both ideological positions rely upon the premise of a conflict between Galician and Spanish, and hence advocate policies which essentialize languages: either they aim at a bilingualism which is in fact a form of double monolingualism (in Galician and Spanish perceived as separate entities) or at Galician monolingualism (also perceiving Galician as a separate entity which is indexical of an equally essentialized Galician identity). Del Valle (2000: 123), on the other hand, argues that the language use of many Galicians is grounded in a 'linguistic culture of heteroglossia', which is more indexical of Galicia's multifaceted identity. It can be seen in the linguistic behaviour of many Galicians who negotiate multiple norms and varieties, including the following: 'the *lusista* (Portuguese-like) standard, official Standard Galician, Standard Spanish, Galician Spanish, Galician varieties influenced by Spanish, and local varieties, including Eastern dialects adjacent to the Leonese dialectal area and Southern dialects adjacent to Northern Portugal', with lots of code-switching and mixing between these varieties (del Valle, 2000: 127).

Del Valle (2000: 127) describes Galicia as a 'community in which the availability of several norms of linguistic behaviour constitutes a source of ethnic identity'. The sociohistorical explanation for this somewhat unusual state of affairs includes such factors as its political and economic dependence on Madrid, its geographical proximity to Portugal, as well as its large-scale emigration to other European countries and the American continent. As an illustration, del Valle (2000: 130) mentions the campaign slogan used by the nationalist coalition *Bloque Nacionalista Galego* (Galician Nationalist Block) during the parliamentary elections of 1997, in which it obtained an unprecedented 25.5% of the vote: *Porque nos interesa este País* (Because we care about this nation). In Woolard's terminology, this slogan is a 'bivalent' expression that is identical in both Galician and Spanish. In conclusion, del Valle (2000: 130) wonders: 'Could this mean that Galician nationalism is quietly assuming the linguistic culture of heteroglossia, and the ambiguity, hybridity and open-endedness of which Galicians are so fond as a source of identity?'.

Despite such openings to the culture of heteroglossia, there is still a clear tension in Galicia between linguistic practices on the one hand and language attitudes and ideologies on the other hand. While the former tend to be quite fluid and involve a lot of code-switching between varieties of both Galician and Spanish, the latter are still more stereotypically associated with traditional and fixed identities. In particular, even though Galician is nowadays used more and more in public spaces such as education and administration, its use as a public language is still marked in comparison with Spanish, and indexical of Galician nationalism and of an essentialized Galician identity (O'Rourke & Ramallo, 2013). It would therefore be important to develop more flexible language policies and language-in-education policies building more directly upon people's heteroglossic practices and at the same time helping to break up the fixed, traditional attitudes and ideologies.

Lessons to be Learnt from the Catalan, Basque and Galician Experience

In this concluding section, I briefly summarize the main points that can be learnt from the Catalan, Basque and Galician experience:

- as in Luxembourg, Catalan has been constructed as the language of integration, especially in preschool and primary education;
- Catalonia's language-in-education policy needs to develop from a rather fixed Catalan-medium system to a more flexible system of multilingual education that prioritizes the needs and interests of all students, and in particular guarantees migrant students' access to learning English;
- both Galicia and the Basque Country have more flexible education systems that offer a choice of medium of instruction, yet further measures are needed to ensure that this does not lead to ghettoization of migrant students (in the Basque Country);
- the discussion in this chapter has also brought out the limitations of the neo-liberal discourse of choice: it is steeped in an either-or 'culture of monoglossia' (del Valle, 2000) that takes insufficient account of people's multilingual repertoires and heteroglossic practices;
- more important than *choice* is the question of *access* for all students, including migrant children, to both the local and global languages that they need for educational and professional success.

11 Conclusion

As more and more children grow up multilingually in our globalized and superdiverse world, it has become imperative for our education systems to reinvent themselves in the form of flexible multilingual education. Much of the debate so far has been focused on languages, in particular the need to defend small 'mother tongues' against the encroachment of global languages such as English, and as a result the human element has gone missing. It is important, therefore, to reconnect with the children, who should be our primary concern, and to construct the new education systems of the future based on the full complexity of their linguistic repertoires. The challenge will be to find the best possible 'bridges' leading them from their home linguistic resources to the academic discourses that they will need in their lives. In this concluding chapter, I summarize the key points that arise from the discussion of these themes in the previous chapters.

The Importance of Access and of Using Non-standard Varieties in Education

The case studies in this book have confirmed the importance of, first, valorizing and building on all students' linguistic resources and, secondly, providing them with access to both minority and majority, local and global languages. They have shown how crucial it is to develop positive attitudes towards vernacular varieties such as African-American English, Singlish and African urban vernaculars. The model here could be Corsican, the teaching of which is based on a philosophy of linguistic tolerance, which is imparted as a key component of all teacher training programmes in Corsica (see Chapter 2). As for the question of access to both local and global languages, we have seen how it is of primary importance for all students, including migrant students – whether internal migrants as in China or transnational migrants as in Catalonia and Luxembourg, for instance.

The discussion of US experiences (especially Arizona) in the area of bi-/multilingual education was our first case study, which laid the foundation for all subsequent ones. It has shown that English-only immersion programmes do not work, especially if they focus primarily on students' acquisition of discrete linguistic skills. It is much more productive to immerse language minority students in rich multilingual environments, where they can develop all their languages, both Spanish and English, for instance, or both Navajo and English. Other areas of the world have been quicker than Arizona in realizing this, as we have seen in the case of Catalonia, where reception classes have recently been reconfigured, away from a restrictive focus on linguistic skills and towards more flexible Content and Language Integrated Learning (CLIL)-types of models and methodologies (see Chapter 10). However, here too there is still a limitation, in that these programmes tend to be monolingual programmes focused on the teaching of Catalan as the language of 'integration' and take very little if any account of the migrant students' home linguistic resources.

The other important point that the discussion of language-in-education policies in the USA has revealed is that dual language education is a highly promising approach, though it needs to become more flexible in terms of language variation and more inclusive of all students. Indeed, if vernacular and non-standard varieties such as African-American English were included in a positive and additive way, then these programmes would be open to much larger numbers of African-American students. Such models of flexible and inclusive dual language or multilingual education would also work well in China, in particular for minority language students, as well as in Singapore and South Africa, on condition that Singlish and the African urban vernaculars are included in a positive way through the use of flexible multilingual pedagogies (such as code-switching). In Hong Kong, the government's recent 'fine-tuning' policy is a step in the right direction: it moves schools from offering *either* Chinese-medium *or* English-medium secondary education towards offering multilingual programmes where Cantonese, Putonghua and English are used as media of instruction for different subjects. One limitation, however, is that the fine-tuning policy applies primarily to secondary education, and it is only now that primary schools, too, are beginning to engage in the process of implementing more flexible models of multilingual education (see Wang & Kirkpatrick, 2013).

What these Asian and African countries have in common is the impact of globalization on their societies and education systems, and the role played by global languages such as English and, in the case of the Asian countries, also Putonghua. The pressures of globalization are felt in Europe, too, where they have led to the development of new European Union (EU) policies on multilingualism and on lesser-used European languages. The final two case studies focus on how various parts of Europe, namely, Luxembourg and the autonomous regions of Spain, have been influenced by these EU policies. The new emphasis on 'small' languages such as Luxembourgish and Catalan, as well as the new role of these languages as languages of 'integration', has had indirect but wide-ranging implications for the rapidly increasing number of migrant students, especially in terms of access to global languages. I have argued for instance that in Catalonia, migrant students, apart from – or as well as – being given extra instruction in Catalan and Spanish, also need high-level access to English. Similarly in Luxembourg, I have shown how students with a Portuguese migration background are initially taught Luxembourgish and German. Throughout primary and secondary education, they are frequently given extra instruction in German but, much more importantly, they would need higher-quality access to French (as a possible language of basic literacy and medium of instruction in primary education) and English (as a subject, and possibly as a medium of instruction at the higher levels of education), since, after all, these are the two most important languages on both the Luxembourgish and the European employment market.

Building on Students' Actual Home Resources

It may be worth emphasizing again here that it is essential to take into account students' *actual* home linguistic resources. Many children grow up in today's globalized world with complex multilingual repertoires. In order to ensure that education systems build on these repertoires, it is necessary to move away from the discourse of ethnolinguistic essentialism linking ethnicity with language (e.g. if you are a person of Portuguese origin living in Luxembourg, then your 'mother tongue' is Portuguese). As we have seen in Chapter 9 (see also Weber, 2009), the linguistic repertoires of many youngsters of Portuguese origin living in Luxembourg comprise French, Luxembourgish and non-standard varieties of mostly northern Portuguese (often mixed with French and sometimes also Luxembourgish). Hence, these are the resources that the Luxembourgish education system needs to build on. Another example, though from a very different sociolinguistic context, is that of Tswanas, Zulus and Xhosas in South Africa, who at school are simply assumed to have standard Setswana, standard isiZulu or standard isiXhosa as their mother tongue, even though for many of them these will be more like foreign languages. Flexible multilingual education would therefore build on these children's actual resources in vernacular varieties and English, rather than the standard varieties (see Chapter 8).

To further illustrate this crucial point, let me give one final example, taken from Sebba's (1993) seminal study of youngsters of Caribbean origin in London. Sebba (1993: 142) discusses the alleged difficulties of using creole in the British education system: it is often claimed that Jamaican Creole would have to be used for children of Jamaican parentage, Dominican for children of Dominican parentage, Guyanese for children of Guyanese parentage, and so on. In fact, however, the actual linguistic repertoires of youth of Caribbean origin in London include mostly Jamaican Creole (as well as London English, of course). In this way, Sebba (1993: 143) insists, 'there is only *one* Caribbean Creole variety which is significant among the peer group'. Flexible multilingual education would build on this language – i.e. Jamaican Creole – even though it is not the 'mother tongue' of many of these students.

From Mother Tongue Education Towards Flexible Multilingual Education

This book has aimed to debunk the myth that mother tongue education is best for all children, including the associated axiom that a high level of proficiency in their 'mother tongue' is needed before a second language (L2) can be used as a medium of instruction. Every aspect of this myth has been shown to be problematic. As already discussed in the previous section, mother tongue education tends to lead to rather fixed multilingual education systems, because politicians, policymakers and teachers often rely on a discourse of ethnolinguistic essentialism in attributing a 'mother tongue' to schoolchildren. In most cases, however, the attribution of a single mother tongue involves at least a simplification of an increasingly complex multilingual reality. The problem is that 'mother tongue' is a politicized concept, and hence not the best concept to base a pedagogical approach on. Thus, for instance, it hardly makes sense to claim that the same system of education in Luxembourg constituted a form of mother tongue education in the 19th century but no longer does so nowadays, simply because Luxembourgish has been upgraded from (being perceived as) a 'dialect' of German to the status of the 'national language' of Luxembourg (see Chapter 9).

We have also seen that mother tongue education systems can be bad for children. The extreme case here is Apartheid education, but there are other examples such as Chinese-medium education in Hong Kong (more specifically, the 1998 streaming policy, forcing large numbers of students to attend mother tongue education with Chinese as the medium of instruction), which helped to construct and reproduce social stratification and inequality (see Chapter 6). A positive response to these problems on the part of the Hong Kong government has been to give secondary schools more flexibility to choose between Chinese and English as the medium of instruction for different subjects, thus moving away from a strict application of mother tongue education. In general, it would seem that a sudden shift in the medium of instruction is difficult to negotiate for many students, and that it is preferable to use a more flexible and gradual shift from one language to the other. Here, it is also important to allow for multilingual pedagogies, including the classroom use of code-switching as a way of scaffolding students' learning, rather than to insist on language separation approaches that attempt to keep each language in an impossible state of 'purity'. Such language separation approaches are still quite common both in mother tongue education programmes and in dual language programmes, so that there is a strong need to introduce new, more flexible models.

Furthermore, we have seen that non-mother tongue education programmes can be highly successful. Examples include the Singaporean education system that successfully used (what at the time of its introduction was) an L2 or foreign language as the medium of instruction for the whole school population (see Chapter 7), or Māori-medium education for Māori children who were L1 speakers of English but who learnt through Māori even though it was an L2 for them (see Chapter 3). It would seem that a major condition for success is that the language needs to be present, at least to some extent, in students' out-of-school environment. Ironically, however, this is not always the case in mother tongue education. Thus, standard Setswana, the assumed mother tongue of Tswana children, is used as a medium of instruction in schools but is *not* present in most children's out-of-school environment. On the contrary, the languages that are present in these children's environment include English and Street Setswana, the urban vernacular that is quite different from standard Setswana. Hence, it is not surprising that the Tswana mother tongue education system has not been very successful (see Chapter 8).

Thus, there is a need to move from rather fixed mother tongue education programmes to more flexible multilingual education. While mother tongue education tends to be focused on the standard variety (the 'mother tongue') ascribed on the basis of children's perceived ethnicity (as part of the discourse of ethnolinguistic essentialism), flexible multilingual education builds on children's actual home linguistic varieties, on the whole of their multilingual repertoires including non-standard varieties, urban vernaculars, etc. Moreover, while mother tongue education tends to provide delayed access to a global language such as English, flexible multilingual education prefers very gradual shifts between local and global languages from an early stage (at least for children with multilingual repertoires). As also emphasized in Edwards (2009: 60), this needs to be done in a positive and additive way, unlike in transitional bilingual education, which solely aims at transitioning students as quickly as possible from their minority language to the dominant language. Importantly, flexible multilingual education also involves the strategic use of multilingual pedagogies such as code-switching, both in order to scaffold students' learning and to make them aware of the differences between the standard variety and their own vernacular varieties.

Furthermore, there is a key difference in the primary aims of flexible multilingual education, as opposed to mother tongue education. The latter is often concerned with the revitalization of a particular local language, which is to be achieved through a struggle against the hegemonic encroachment of (usually) English. In the process, it tends to overlook the needs of particular groups of students such as migrant students. In previous chapters, I have discussed the difficult situation of migrant students in the education systems of francophone Canada (Chapter 3), Luxembourg (Chapter 9) and Catalonia (Chapter 10), which often only offer them reduced access to English. On the other hand, the primary concern of flexible multilingual education is to include all schoolchildren and to provide them with high-quality access to the languages that they need for educational and professional success. While this normally involves both local and global languages, it does not necessarily include the standard varieties of local languages that students are not familiar with – precisely those varieties that mother tongue education is often trying to preserve. The justification for this is, primarily, a concern with what is best for the students themselves and, secondly, a need to balance language maintenance with (inevitable) language variation and change.

The Darker Side of Mother Tongue Education

What is even more worrying about mother tongue education is that there is a darker side to it in at least two respects. First of all, there is the element of compulsion that some mother tongue education programmes involve, either in the form of the imposition of a standard or a restriction of parents' and students' choice. As researchers such as Wroblewski (2012) and Selleck (2013) have pointed out, this may lead to a polarization of communities and may therefore be too high a price to pay for language revitalization. Yet, an element of compulsion can frequently be found in mother tongue education systems, such as in francophone Canada or Catalonia. The fact that the system may impede migrant students' access to a global language such as English is ignored by the mother tongue education advocates, in whose eyes the maintenance of French or the revitalization of Catalan is the overarching goal, besides which everything else pales in significance.

Secondly, with its focus on the standard variety of the assumed 'mother tongue', mother tongue education frequently erases non-standard varieties or 'dialects', which as a result are not seen as worth preserving. This has happened in Singapore, where the focus on the 'official' mother tongue – Mandarin in the case of the Chinese community – has involved the deliberate eradication of all other varieties of Chinese (see Chapter 7). Somewhat surprisingly, even academics tend to look upon this as a highly successful language policy to the extent that it has managed to supplant the different varieties – Hokkien, Teochew, Cantonese, etc. – with the standard variety, Mandarin. The same is happening in China, where nation-building efforts involve the imposition of standard Chinese – here referred to as Putonghua – and the suppression of the other varieties of Chinese (see Chapter 6). In light of the political nature of the distinction between language and dialect, these are very disturbing policies and attitudes that seem to be encouraged by mother tongue education: only the standard variety is perceived as being in need of protection and preservation, whereas non-standard varieties are largely erased and considered to be worthless. We have seen yet another example of this in the chapter on South Africa, where some mother tongue advocates object to the use of mixed Xhosa–English varieties in the classroom – though these correspond to many urban children's actual home linguistic resources – and aim to enforce instead the use of a 'pure', standard variety of Xhosa, even though this may seem like a foreign language to many students.

It should be clear that I am not arguing against mother tongue education as such; I am arguing for a more flexible application of the mother tongue education principle. In the case of the Xhosa students discussed above, there is a need to build on their mixed Xhosa–English varieties. In classrooms with a more heterogeneous school population, there is a need for resolutely multilingual approaches right from the initial stages of education. In all cases, there is also a need for flexible multilingual pedagogies, to which I turn in the following section.

Towards Flexible Multilingual Pedagogies

My repeated call in this book for more flexible multilingual pedagogies is echoed by other researchers such as Lin (2012, 2013). Lin argues, with special reference to Asian contexts, that there is an urgent need to move beyond monolingually informed programmes such as total immersion in an L2 (usually English), which is often referred to in Asian educational discourses as 'bilingualism through monolingualism'. The idea here is to immerse students in English language programmes with the hope that as a result they will become balanced bilinguals in English and their Asian 'mother tongue'. Instead, Lin argues that it would be pedagogically more beneficial to implement flexible multilingual programmes building on students' home linguistic resources (both standard and vernacular), as well as their out-of-school knowledge and experiences. According to Lin (2012: 99–100), the most promising approaches are 'multiple flexible pedagogical approaches that draw on multilingual and multimodal resources in English academic content classrooms'.

Therefore, Lin firmly rejects skills-based English language instruction models of the type used in Arizona, and insists on the importance of strong content-based English programmes. This is where flexible multilingual pedagogy links up with experience-based and 'participatory' approaches, which are inspired by the work of Paulo Freire and are increasingly used in the field of adult language education and English for Speakers of Other Languages (ESOL; see e.g. Cooke & Winstanley, 2012; Hamilton et al., 2012; Mallows, 2012; also Freire, 1970).

Lin also advocates breaking away from language separation (or, as she calls them, 'discrete language') models and urges instead the adoption by teachers of code-switching and other bridging and scaffolding strategies. Building on Gibbons' (2009) work, she emphasizes the importance for students of learning in a multilingual 'challenge zone', in which

> the curriculum is amplified, not simplified: teachers use 'message abundancy' (i.e. key ideas are presented in many different ways, including visuals, multimodalities and multiple linguistic resources). (Lin, 2012: 98)

I will just add here that the use of code-switching, bridging and scaffolding strategies, with their reliance on students' home linguistic varieties, is a way of drawing upon students' 'funds of knowledge' (González et al., 2005; Martin-Jones & Saxena, 2003; Moje, 2008; Moll et al., 1992) and thus connecting home and school knowledge. It helps to develop students' bi- or multiliteracies; for instance, they can be encouraged to write multilingual and multimodal 'identity texts' that 'hold a mirror up to students in which their identities are reflected back in a positive light' (Cummins, 2006: 60; see also Cummins et al., 2005; Cummins & Early, 2011). Furthermore, it can foster the use of exploratory talk in the classroom, which has been shown to be very important for deep learning (see the discussion in Chapter 3; also Mercer, 2000, 2004; Mercer & Hodgkinson, 2008; Mercer & Littleton, 2007).

Difficulties in Implementing Flexible Multilingual Education

The implementation of flexible multilingual education faces major pedagogical and attitudinal obstacles, primarily in the areas of teacher education and materials development. Some of these issues are shared by both flexible multilingual education and mother tongue education programmes, and they have been exacerbated by what could be referred to as 'the challenge of super-diverse classrooms'.

Indeed, in many classrooms of today's globalized world, there may be students with a wide range of different home languages, which makes mother tongue education increasingly difficult to implement. However, what is quite typical of such superdiverse environments is that the students tend to use lingua francas among themselves. These youth languages or urban vernaculars can usefully be drawn upon by teachers as resources for learning and be used as bridges into literacy (Weber, 2009: 150–156; Weber & Horner, 2012a: 130–132). As we have seen, this implies a move away from a strict application of mother tongue education and towards a more flexible approach to multilingual education of the type that this book argues for. In superdiverse classrooms, only flexible multilingual education can provide effective education for all students.

While increasingly needed, flexible multilingual education building on students' vernaculars is also difficult to implement because of the negative attitudes towards these varieties or languages that exist in many societies and are shared by many teachers. As a way of counteracting such negative attitudes, the importance of a good teacher education for all teachers, both language and content teachers, cannot be overestimated. It needs to include well-informed modules on the nature of language variation, the mechanisms of language contact and the inevitability of language change, with the hope that an understanding of these sociolinguistic processes will foster in educators an attitude of linguistic respect and tolerance.

But such developments are limited by the fact that very often teacher education is controlled by politicians rather than academics. Thus, we have seen in Chapter 5 how Arizona has introduced a skills-based approach for English language learners that, instead of focusing on content and meaning, aims at teaching isolated linguistic skills in the dominant language only, and how its teacher preparation endorsement in Structured English Immersion may inculcate a deficit view of these students in trainee teachers. Though numerous researchers and practitioners have shown that such an approach has negative effects, this has not (yet) altered politicians' determination to enforce the policy.

A further obstacle to the implementation of flexible multilingual education is in the related area of materials development. It is an unfortunate fact that there is a dearth of learning and teaching materials in many lesser-used languages, simply because they are not economically viable. Yet, it is difficult for teachers to teach in a particular language if there are no – or few

– materials available in that language. Therefore, researchers have focused on the production and pedagogical use of innovative materials such as the following: dual language books, which can lead students both to biliteracy and greater language awareness (e.g. Sneddon, 2008), and 'multivariety' text-books, which incorporate authentic texts such as literary texts, newspaper articles, advertisements, etc., in a number of different varieties (see Edwards, 2009: 107–108). An example of the latter is the *Pogledi* ('Views') textbook, created in 2000 for schools in the whole of Bosnia-Herzegovina, where there are three mutually intelligible official languages (Bosnian, Croatian and Serbian; Busch & Schick, 2007). *Pogledi* includes texts in all three official languages, which hopefully can contribute to a new mutual understanding in a part of the world that suffered from some of the worst ethnic conflicts of the 20th century. Multivariety textbooks could also be useful in other parts of the world such as South Africa, where they could include authentic texts in the closely related Nguni or Sotho languages (cf. the discussion in Chapter 8). Another way of increasing the amount of high-quality reading materials available in smaller languages would be co-publishing initiatives, as part of which different language versions of children's picture books could be produced, thus making the smaller language versions more economically viable (Edwards, 2009: 110).

Translation, too, can be helpful in the process of producing additional learning materials for lesser-used languages. Yet, publishers tend to focus on translation into larger languages and to ignore the smaller ones. This is the case for instance in South Africa, where many books are translated into the larger official languages (isiZulu, isiXhosa, Setswana, Sesotho) but far fewer books are translated into the other, smaller official languages (Sepedi, siSwati, Xitsonga, Tshivenda, isiNdebele). Edwards and Ngwaru (2011a, 2011b) point out that an extra challenge for translation into the smaller lan-guages is that they have only undergone varying degrees of standardization. This argument applies even more to the case of the new urban vernaculars: if they are to be used as media of instruction in schools and if teaching materials are produced in these languages, they, too, will need to undergo a process of at least partial standardization, which in turn will again create a gap between the newly fixed school language and the fluid, constantly changing youth language used outside school. In this way, school inevitably always lags behind actual language use, though this should certainly not be construed as an argument for doing nothing and keeping the status quo.

In any case, there is a need to keep in mind that many children in today's globalized cities are multilingual, and hence it would be counterproductive to imprison them within fixed essentialized identities linked to only one culture and language, whether standard or vernacular. Ultimately, what matters most is educators' attitude of care towards the students, towards *all* their languages and cultures. According to García *et al.* (2013), such an attitude of care comprises the following four facets:

- educators build on students' fluid multilingual practices
- they connect with students' cultural resources (cf. Moll *et al.* 1992 on 'funds of knowledge')
- they co-construct meaningful instruction through the involvement of members of the local community
- instead of relying upon standardized testing, they use dynamic assessment (e.g. Lantolf & Poehner, 2004)

The result is the creation of a 'third space' (Gutiérrez, 2008; Gutiérrez *et al.*, 1999) that allows for effective learning and empowers students. García *et al.*, in their preference for 'trans-' compounds, refer to the above as 'transcaring' strategies and label them 'translanguaging', '*transculturación*', 'transcollaboration' and 'transaction' (of learning through dynamic assessment), though it is not clear what is gained by this terminology, in particular since third space pedagogy always involves straddling varieties, languages or cultures, and transcending boundaries, whether ethnic, class or gender.

Flexible Multilingual Education for All

We live in an era of globalization, migration and superdiversity, in which multilingualism rather than monolingualism has become the norm. As a result, for instance, linguistic human rights discourses or political programmes of linguistic normalization are of less and less value nowadays, as they tend to be focused upon one single minority language, which they see as being in conflict with other languages; in fact, such discourses can even be dangerous in that they potentially lead to a polarization of communities. What we need instead is a shift in focus towards multilingualism as bringing people and communities together, towards a view of languages as complementing and enriching each other. This linguistic richness is constituted not so much by neatly bounded, standard 'languages' as by people's much more fluid and heteroglossic practices that usually also comprise vernacular and non-standard varieties.

In education, too, the days of monolingual as well as fixed bi-/multilingual education are hopefully numbered. Their underlying assumptions, such as that the same size fits all or that languages can be neatly separated, have become increasingly outdated and problematic in the contemporary world. As this book has argued, there is a need for more flexible and inclusive multilingual education systems that break through the narrow view of multilingualism as (a small number of) parallel monolingualisms. Assumptions such as the above-mentioned ones can lead to some students being seen from a deficit perspective; instead, all of them, including speakers of minority languages or non-standard varieties, should be seen as having the potential to benefit from flexible multilingual education. As Snell (2013: 123) warns, if some children 'come to school with less linguistic and cultural capital, and do not find there the means or motivation to increase it through educational investment, it is likely that social inequalities will be reproduced'. Hence the urgent need for more nuanced and more equitable multilingual solutions, with education systems building on all students' home linguistic resources in a positive and additive way, and providing access to both the local and global languages that students need for their educational and professional success. It is important for the different stakeholders (students, parents, teachers, educators, researchers, policymakers, politicians) to work together towards this goal, because – to adapt the advertising slogan of a well-known cosmetics firm – 'our children are worth it'.

References

Adegbija, E. (2004) Language policy and planning in Nigeria. *Current Issues in Language Planning* 5, 181–246.

Aidil Subhan, M. (2007) Planning for Malay language in education: Lessons of history and present ecology. In V. Vaish, S. Gopinathan and Y. Liu (eds) *Language, Capital, Culture: Critical Studies of Language and Education in Singapore* (pp. 157–174). Rotterdam: Sense Publishers.

Alexander, N. (1992) South Africa: Harmonizing Nguni and Sotho. In N. Crawhall (ed.) *Democratically Speaking: International Perspectives on Language Planning* (pp. 56–68). Cape Town: National Language Project.

Alexander, N. (2000) Why the Nguni and Sotho languages in South Africa should be harmonized. In K. Deprez and T. du Plessis (eds) *Multilingualism and Government* (pp. 171–175). Pretoria: van Schaik.

Alexander, N. (2001) Die noodsak van universiteite vir die oorlewing van die niedominante tale in Suid-Afrika, In H. Giliomee and L. Schlemmer (eds) *Kruispad: Die toekoms van Afrikaans as openbare taal* (pp. 8–14). Cape Town: Tafelberg.

Alexander, N. (2006) Socio-political factors in the evolution of language policy in post-Apartheid South Africa. In M. Pütz, J. Fishman and J. Neff-van Aertselaer (eds) *'Along the Routes to Power': Explorations of Empowerment through Language* (pp. 241–260). Berlin: Mouton de Gruyter.

Alsagoff, L. (2007) Singlish: Negotiating culture, capital and identity. In V. Vaish, S. Gopinathan and Y. Liu (eds) *Language, Capital, Culture: Critical Studies of Language and Education in Singapore* (pp. 25–46). Rotterdam: Sense Publishers.

Alsagoff, L. (2010) Hybridity in ways of speaking: The glocalization of English in Singapore. In L. Lim, A. Pakir and L. Wee (eds) *English in Singapore: Modernity and Management* (pp. 109–130). Hong Kong: Hong Kong University Press.

Anderson, B. (1991) *Imagined Communities: Reflections on the Origin and Spread of Nationalism*. London: Verso.

Annamalai, E. (2004) Medium of power: The question of English in education in India. In J. Tollefson and A. Tsui (eds) *Medium of Instruction Policies: Which Agenda? Whose Agenda?* (pp. 177–194). Mahwah, NJ: Erlbaum.

Arias, M.B. (2012) Language policy and teacher preparation: The implications of a restrictive language policy on teacher preparation. In M.B. Arias and C. Faltis (eds) *Implementing Educational Language Policy in Arizona: Legal, Historical and Current Practices in Structured English Immersion* (pp. 3–20). Bristol: Multilingual Matters.

Baker, C. (2006) *Foundations of Bilingual Education and Bilingualism* (4th edn). Clevedon: Multilingual Matters.

Baker, C. (2007) Becoming bilingual through bilingual education. In P. Auer and L. Wei (eds) *Handbook of Multilingualism and Multilingual Education* (pp. 130–152). Berlin: Mouton de Gruyter.

Banda, F. (2000) The dilemma of the mother tongue: Prospects for bilingual education in South Africa. *Language, Culture and Curriculum* 13, 51–66.

Banda, F. (2010) Defying monolingual education: Alternative bilingual discourse practices in selected coloured schools in Cape Town. *Journal of Multilingual and Multicultural Development* 31, 221–235.

Bannerji, H. (2000) *The Dark Side of the Nation: Essays on Multiculturalism, Nationalism, and Gender.* Toronto: Canadian Scholars' Press.

Baugh, J. (1998) Linguistics, education, and the law: Educational reform for African-American language minority students. In S.S. Mufwene, J.R. Rickford, G. Bailey and J. Baugh (eds) *African-American English: Structure, History and Use* (pp. 282–301). New York: Routledge.

Bentahila, A. and Davies, E. (1993) Language revival: Restoration or transformation? *Journal of Multilingual and Multicultural Development* 14, 355–373.

Berg, C. and Weis, C. (2005) *Sociologie de l'enseignement des langues dans un environnement multilingue. Rapport national en vue de l'élaboration du profil des politiques linguistiques éducatives luxembourgeoises.* Luxembourg: Ministère de l'Education nationale et de la Formation professionnelle et Centre d'Etudes sur la situation des jeunes en Europe (CESIJE).

Beswick, J. (2007) *Regional Nationalism in Spain: Language Use and Ethnic Identity in Galicia.* Bristol: Multilingual Matters.

Blackledge, A. and Creese, A. (2010) *Multilingualism: A Critical Perspective.* London: Continuum.

Bloch, C., Guzula, X. and Nkence, N. (2010) Towards normalizing South African classroom life: The ongoing struggle to implement mother-tongue based bilingual education. In K. Menken and O. García (eds) *Negotiating Language Policies in Schools* (pp. 88–106). Abingdon: Routledge.

Blommaert, J. (2010) *The Sociolinguistics of Globalization.* Cambridge: Cambridge University Press.

Bokhorst-Heng, W. (1999) Singapore's *Speak Mandarin Campaign*: Language ideological debates and the imagining of the nation. In J. Blommaert (ed.) *Language Ideological Debates* (pp. 235–265). Berlin: Mouton de Gruyter.

Bokhorst-Heng, W. and Wee, L. (2007) Language planning in Singapore: On pragmatism, communitarianism and personal names. *Current Issues in Language Planning* 8, 324–343.

Bourdieu, P. (1991) *Language and Symbolic Power.* Cambridge, MA: Harvard University Press.

Bourne, J. (2007) Reflections and suggestions for ways forward. In J. Conteh, P. Martin and L. Helavaara Robertson (eds) *Multilingual Learning: Stories from Schools and Communities in Britain* (pp. 135–144). Stoke-on-Trent: Trentham Books.

Braam, D. (2004) Community perception of change in a school's language policy. *PRAESA Occasional Papers* (University of Cape Town) 21.

Brock-Utne, B. (2005) Language-in-education policies and practices in Africa with a special focus on Tanzania and South Africa – insights from research in progress. In A.M.Y. Lin and P. Martin (eds) *Decolonization, Globalization: Language-in-Education Policy and Practice* (pp. 173–193). Clevedon: Multilingual Matters.

Brutt-Griffler, J. (2006) Language endangerment, the construction of indigenous languages and world English. In M. Pütz, J. Fishman and J. van Aertselaer (eds) 'Along the Routes to Power': Explorations of Empowerment through Language (pp. 35–53). Berlin: Mouton de Gruyter.

Budach, G. and Bardtenschlager, H. (2008) Est-ce que ce n'est pas trop dur? Enjeux et expériences de l'alphabétisation dans un projet de double immersion. Glottopol 11, 148–70.

Budach, G., Erfurt, J. and Kunkel, M. (eds) (2008) Ecoles plurilingues – Multilingual Schools: Konzepte, Institutionen und Akteure. Frankfurt/Main: Peter Lang.

Burnaby, B. (1996) Language policies in Canada. In M. Herriman and B. Burnaby (eds) Language Policies in English-Dominant Countries (pp. 159–219). Clevedon: Multilingual Matters.

Busch, B. (2010) School language profiles: Valorizing linguistic resources in heteroglossic situations in South Africa. Language and Education 24, 283–294.

Busch, B. and Schick, J. (2007) Educational materials reflecting heteroglossia: Disinventing ethnolinguistic differences in Bosnia-Herzegovina. In S. Makoni and A. Pennycook (eds) Disinventing and Reconstituting Languages (pp. 216–232). Clevedon: Multilingual Matters.

Cavallero, F. and Serwe, S.K. (2010) Language use and language shift among the Malays in Singapore. Applied Linguistics Review 1, 129–170.

Cenoz, J. (2008) Achievements and challenges in bilingual and multilingual education in the Basque Country. AILA Review 21, 13–30.

Cenoz, J. (2009) Towards Multilingual Education: Basque Educational Research from an International Perspective. Bristol: Multilingual Matters.

Cheshire, J., Edwards, V., Munstermann, H. and Weltens, B. (eds) (1989) Dialect and Education: Some European Perspectives. Clevedon: Multilingual Matters.

Chick, K. (1996) Safe-talk: Collusion in apartheid education. In H. Coleman (ed.) Society and the Language Classroom (pp. 21–39). Cambridge: Cambridge University Press.

Chick, K. (2001) Constructing a multicultural national identity: South African classrooms as sites of struggle between competing discourses. Working Papers in Educational Linguistics 17, 27–45.

Chick, K. and Wade, R. (1997) Restandardization in the direction of a new English: Implications for access and equity. Journal of Multilingual and Multicultural Development 18, 271–284.

Clyne, M. (2008) The monolingual mindset as an impediment to the development of plurilingual potential in Australia. Sociolinguistic Studies 2, 347–365.

Combs, M.C. (2012) Everything on its head: How Arizona's Structured English Immersion policy re-invents theory and practice. In M.B. Arias and C. Faltis (eds) Implementing Educational Language Policy in Arizona: Legal, Historical and Current Practices in Structured English Immersion (pp. 59–85). Bristol: Multilingual Matters.

Conklin, N.F. and Lourie, M.A. (1983) A Host of Tongues: Language Communities in the United States. New York: The Free Press.

Cook, S. (2009) Street Setswana vs. School Setswana: Language policies and the forging of identities in South African classrooms. In J.A. Kleifgen and G.C. Bond (eds) The Languages of Africa and the Diaspora: Educating for Language Awareness (pp. 96–116). Bristol: Multilingual Matters.

Corona, V., Moore, E. and Unamuno, V. (2008) Linguistic reception in Catalonia: Challenges and contradictions. In G. Budach, J. Erfurt and M. Kunkel (eds) Ecoles *plurilingues – Multilingual Schools: Konzepte, Institutionen und Akteure* (pp. 121–145). Frankfurt/Main: Peter Lang.

Corona, V., Nussbaum, L. and Unamuno, V. (2013) The emergence of new linguistic repertoires among Barcelona's youth of Latin American origin. *International Journal of Bilingual Education and Bilingualism* 16, 182–194.

Coulmas, F. (2002) Language policy in modern Japanese education. In J.W. Tollefson (ed.) *Language Policies in Education: Critical Issues* (pp. 203–223). Mahwah, NJ: Erlbaum.

Council of Europe (2005) *Rapport du groupe d'experts: Grand-Duché de Luxembourg. Profil des politiques linguistiques éducatives.* Strasbourg: Division des Politiques linguistiques.

Crawford, J. (2000) *At War with Diversity: US Language Policy in an Age of Anxiety.* Clevedon: Multilingual Matters.

Crawford, J. (2004) *Educating English Learners: Language Diversity in the Classroom* (5th edn). Los Angeles, CA: Bilingual Educational Services.

Creese, A. (2005) *Teacher Collaboration and Talk in Multilingual Classrooms.* Clevedon: Multilingual Matters.

Cummins, J. (2000) *Language, Power and Pedagogy: Bilingual Children in the Crossfire.* Clevedon: Multilingual Matters.

Cummins, J. (2006) Identity texts: The imaginative construction of self through multiliteracies pedagogy. In O. García, T. Skutnabb-Kangas and M.E. Torres-Guzmán (eds) *Imagining Multilingual Schools: Languages in Education and Glocalization* (pp. 51–68). Clevedon: Multilingual Matters.

Cummins, J., Bismilla, V., Chow, P., Cohen, S., Giampapa, F., Leoni, L., Sandhu, P. and Sastri, P. (2005) Affirming identity in multilingual classrooms. *Educational Leadership* 63, 38–43.

Cummins, J. and Early, M. (2011) *Identity Texts: The Collaborative Creation of Power in Multilingual Schools.* Stoke-on-Trent: Trentham Books.

Davis, K.A. (1994) *Language Planning in Multilingual Contexts: Policies, Communities, and Schools in Luxembourg.* Amsterdam: Benjamins.

Davis, K.A. (2009) Agentive youth research: Towards individual, collective and policy transformations. In T.G. Wiley, J.S. Lee and R.W. Rumberger (eds) *The Education of Language Minority Immigrants in the United States* (pp. 202–239). Bristol: Multilingual Matters.

de Jong, E.J. (2011) *Foundations of Multilingualism for Education: From Principles to Practice.* Philadelphia, PA: Caslon Publishing.

de Jong, E.J., Arias, M.B. and Sánchez, M.T. (2010) Undermining teacher competencies: Another look at the impact of restrictive language policies. In P. Gándara and M. Hopkins (eds) *Forbidden Language: English Learners and Restrictive Language Policies* (pp. 118–136). New York: Teachers College Press.

de Klerk, G. (2002) Mother-tongue education in South Africa: The weight of history. *International Journal of the Sociology of Language* 154, 29–46.

de Korne, H. (2010) Indigenous language education policy: Supporting community-controlled immersion in Canada and the US. *Language Policy* 9, 115–141.

de Korne, H. (2012) Towards new ideologies and pedagogies of multilingualism: Innovations in interdisciplinary language education in Luxembourg. *Language and Education* 26, 479–500.

de Korne, H. (2013) Allocating authority and policing competency: Indigenous language teacher certification in the United States. *Working Papers in Educational Linguistics* 28, 23–41.

del Valle, J. (2000) Monoglossic policies for a heteroglossic culture: Misinterpreted multilingualism in modern Galicia. *Language and Communication* 20, 105–132.

Deterding, D. (2007) *Singapore English*. Edinburgh: Edinburgh University Press.

Deumert, A. (2005) The unbearable lightness of being bilingual: English–Afrikaans language contact in South Africa. *Language Sciences* 27, 113–135.

Deumert, A. (2010) *Klk cc* ... Supporting indigenous literacies in the digital space. Report. Cape Town: Department of Linguistics, University of Cape Town.

Deumert, A. (2013) Xhosa in town (revisited) – space, place and language. *International Journal of the Sociology of Language* 222, 51–75.

Ding, H. and Yu, L. (2013) The dilemma: A study of bilingual education policy in Yi minority schools in Liangshan. *International Journal of Bilingual Education and Bilingualism* 16, 451–470.

Dixon, L.Q. (2009) Assumptions behind Singapore's language-in-education policy: Implications for language planning and second language acquisition. *Language Policy* 8, 117–137.

Dong, J. (2009) 'Isn't it enough to be a Chinese speaker': Language ideology and migrant identity construction in a public school in Beijing. *Language and Communication* 29, 115–26.

Dong, J. (2010) The enregisterment of Putonghua in practice. *Language and Communication* 30, 265–275.

Dong, J. (2011) *Discourse, Identity and China's Internal Migration: The Long March to the City*. Bristol: Multilingual Matters.

Dowling, T. (2011) 'Stressed and sexy': Lexical borrowing in Cape Town Xhosa. *International Journal of Multilingualism* 8, 345–366.

Duchêne, A. and Heller, M. (eds) (2007) *Discourses of Endangerment: Ideology and Interest in the Defence of Languages*. London: Continuum.

Duchêne, N. (2012) Aménagement linguistique, éducation et cohésion sociale en contexte multiculturel: Le débat sur la langue française au Québec. *Language Problems and Language Planning* 36, 237–251.

Duff, P. (2008) Heritage language education in Canada. In D. Brinton, O. Kagan and S. Bauckus (eds) *Heritage Language Education* (pp. 71–90). New York: Routledge.

Dyers, C. (2009) From *ibaru* to *amajoin*: Translocation and language in a new South African township. *Language and Intercultural Communication* 9, 256–270.

Echeverria, B. (2003) Schooling, language and ethnic identity in the Basque Autonomous Community. *Anthropology and Education Quarterly* 34, 351–372.

Echeverria, B. (2010) For whom does language death toll? Cautionary notes from the Basque case. *Linguistics and Education* 21, 197–209.

Edwards, J. (1989) *Language and Disadvantage* (2nd edn). London and Jersey City, NJ: Whurr Publishers.

Edwards, J. (2009) *Language and Identity*. Cambridge: Cambridge University Press.

Edwards, V. (2009) *Learning to be Literate: Multilingual Perspectives*. Bristol: Multilingual Matters.

Edwards, V. and Ngwaru, J.M. (2011a) African language publishing for children in South Africa: Challenges for translators. *International Journal of Bilingual Education and Bilingualism* 14, 589–602.

Edwards, V. and Ngwaru, J.M. (2011b) Multilingual education in South Africa: The role of publishers. *Journal of Multilingual and Multicultural Development* 32, 435–450.

Edwards, V. and Redfern, A. (1992) *The World in a Classroom: Language in Education in Britain and Canada*. Clevedon: Multilingual Matters.

Escobar Urmeneta, C. and Unamuno, V. (2008) Languages and language learning in Catalan schools: From the bilingual to the multilingual challenge. In C. Hélot and A.-M. de Mejía (eds) *Forging Multilingual Spaces: Integrated Perspectives on Majority and Minority Bilingual Education* (pp. 228–255). Bristol: Multilingual Matters.

Fehlen, F. (2009) *BaleineBis. Une enquête sur un marché linguistique multilingue en profonde mutation. Luxemburgs Sprachenmarkt im Wandel* (Recherche Etude Documentation 12). Luxembourg: SESOPI Centre Intercommunautaire.

Feng, A. (2005) Bilingualism for the minor or the major? An evaluative analysis of parallel conceptions in China. *International Journal of Bilingual Education and Bilingualism* 8, 529–551.

Feng, A. (2007) Intercultural space for bilingual education. In A. Feng (ed.) *Bilingual Education in China: Practices, Policies and Concepts* (pp. 259–286). Clevedon: Multilingual Matters.

Fishman, J.A. (1992) The displaced anxieties of Anglo-Americans. In J. Crawford (ed.) *Language Loyalties: A Source Book on the Official English Controversy* (pp. 165–170). Chicago, IL: Chicago University Press.

Fong, V. (2004) The verbal cluster. In L. Lim (ed.) *Singapore English: A Grammatical Description* (pp. 75–104). Amsterdam: Benjamins.

Freire, P. (1970) *Pedagogy of the Oppressed.* New York: Herder and Herder.

Gándara, P. and Orfield, G. (2012) Why Arizona matters: The historical, legal, and political contexts of Arizona's instructional policies and US linguistic hegemony. *Language Policy* 11, 7–19.

Gao, F. (2011) Linguistic capital: Continuity and change in educational language policies for South Asians in Hong Kong primary schools. *Current Issues in Language Planning* 12, 251–263.

García, O. (2009) *Bilingual Education in the 21st Century: A Global Perspective.* Chichester: Wiley-Blackwell.

García, O., Woodley, H.H., Flores, N., with Chu, H. (2013) Latino emergent bilingual youth in high schools: Transcaring strategies for academic success. *Urban Education* 48, 798–827.

Garzón, L. (2011) Second generation Argentineans: Between identity and mobilization. In A. Alarcón and L. Garzón (eds) *Language, Migration and Social Mobility in Catalonia* (pp. 33–62). Leiden and Boston, MA: Brill.

Genesee, F. (2008) Dual language in the global village. In T. Williams Fortune and D.J. Tedick (eds) *Pathways to Multilingualism: Evolving Perspectives on Immersion Education* (pp. 22–45). Clevedon: Multilingual Matters.

Gibbons, P. (2009) *English Learners, Academic Literacy, and Thinking: Learning in the Challenge Zone.* Portsmouth, NH: Heinemann.

Giliomee, H. (2003) The rise and possible demise of Afrikaans as a public language. *PRAESA Occasional Papers* (University of Cape Town) 14.

Gogolin, I. (1994) *Der monolinguale Habitus der multilingualen Schule.* Münster: Waxmann.

González, N., Moll, L. and Amanti, C. (eds) (2005) *Funds of Knowledge: Theorizing Practices in Households and Classrooms.* Mahwah, NJ: Erlbaum.

Grin, F. and Korth, B. (2005) On the reciprocal influence of language policies and language education: The case of English in Switzerland. *Language Policy* 4, 67–85.

Gu, M. and Patkin, J. (2013) Heritage and identity: Ethnic minority students from South Asia in Hong Kong. *Linguistics and Education* 24, 131–141

Gupta, A.F. (2010) Singapore Standard English revisited. In L. Lim, A. Pakir and L. Wee (eds) *English in Singapore: Modernity and Management* (pp. 57–89). Hong Kong: Hong Kong University Press.

Gutiérrez, K.D. (2008) Developing a sociocritical literacy in the third space. *Reading Research Quarterly* 43, 148–164.

Gutiérrez, K.D., Baquedano-López, P. and Tejeda, C. (1999) Rethinking diversity: Hybridity and hybrid language practices in the third space. *Mind, Culture and Activity* 6, 286–303.

Hambye, P. and Richards, M. (2012) The paradoxical visions of multilingualism in education: The ideological dimension of discourses on multilingualism in Belgium and Canada. *International Journal of Multilingualism* 9, 165–188.

Hamilton, M., Tett, L. and Crowther, J. (eds) (2012) *More Powerful Literacies*. Leicester: NIACE.

Harris, R., Leung, C. and Rampton, B. (2002) Globalization, diaspora and language education in England. In D. Block and D. Cameron (eds) *Globalization and Language Teaching* (pp. 29–46). London: Routledge.

Haselbach, D. (1999) Group rights, and 'soft' nationalism: A response to Miquel Strubell. In S. Wright (ed.) *Language, Democracy and Devolution in Catalonia* (pp. 57–61). Clevedon: Multilingual Matters.

Hashimoto, K. (2009) Cultivating 'Japanese who can use English': Problems and contradictions in government policy. *Asian Studies Review* 33, 21–42.

Heller, M. (2001) Legitimate language in a multilingual school. In M. Heller and M. Martin-Jones (eds) *Voices of Authority: Education and Linguistic Difference* (pp. 381–402). Westport, CT: Ablex.

Heller, M. (2006) *Linguistic Minorities and Modernity: A Sociolinguistic Ethnography* (2nd edn). London: Continuum.

Hélot, C. (2003) Language policy and the ideology of bilingual education in France. *Language Policy* 2, 255–277.

Hélot, C. (2008a) 'Mais d'où est-ce qu'il sort ce bilinguisme?' La notion de bilinguisme dans l'espace scolaire français. In G. Budach, J. Erfurt and M. Kunkel (eds) *Ecoles plurilingues – Multilingual Schools: Konzepte, Institutionen und Akteure* (pp. 55–80). Frankfurt/Main: Peter Lang.

Hélot, C. (2008b) Bilingual education in France: School policies versus home practices. In C. Hélot and A.-M. de Mejía (eds) *Forging Multilingual Spaces: Integrated Perspectives on Majority and Minority Bilingual Education* (pp. 203–227). Bristol: Multilingual Matters.

Hélot, C. and Young, A. (2005) The notion of diversity in language education: Policy and practice at primary level in France. *Language, Culture and Curriculum* 18, 242–257.

Hernández-Carr, A. (2011) Second generation Moroccan migrants in Catalonia: Language, employment and social inclusion. In A. Alarcón and L. Garzón (eds) *Language, Migration and Social Mobility in Catalonia* (pp. 95–122). Leiden and Boston, MA: Brill.

Herriman, M. (1996) Language policy in Australia. In M. Herriman and B. Burnaby (eds) *Language Policies in English-Dominant Countries* (pp. 35–61). Clevedon: Multilingual Matters.

Hill, J.H. (2001) The racializing function of language panics. In R. Dueñas Gonzales with J. Melis (eds) *Language Ideologies: Critical Perspectives on the Official English Movement* Vol. 2 (pp. 245–267). Urbana, IL: National Council of Teachers.

Hill, R. and May, S. (2011) Exploring biliteracy in Māori-medium education: An ethnographic perspective. In T. McCarty (ed.) *Ethnography and Language Policy* (pp. 161–183). New York: Routledge.

Hino, N. (2009) The teaching of English as an international language in Japan: An answer to the dilemma of indigenous values and global needs in the Expanding Circle. *AILA Review* 22, 103–119.

Hornberger, N. (1995) Five vowels or three? Linguistics and politics in Quechua language planning in Peru. In J. Tollefson (ed.) *Power and Inequality in Language Education* (pp. 187–205). Cambridge: Cambridge University Press.

Hornberger, N. (2006) Voice and biliteracy in indigenous language revitalization: Contentious educational practices in Quechua, Guarani and Māori contexts. *Journal of Language, Identity and Education* 5, 277–292.

Hornberger, N. and Chick, K. (2001) Co-constructing school safetime: Safetalk practices in Peruvian and South African classrooms. In M. Heller and M. Martin-Jones (eds) *Voices of Authority: Education and Linguistic Difference* (pp. 31–56). Westport, CT: Ablex.

Hornberger, N. and King, K.A. (1998) Authenticity and unification in Quechua language planning. *Language, Culture and Curriculum* 11, 390–410.

Hornberger, N. and López, L.E. (1998) Policy, possibility and paradox: Indigenous multi-lingualism and education in Peru and Bolivia. In J. Cenoz and F. Genesee (eds) *Beyond Bilingualism: Multilingualism and Multilingual Education* (pp. 206–242). Clevedon: Multilingual Matters.

Horner, K. (2004) Negotiating the Language-Identity Link: Media Discourse and Nation-building in Luxembourg. PhD dissertation, State University of New York at Buffalo. Ann Arbor: UMI.

Horner, K. (2005) Reimagining the nation: Discourses of language purism in Luxembourg. In N. Langer and W.V. Davies (eds) *Linguistic Purism in the Germanic Languages* (pp. 166–185). Berlin: de Gruyter.

Horner, K. (2007a) Global challenges to nationalist ideologies: Language and education in the Luxembourg press. In S. Johnson and A. Ensslin (eds) *Language in the Media: Representations, Identities, Ideologies* (pp. 130–146). London: Continuum.

Horner, K. (2007b) Language and Luxembourgish national identity: Ideologies of hybridity and purity in the past and present. In S. Elspaß, N. Langer, J. Scharloth and W. Vandenbussche (eds) *Germanic Language Histories 'from below' (1700–2000)* (pp. 363–378). Berlin: Walter de Gruyter.

Horner, K. (2009a) Language, citizenship and Europeanization: Unpacking the discourse of integration. In G. Hogan-Brun, C. Mar-Molinero and P. Stevenson (eds) *Discourses on Language and Integration: Critical Perspectives on Language Testing Regimes in Europe* (pp. 109–128). Amsterdam: Benjamins.

Horner, K. (2009b) Regimenting language, mobility and citizenship in Luxembourg. In G. Extra, M. Spotti and P. Van Avermaet (eds) *Language Testing, Migration and Citizenship: Cross-National Perspectives* (pp. 148–166). London: Continuum.

Horner, K. and Weber, J.-J. (2008) The language situation in Luxembourg. *Current Issues in Language Planning* 9, 69–128.

Horner, K. and Weber, J.-J. (2010) Small languages, education and citizenship: The para-doxical case of Luxembourgish. *International Journal of the Sociology of Language* 205, 179–192.

Horner, K. and Weber, J.-J. (2013) Recent developments in language policy in Luxembourg. In R.B. Kaplan, R.B. Baldauf and N. Kamwangamalu (eds) *Language Planning in Europe: Cyprus, Iceland and Luxembourg* (pp. 28–32). Abingdon: Routledge.

Ioannidou, E. (2007) 'This ain't my real language, miss': The use of the Cypriot Dialect and Standard Modern Greek in a typical classroom interaction. In A. Papapavlou and P. Pavlou (eds) *Sociolinguistic and Pedagogical Dimensions of Dialects in Education* (pp. 165–191). Newcastle: Cambridge Scholars Publishing.

Ioannidou, E. (2012) Language policy in Greek Cypriot education: Tensions between national and pedagogical values. *Language, Culture and Curriculum* 25, 215–230.

Jaffe, A. (2005) La polynomie dans une école bilingue corse: bilan et défis. *Marges linguistiques* 10, 282–300. See www.revue-texto.net/Archives/Archives.html (accessed: 10-10-2010).

Jaffe, A. (2007) Codeswitching and stance: Issues in interpretation. *Journal of Language, Identity and Education* 6, 53–77.

Jaffe, A. (2008) Language ecologies and the meaning of diversity: Corsican bilingual education and the concept of 'polynomie'. In A. Creese, P. Martin and A. Blackledge (eds) *Encyclopedia of Language and Education, vol. 9: Ecology of Language* (pp. 225–237). New York: Springer.

Jaffe, A. (2011) Critical perspectives on language-in-education policy: The Corsican example. In T. McCarty (ed.) *Ethnography and Language Policy* (pp. 205–229). New York: Routledge.

Jaffe, A. (2013) Minority language learning and communicative competence: Models of identity and participation in Corsican adult language courses. *Language and Communication* 13, 450–462.

Jones, D.V. and Martin-Jones, M. (2004) Bilingual education and language revitalization in Wales: Past achievements and current issues. In J. Tollefson and A. Tsui (eds) *Medium of Instruction Policies: Which Agenda? Whose Agenda?* (pp. 43–70). Mahwah, NJ: Erlbaum.

Kadenge, M. and Nkomo, D. (2011) The politics of the English language in Zimbabwe. *Language Matters* 42, 248–263.

Kamwangamalu, N.M. (2001) The language planning situation in South Africa. *Current Issues in Language Planning* 2, 361–445.

Khubchandani, L. (2003) Defining mother tongue education in plurilingual contexts. *Language Policy* 2, 239–254.

King, K.A. (2001) *Language Revitalization Processes and Prospects: Quichua in the Ecuadorian Andes*. Clevedon: Multilingual Matters.

King, K.A. and Haboud, M. (2011) International migration and Quichua language shift in the Ecuadorian Andes. In T. McCarty (ed.) *Ethnography and Language Policy* (pp. 139–159). New York: Routledge.

Klein, C. (2007) The valuation of plurilingual competences in an open European labour market. *International Journal of Multilingualism* 4, 262–281.

Kraus, P. (2008) *A Union of Diversity: Language, Identity and Polity-Building in Europe*. Cambridge: Cambridge University Press.

Labov, W. (2008) Unendangered dialects, endangered people. In K.A. King, N. Schilling-Estes, L. Fogle, J.J. Lou and B. Soukup (eds) *Sustaining Linguistic Diversity* (pp. 219–238). Washington DC: Georgetown University Press.

Lakoff, R. (2000) *The Language War*. Berkeley, CA: University of California Press.

Lam, A.S.L. (2007) Bilingual or multilingual education in China: Policy and learner experience. In A. Feng (ed.) *Bilingual Education in China: Practices, Policies and Concepts* (pp. 13–33). Clevedon: Multilingual Matters.

Lam, A.S.L. and Wang, W. (2008) Negotiating language value in multilingual China. In P. Tan and R. Rubdy (eds) *Language as Commodity* (pp. 146–170). London: Continuum.

Lamarre, P. and Dagenais, D. (2004) Language practices of trilingual youth in two Canadian cities. In C. Hoffmann and J. Ytsma (eds) *Trilingualism in Family, School and Community* (pp. 53–74). Clevedon: Multilingual Matters.

Lamarre, P. and Lamarre, S. (2009) Montréal 'on the move': Pour une approche ethnographique non-statique de l'étude des pratiques langagières de jeunes multilingues.

In T. Bulot (ed.) *Formes et normes sociolinguistiques: Ségrégations et discriminations urbaines* (pp. 105–134). Paris: L'Harmattan.

Lantolf, J.P. and Poehner, M.E. (2004) Dynamic assessment of L2 development: Bringing the past into the future. *Journal of Applied Linguistics* 1, 49–72.

Lasagabaster, D. (2009) Multilingual educational systems: An added challenge for immigrant students. In J. Miller (ed.) *Culturally and Linguistically Diverse Classrooms: New Dilemmas for Teachers* (pp. 18–35). Bristol: Multilingual Matters.

Laversuch, I.M. (2008) An unequal balance: The Seychelles' trilingual language policy. *Current Issues in Language Planning* 9, 375–394.

Li, D.C.S. (2008) Understanding mixed code and classroom code-switching: Myths and realities. *New Horizons in Education* 56, 75–87.

Li, D.C.S. (2011) Improving the standards and promoting the use of English in Hong Kong: Issues, problems and prospects. In A. Feng (ed.) *English Language Education across Greater China* (pp. 95–113). Bristol: Multilingual Matters.

Li, L., Zhao, S. and Yeung, A.S. (2012) Chinese language reform in Singapore: Teacher perceptions of instructional approaches and curriculum implementation. *International Journal of Bilingual Education and Bilingualism* 15, 533–548.

Liddicoat, A.J. (2013) *Language-in-education Policies: The Discursive Construction of Intercultural Relations*. Bristol: Multilingual Matters.

Lim, L. (2009) Beyond fear and loathing in SG: The real mother tongues and language policies in multilingual Singapore. *AILA Review* 22, 52–71.

Lim, L. (2010) Migrants and 'mother tongues': Extralinguistic forces in the ecology of English in Singapore. In L. Lim, A. Pakir and L. Wee (eds) *English in Singapore: Modernity and Management* (pp. 19–54). Hong Kong: Hong Kong University Press.

Lin, A.M.Y. (1999) Doing-English-lessons in the reproduction or transformation of social worlds? *TESOL Quarterly* 33, 393–412.

Lin, A.M.Y. (2001) Symbolic domination and bilingual classroom practices in Hong Kong. In M. Heller and M. Martin-Jones (eds) *Voices of Authority: Education and Linguistic Difference* (pp. 139–168). Westport, CT: Ablex.

Lin, A.M.Y. (2005) Critical, transdisciplinary perspectives on language-in-education policy and practice in postcolonial contexts: The case of Hong Kong. In A. Lin and P. Martin (eds) *Decolonization, Globalization: Language-in-Education Policy and Practice* (pp. 38–54). Clevedon: Multilingual Matters.

Lin, A.M.Y. (2006) Beyond linguistic purism in language-in-education policy and practice: Exploring bilingual pedagogies in a Hong Kong science classroom. *Language and Education* 20, 287–305.

Lin, A.M.Y. (2012) Multilingual and multimodal resources in genre-based pedagogical approaches to L2 English content classrooms. In C. Leung and B.V. Street (eds) *English: A Changing Medium for Education* (pp. 79–103). Bristol: Multilingual Matters.

Lin, A.M.Y. (2013) Toward paradigmatic change in TESOL methodologies: Building plurilingual pedagogies from the ground up. *TESOL Quarterly* 47, 521–545.

Lin, A.M.Y. and Man, E.Y.F. (2009) *Bilingual Education: Southeast Asian Perspectives*. Hong Kong: Hong Kong University Press.

Lo Bianco, J. (2007) Advantage and identity: Neat discourse, loose connection. Singapore's medium of instruction policy. In V. Vaish, S. Gopinathan and Y. Liu (eds) *Language, Capital, Culture: Critical Studies of Language and Education in Singapore* (pp. 5–21). Rotterdam: Sense Publishers.

Lo Bianco, J. and Rhydwen, M. (2001) Is the extinction of Australia's indigenous languages inevitable? In J.A. Fishman (ed.) *Can Threatened Languages be Saved?* (pp. 391–422). Clevedon: Multilingual Matters.

Long, M.H. and Adamson, H.D. (2012) SLA research and Arizona's Structured English Immersion policies. In M.B. Arias and C. Faltis (eds) *Implementing Educational Language Policy in Arizona: Legal, Historical and Current Practices in Structured English Immersion* (pp. 39–55). Bristol: Multilingual Matters.

Lytra, V., Martin, P., Barac, T. and Bhatt, A. (2010) Investigating the intersection of multilingualism and multimodality in Turkish and Gujarati literacy classes. In V. Lytra and P. Martin (eds) *Sites of Multilingualism: Complementary Schools in Britain Today* (pp. 19–31). Stoke-on-Trent: Trentham Books.

McCarty, T.L. (2004) Dangerous difference: A critical-historical analysis of language education policies in the United States. In J. Tollefson and A. Tsui (eds) *Medium of Instruction Policies: Which Agenda? Whose Agenda?* (pp. 71–93). Mahwah, NJ: Erlbaum.

McCarty, T.L. (2012) Enduring inequities, imagined futures – Circulating policy discourses and dilemmas in the anthropology of education. *Anthropology and Education Quarterly* 43, 1–12.

McCarty, T.L. (2013) *Language Planning and Policy in Native America: History, Theory, Praxis.* Bristol: Multilingual Matters.

McCarty, T.L., Romero-Little, M.E. and Zepeda, O. (2008) Indigenous language policies in social practice: The Case of Navajo. In K.A. King, N. Schilling-Estes, L. Fogle, J.J. Lou and B. Soukup (eds) *Sustaining Linguistic Diversity: Endangered and Minority Languages and Language Varieties* (pp. 159–172). Washington, DC: Georgetown University Press.

McDonald, M. (1989) *We Are Not French! Language, Culture and Identity in Brittany.* London: Routledge.

McLaughlin, F. (ed.) (2009) *The Languages of Urban Africa.* London: Continuum.

McNamara, T. (2009) The spectre of the Dictation Test: Language testing for immigrants and citizenship in Australia. In G. Extra, M. Spotti and P. Van Avermaet (eds) *Language Testing, Migration and Citizenship: Cross-National Perspectives* (pp. 224–241). London: Continuum.

McWhorter, J. (1998) *The Word on the Street: Fact and Fable about American English.* New York: Plenum.

Makoni, S. (2011) A critical analysis of the historical contemporary status of minority languages in Zimbabwe. *Current Issues in Language Planning* 12, 437–455.

Makoni, S., Brutt-Griffler, J. and Mashiri, P. (2007) The use of 'indigenous' and urban vernaculars in Zimbabwe. *Language in Society* 36, 25–49.

Makoni, S., Dube, B. and Mashiri, P. (2006) Zimbabwe colonial and post-colonial language policy and planning practices. *Current Issues in Language Planning* 7, 377–414.

Makoni, S., Makoni, B. and Rosenberg, A. (2010) The wordy worlds of popular music in Eastern and Southern Africa· Possible implications for language-in-education policy. *Journal of Language, Identity and Education* 9, 1–16.

Makoni, S. and Mashiri, P. (2007) Critical historiography: Does language planning in Africa need a construct of language as part of its theoretical apparatus? In S. Makoni and A. Pennycook (eds) *Disinventing and Reconstituting Languages* (pp. 62–89). Clevedon: Multilingual Matters.

Mallows, D. (ed.) (2012) *Innovations in English Language Teaching for Migrants and Refugees.* London: British Council.

Martin, P. (2005) 'Safe' language practices in two rural schools in Malaysia: Tensions between policy and practice. In A. Lin and P. Martin (eds) *Decolonization, Globalization: Language-in-Education Policy and Practice* (pp. 74–97). Clevedon: Multilingual Matters.

Martin-Jones, M. and Saxena, M. (2003) Bilingual resources and 'funds of knowledge' for teaching and learning in multi-ethnic classrooms in Britain. In A. Creese and

P. Martin (eds) *Multilingual Classroom Ecologies: Inter-relationships, Interactions and Ideologies* (pp. 107–122). Clevedon: Multilingual Matters.

May, S. (2001) *Language and Minority Rights.* Harlow: Pearson Longman.

May, S. and Hill, R. (2008) Māori-medium education: Current issues and challenges. In N. Hornberger (ed.) *Can Schools Save Indigenous Languages? Policy and Practice on Four Continents* (pp. 66–98). Basingstoke: Palgrave.

Menken, K. (2008) *English Learners Left Behind: Standardized Testing as Language Policy.* Bristol: Multilingual Matters.

Mercer, N. (2000) *Words and Minds: How We Use Language to Think Together.* London: Routledge.

Mercer, N. (2004) Sociocultural discourse analysis: Analysing classroom talk as a social mode of thinking. *Journal of Applied Linguistics* 1, 137–168.

Mercer, N. and Littleton, M. (2007) *Dialogue and the Development of Children's Thinking: A Socio-cultural Approach.* London: Routledge.

Mercer, N. and Hodgkinson, S. (eds) (2008) *Exploring Talk in School.* London: Sage.

Mesthrie, R. and Upton, C. (2013) Englishes in a multilingual South Africa. *English Today* 29, 2.

Mohanty, A.K. (2006) Multilingualism of the unequals and predicaments of education in India: Mother tongue or other tongue? In O. García, T. Skutnabb-Kangas and M.E. Torres-Guzmán (eds) *Imagining Multilingual Schools: Languages in Education and Glocalization* (pp. 262–283). Clevedon: Multilingual Matters.

Mohanty, A.K. (2010) Languages, inequality and marginalization: Implications of the double divide in Indian multilingualism. *International Journal of the Sociology of Language* 205, 131–154.

Moje, E.B. (2008) Everyday funds of knowledge and school discourses. In M. Martin-Jones and A.M. de Mejia (eds) *Encyclopedia of Language and Education Vol. 3* (pp. 341–355). Berlin: Springer.

Moll, L., Amanti, C., Neff, D. and González, N. (1992) Funds of knowledge for teaching: Using a qualitative approach to connect homes and classrooms. *Theory into Practice* 31, 132–141.

Moore, H. (2000) Language policies as virtual realities: Two Australian examples. In T. Ricento (ed.) *Ideology, Politics, and Language Policies: Focus on English* (pp. 25–47). Amsterdam: Benjamins.

Murray, S. (2002) Language issues in South African education: An overview. In R. Mesthrie (ed.) *Language in South Africa* (pp. 434–447). Cambridge: Cambridge University Press.

Musk, N. (2006) *Performing Bilingualism in Wales with the Spotlight on Welsh: A Study of Language Policy and the Language Practices of Young People in Bilingual Education.* PhD dissertation, Linköping: Linköping University.

Musk, N. (2010) Bilingualisms-in-practice at the meso level: An example from a bilingual school in Wales. *International Journal of the Sociology of Language* 202, 41–62.

Musk, N. (2012) Performing bilingualism in Wales: Arguing the case for empirical and theoretical eclecticism. *Pragmatics* 22, 651–669.

Ncoko, S.O.S., Osman, R. and Cockcroft, K. (2000) Codeswitching among multilingual learners in primary schools in South Africa: An exploratory study. *International Journal of Bilingual Education and Bilingualism* 3, 225–241.

Newman, M., Patiño-Santos, A. and Trenchs-Parera, M. (2013) Linguistic reception of Latin American students in Catalonia and their responses to educational language policies. *International Journal of Bilingual Education and Bilingualism* 16, 195–209.

Ngugi wa Thiong'o (1986) *Decolonizing the Mind: The Politics of Language in African Literature*. Oxford: James Currey.

Oakes, L. and Warren, J. (2007) *Language, Citizenship and Identity in Quebec*. Basingstoke: Palgrave.

Olson, K. (2012) The politics of preservice teachers. In M.B. Arias and C. Faltis (eds) *Implementing Educational Language Policy in Arizona: Legal, Historical and Current Practices in Structured English Immersion* (pp. 164–181). Bristol: Multilingual Matters.

Orman, J. (2008) *Language Policy and Nation-Building in Post-Apartheid South Africa*. Dordrecht: Springer.

O'Rourke, B. (2011) *Galician and Irish in the European Context: Attitudes towards Weak and Strong Minority Languages*. Basingstoke: Palgrave.

O'Rourke, B. and Ramallo, F. (2011) The native–non-native dichotomy in minority language contexts: Comparisons between Irish and Galician. *Language Problems and Language Planning* 35, 139–159.

O'Rourke, B. and Ramallo, F. (2013) Competing ideologies of linguistic authority amongst new speakers in contemporary Galicia. *Language in Society* 42, 287–305.

Otsuji, E. and Pennycook, A. (2011) Social inclusion and metrolingual practices. *International Journal of Bilingual Education and Bilingualism* 14, 413–426.

Pakir, A. (2008) Bilingual education in Singapore. In J. Cummins and N. Hornberger (eds) *Encyclopedia of Language and Education* Vol. 5 (2nd edn) (pp. 191–203). New York: Springer.

Palmer, D. (2010) Race, power and equity in a multiethnic urban elementary school with a dual-language 'strand' program. *Anthropology and Education Quarterly* 41, 94–114.

Parodi, C. (2008) Stigmatized Spanish inside the classroom and out: A model of language teaching to heritage speakers. In D.M. Brinton, O. Kagan and S. Bauckus (eds) *Heritage Language Education* (pp. 199–214). New York: Routledge.

Pavlenko, A. and Blackledge, A. (2004) Introduction: New theoretical approaches to the study of negotiation of identities in multilingual contexts. In A. Pavlenko and A. Blackledge (eds) *Negotiation of Identities in Multilingual Contexts* (pp. 1–33). Clevedon: Multilingual Matters.

Pennycook, A. (2002) Language policy and docile bodies: Hong Kong and governmentality. In J. Tollefson (ed.) *Language Policies in Education: Critical Issues* (pp. 91–110). Mahwah, NJ: Erlbaum.

Petrovic, J. and Majumdar, S. (2010) Language planning for equal educational opportunity in multilingual states: The case of India. *International Multilingual Research Journal* 4, 1–19.

Pettinger, P. and Heggen, L. (2012) Plaidoyer pour une école bilingue. *Forum für Politik, Gesellschaft und Kultur* 324: 41–43.

Poon, A.Y.K. (2010) Language use, and language policy and planning in Hong Kong. *Current Issues in Language Planning* 11, 1–66.

Poon, A.Y.K. (2013) Will the new fine-tuning medium-of-instruction policy alleviate the threat of dominance of English-medium instruction in Hong Kong? *Current Issues in Language Planning* 14, 34–51.

Probyn, M. (2005) Language and the struggle to learn: The intersection of classroom realities, language policy, and neo-colonial and globalization discourses in South African schools. In A. Lin and P. Martin (eds) *Decolonization, Globalization: Language-in-Education Policy and Practice* (pp. 153–172). Clevedon: Multilingual Matters.

Probyn, M. (2008) Policy, practice and power: Language ecologies of South African classrooms. In A. Creese, P. Martin and N. Hornberger (eds) *Encyclopedia of Language and Education* Vol. 9 (2nd edn) (pp. 207–223). New York: Springer.

Probyn, M. (2009) 'Smuggling the vernacular into the classroom': Conflicts and tensions in classroom codeswitching in township/rural schools in South Africa. *International Journal of Bilingual Education and Bilingualism* 12, 123–136.

Pujolar, J. (2010) Immigration and language education in Catalonia: Between national and social agendas. *Linguistics and Education* 21, 229–243.

Pujolar, J. and Gonzàlez, I. (2013) Linguistic 'mudes' and the de-ethnicization of language choice in Catalonia. *International Journal of Bilingual Education and Bilingualism* 16, 138–152.

Ramallo, F. (2007) Sociolinguistics of Spanish in Galicia. *International Journal of the Sociology of Language* 184, 21–36.

Rao, P.K.S., Shanbal, J.C. and Khurana, S. (2010) Bilingualism and biliteracy in India: Implications for education. In J.E. Petrovic (ed.) *International Perspectives on Bilingual Education: Policy, Practice, and Controversy* (pp. 95–129). Charlotte, NC: Information Age Publishing.

Rickford, J.R. (2005) Using the vernacular to teach the standard. In J.D. Ramirez, T.G. Wiley, G. de Klerk, E. Lee and W.E. Wright (eds) *Ebonics: The Urban Education Debate* (2nd edn) (pp. 18–40). Clevedon: Multilingual Matters.

Rios-Aguilar, C., Gonzáles Canché, M.S. and Sabetghadam, S. (2012) Evaluating the impact of restrictive language policies: The Arizona 4-hour English language development block. *Language Policy* 11, 47–80.

Rubdy, R. (2001) Creative destruction: Singapore's Speak Good English movement. *World Englishes* 3, 341–355.

Rubdy, R. (2007) Singlish in the school: An impediment or a resource? *Journal of Multilingual and Multicultural Development* 28, 308–324.

Rubdy, R. and McKay, S. Lee (2013) 'Foreign workers' in Singapore: Conflicting discourses, language politics and the negotiation of immigrant identities. *International Journal of the Sociology of Language* 222, 157–185.

Rubinstein-Avila, E. (2002) Problematizing the 'dual' in a dual-immersion program: A portrait. *Linguistics and Education* 13, 65–87.

Schiffman, H. (2007) Tamil language policy in Singapore: The role of implementation. In V. Vaish, S. Gopinathan and Y. Liu (eds) *Language, Capital, Culture: Critical Studies of Language and Education in Singapore* (pp. 209–226). Rotterdam: Sense Publishers.

Schmid, C.L. (2001) *The Politics of Language: Conflict, Identity and Cultural Pluralism in Comparative Perspective*. Oxford: Oxford University Press.

Schwarzenbach, R. (2011) 'JA zur Mundart im Kindergarten': Sprachbildung als Politikum: zur Zürcher Volksabstimmung vom 15. Mai 2011. *SchweizerDeutsch. Zeitschrift für Sprache in der deutschen Schweiz* 3–7.

Scollon, R. and Scollon, S.W. (2003) *Discourses in Place: Language in the Material World*. London: Routledge.

Sebba, M. (1993) *London Jamaican*. London: Longman.

Selleck, C.L.R. (2013) Inclusive policy and exclusionary practice in secondary education in Wales. *International Journal of Bilingual Education and Bilingualism* 16, 20–41.

Setati, M., Adler, J., Reed, Y. and Bapoo, A. (2002) Incomplete journeys: Code-switching and other language practices in mathematics, science and English language classrooms in South Africa. *Language and Education* 16, 128–149.

Shohamy, E. (2008) At what cost? Methods of language revival and protection. In K.A. King, N. Schilling-Estes, L. Fogle, J.J. Lou and B. Soukup (eds) *Sustaining Linguistic Diversity* (pp. 205–218). Washington, DC: Georgetown University Press.

Siegel, J. (1999) Stigmatized and standardized varieties in the classroom: Interference or separation. *TESOL Quarterly* 33, 701–728.

Siegel, J. (2006) Language ideologies and the education of speakers of marginalized language varieties: Adopting a critical awareness approach. *Linguistics and Education* 17, 157–174.

Siegel, J. (2010) *Second Dialect Acquisition*. Cambridge: Cambridge University Press.

Slabbert, S. and Finlayson, R. (2002) Code-switching in South African townships. In R. Mesthrie (ed.) *Language in South Africa* (pp. 235–248). Cambridge: Cambridge University Press.

Sneddon, R. (2008) Magda and Albana: Learning to read with dual language books. *Language and Education* 22, 137–154.

Snell, J. (2013) Dialect, interaction and class positioning at school: From deficit to difference to repertoire. *Language and Education* 27, 110–128.

So, D.W.C. (2000) Achieving biliteracy and trilingualism without MOI-based bifurcation of the schools: A plea for third alternatives. In D.C.S. Li, A.M.Y. Lin and W.K. Tsang (eds) *Language and Education in Postcolonial Hong Kong* (pp. 9–33). Hong Kong: Linguistic Society of Hong Kong.

Stotz, D. (2006) Breaching the peace: Struggles around multilingualism in Switzerland. *Language Policy* 5, 247–265.

Stroud, C. and Wee, L. (2006) Anxiety and influence in the language classroom. *RELC Journal* 37, 299–307.

Stroud, C. and Wee, L. (2007) Consuming identities: Language planning and policy in Singaporean late modernity. *Language Policy* 6, 253–279.

Stroud, C. and Wee, L. (2010) Language policy and planning in Singaporean late modernity. In L. Lim, A. Pakir and L. Wee (eds) *English in Singapore: Modernity and Management* (pp. 181–204). Hong Kong: Hong Kong University Press.

Stroud, C. and Wee, L. (2012) *Style, Identity and Literacy: English in Singapore*. Bristol: Multilingual Matters.

Strubell, M. (1999) Language, democracy and devolution in Catalonia. In S. Wright (ed.) *Language, Democracy and Devolution in Catalonia* (pp. 4–38). Clevedon: Multilingual Matters.

Strubell, M. (2001) Catalan a decade later. In J.A. Fishman (ed.) *Can Threatened Languages be Saved?* (pp. 260–283). Clevedon: Multilingual Matters.

Stull, G. (2012) Language, borders and education: Language policy and the making of New Mexico and Arizona. *Working Papers in Educational Linguistics* 27, 19–27.

Sunuodula, M. and Feng, A. (2011) Learning English as a third language by Uyghur students in Xinjiang: A blessing in disguise? In A. Feng (ed.) *English Language Education across Greater China* (pp. 260–283). Bristol: Multilingual Matters.

Tam, A.C.F. (2011) Does the switch of medium of instruction facilitate the language learning of students? A case study of Hong Kong from teachers' perspective. *Language and Education* 25, 399–417.

Tollefson, J.W. and Tsui, A.B.M. (2004) *Medium of Instruction Policies: Which Agenda? Whose Agenda?* Mahwah, NJ: Erlbaum.

Trenchs-Parera, M. and Patiño-Santos, A. (2013) Language attitudes of Latin American newcomers in three secondary school reception classes in Catalonia. In J. Arnau (ed.) *Reviving Catalan at School: Challenges and Instructional Approaches* (pp. 49–71). Bristol: Multilingual Matters.

Trudgill, P. (1975) *Accent, Dialect and the School*. London: Hodder Arnold.

Tsang, W.K. (2008) *The Effect of Medium-of-Instruction Policy on Education Advancement*. Hong Kong: The Chinese University of Hong Kong.

Tsui, A.B.M. (2007) Language policy and the construction of identity: The case of Hong Kong. In A.B.M. Tsui and J.W. Tollefson (eds) *Language Policy, Culture and Identity in Asian Contexts* (pp. 121–141). Mahwah, NJ: Erlbaum.

Tsung, L. (2009) *Minority Language, Education and Communities in China*. Basingstoke: Palgrave.

Urla, J. (2012) *Reclaiming Basque: Language, Nation, and Cultural Activism*. Reno, NV: University of Nevada Press.

Vaish, V. (2005) A peripherist view of English as a language of decolonization in post-colonial India. *Language Policy* 4, 187–206.

Vaish, V. (2010) Pedagogy, culture and globalization in India. In V. Vaish (ed.) *Globalization of Language and Culture in Asia: The Impact of Globalization Processes on Language* (pp. 120–138). London: Continuum.

Vaish, V. (2013) Questioning and oracy in a reading program. *Language and Education* 27, 526–541.

Vaish, V., Tan, T.K., Bokhorst-Heng, W.D. Hogan, D. and Kang, T. (2010) Language and social capital in Singapore. In L. Lim, A. Pakir and L. Wee (eds) *English in Singapore: Modernity and Management* (pp. 159–180). Hong Kong: Hong Kong University Press.

Valdés, G. (1997) Dual-language immersion programs: A cautionary note concerning the education of language-minority students. *Harvard Educational Review* 67, 391–429.

Valdés, G., Gonzalez, S.V., Lopez Garcia, D. and Marquez, P. (2008) Heritage languages and ideologies of language: Unexamined challenges. In D.M. Brinton, O. Kagan and S. Bauckus (eds) *Heritage Language Education* (pp. 107–130). New York: Routledge.

van Avermaet, P., van Houtte, M. and van den Branden, K. (2011) Promoting equity and excellence in education: An overview. In K. van den Branden, P. van Avermaet and M. van Houtte (eds) *Equity and Excellence in Education: Towards Maximal Learning Opportunities for all Students* (pp. 1–20). Abingdon: Routledge.

Vertovec, S. (2007) Superdiversity and its implications. *Ethnic and Racial Studies* 30, 1024–1054.

Vila i Moreno, F.X. (2010) Making choices for sustainable social plurilingualism: Some reflections from the Catalan language area. In J.E. Petrovic (ed.) *International Perspectives on Bilingual Education: Policy, Practice, and Controversy* (pp. 131–152). Charlotte, NC: Information Age Publishing.

Wang, L. and Kirkpatrick, A. (2013) Trilingual education in Hong Kong primary schools: A case study. *International Journal of Bilingual Education and Bilingualism* 16, 100–116.

Warren, J. and Oakes, L. (2011) Language policy and citizenship in Quebec: French as a force for unity in a diverse society? In C. Norrby and J. Hajek (eds) *Uniformity and Diversity in Language Policy: Global Perspectives* (pp. 7–21). Bristol: Multilingual Matters.

Watts, R.J. (1999) The ideology of dialect in Switzerland. In J. Blommaert (ed.) *Language Ideological Debates* (pp. 67–103). Berlin: Mouton de Gruyter.

Weber, J.-J. (2009) *Multilingualism, Education and Change*. Frankfurt/Main: Peter Lang.

Weber, J.-J. (2010) Foreign language provision at secondary level in Luxembourg. *Sociolinguistica* 24, 1–12.

Weber, J.-J. and Horner, K. (2010) Orwellian doublethink: Keywords in Luxembourgish and European language-in-education policy discourses. *Language Policy* 9, 241–256.

Weber, J.-J. and Horner, K. (2012a) *Introducing Multilingualism: A Social Approach*. Abingdon: Routledge.

Weber, J.-J. and Horner, K. (2012b) The trilingual Luxembourgish school system in historical perspective: Progress or regress? *Language, Culture and Curriculum* 25, 3–15.

Wee, L. (2002) When English is not a mother tongue: Linguistic ownership and the Eurasian community in Singapore. *Journal of Multilingual and Multicultural Development* 23, 282–295.

Wee, L. (2004) Reduplication and discourse particles. In L. Lim (ed.) *Singapore English: A Grammatical Description* (pp. 105–126). Amsterdam: Benjamins.

Wee, L. (2008) Linguistic instrumentalism in Singapore. In P. Tan and R. Rubdy (eds) *Language as Commodity: Global Structures, Local Marketplaces* (pp. 31–43). London: Continuum.

Wee, L. (2010) 'Burdens' and 'handicaps' in Singapore's language policy: On the limits of language management. *Language Policy* 9, 97–114.

Wee, L. (2011) Metadiscursive convergence in the Singlish debate. *Language and Communication* 31, 75–85.

Wee, L. (2013) Governing English in Singapore: Some challenges for Singapore's language policy. In L. Wee, R.B.H. Goh and L. Lim (eds) *The Politics of English: South Asia, Southeast Asia and the Asia Pacific* (pp. 105–124). Amsterdam: Benjamins.

Wee, L. and Bokhorst-Heng, W. (2005) Language policy and nationalist ideology: Statal narratives in Singapore. *Multilingua* 24, 159–183.

Wiley, T.G. (2002) Accessing language rights in education: A brief history of the US context. In J. Tollefson (ed.) *Language Policies in Education: Critical Issues* (pp. 39–64). Mahwah, NJ: Erlbaum.

Wiley, T.G. and Lukes, M. (1996) English-only and standard English ideologies in the U.S. *TESOL Quarterly* 30, 511–535.

Wille, C., de Bres, J. and Franziskus, A. (2012) Interkulturelle Arbeitswelten in Luxemburg. Mehrsprachigkeit und kulturelle Vielfalt am Arbeitsplatz von Grenzgängern. *Interculture Journal* 11/17, 73–90.

Willems, H. and Milmeister, P. (2006) Migration und Integration. In W.H. Lorig and M. Hirsch (eds) *Das politische System Luxemburgs: eine Einführung* (pp. 62–92). Wiesbaden: VS Verlag für Sozialwissenschaften.

Williams, E. (2006) *Bridges and Barriers: Language in African Education and Development.* Manchester: St Jerome Publishing.

Winstanley, B. and Cooke, M. (2012) Participatory approaches to ESOL. Paper given at Adult ESOL in Multilingual Britain Seminar, University of Leeds, 13 July 2012.

Wolf, H.-G. and Igboanusi, H. (2006) Empowerment through English – a realistic view of the educational promotion of English in post-colonial contexts: The case of Nigeria. In M. Pütz, J.A. Fishman and J. Neff-van Aertselaer (eds) *'Along the Routes to Power': Explorations of Empowerment through Language* (pp. 333–356). Berlin: Mouton de Gruyter.

Wolfram, W. (2010) Dialect awareness, cultural literacy and the public interest. In M. Farr, L. Seloni and J. Song (eds) *Ethnolinguistic Diversity and Education* (pp. 129–149). New York: Routledge.

Wolfram, W. and Schilling-Estes, N. (1998) *American English: Dialects and Variation.* Oxford: Blackwell.

Woolard, K.A. (1986) The politics of language status planning: 'Normalization' in Catalonia. In N. Schweda-Nicholson (ed.) *Languages in the International Perspective* (pp. 91–102). Norwood, NJ: Ablex.

Woolard, K.A. (1999) Simultaneity and bivalency as strategies in bilingualism. *Journal of Linguistic Anthropology* 8, 3–29.

Woolard, K.A. (2008) Language and identity choice in Catalonia: The interplay of contrasting ideologies of linguistic authority. In K. Süselbeck, U. Mühlschlegel and

P. Masson (eds) *Lengua, nación e identidad: La regulación del plurilingüismo en España y América Latina* (pp. 303–323). Berlin: Ibero-Amerikanisches Institut P.K.

Wright, S. (2004) *Language Policy and Language Planning: From Nationalism to Globalisation.* Basingstoke: Palgrave.

Wroblewski, M. (2012) Amazonian Kichwa Proper: Ethnolinguistic domain in Pan-Indian Ecuador. *Journal of Linguistic Anthropology* 22, 64–86.

Yiakoumetti, A. (2006) A bidialectal programme for the learning of Standard Modern Greek in Cyprus. *Applied Linguistics* 27, 295–317.

Zhou, M. (2005) Legislating literacy for linguistic and ethnic minorities in contemporary China. *Current Issues in Language Planning* 6, 102–121.

Author Index

Subject Index